Jenkins 2.x Continuous Integration Cookbook

Third Edition

Over 90 recipes to produce great results using pro-level practices, techniques, and solutions

Mitesh Soni
Alan Mark Berg

BIRMINGHAM - MUMBAI

Jenkins 2.x Continuous Integration Cookbook

Third Edition

First published: June 2012

Second edition: January 2015

Third edition: October 2017

Production reference: 1261017

Published by Packt Publishing Ltd.
Livery Place
35 Livery Street
Birmingham
B3 2PB, UK.
ISBN 978-1-78829-794-3

www.packtpub.com

Credits

Authors
Mitesh Soni
Alan Mark Berg

Reviewers
Juan Vicente Herrera Ruiz de Alejo
Javier Delgado
Tim Ysewyn

Commissioning Editor
Vijin Boricha

Acquisition Editor
Chandan Kumar

Content Development Editor
Deepti Thore

Technical Editor
Sneha Hanchate

Copy Editors
Laxmi Subramanian
Safis Editing

Project Coordinator
Shweta H Birwatkar

Proofreader
Safis Editing

Indexer
Tejal Daruwale Soni

Graphics
Tania Dutta

Production Coordinator
Deepika Naik

About the Authors

Mitesh Soni is an avid learner with 10 years of experience in the IT industry. He is an SCJP, SCWCD, VCP, IBM Urbancode, and IBM Bluemix certified professional and Certified Scrum Master. He loves DevOps and cloud computing and he also has an interest in programming in Java. He finds design patterns fascinating. He believes a picture is worth a thousand words.

He occasionally contributes to etutorialsworld.com. He loves to play with kids, fiddle with his camera, and take photographs at Indroda Park. He is addicted to taking pictures without knowing many technical details. He lives in the capital of Mahatma Gandhi's home state.

Mitesh has also authored the following books with Packt:

- *Jenkins Essentials, Second Edition*
- *DevOps Bootcamp*
- *Implementing DevOps with Microsoft Azure*
- *DevOps for Web Development*
- *Jenkins Essentials*
- *Learning Chef*

"I've missed more than 9,000 shots in my career. I've lost almost 300 games. 26 times, I've been trusted to take the game-winning shot and missed. I've failed over and over and over again in my life. And that is why I succeed."

— *Michael Jordan.*

Alan Mark Berg, BSc, MSc, PGCE, has been the lead developer at Central Computer Services at the University of Amsterdam since 1998. He is currently working in an Innovation Work Group that accelerates the creation of new and exciting services. In his famously scarce spare time, he writes. Alan has a bachelor's degree, two master's degrees, a teaching qualification, and quality assurance certifications. He has also coauthored two Packt Publishing books about Sakai (`http://sakaiproject.org`), a highly successful open source learning
management platform used by millions of students around the world. He has won a couple of awards, including the Sakai Fellowship and Teaching With Sakai Innovation Award (TWSIA).

Alan enjoys working with talent; this forces him to improve his own competencies. This motivation is why Alan enjoys working in energetic, open source communities of interest. At the time of writing, he is on the board of directors of the Apereo Foundation and is the community offi cer for its Learning Analytics Initiative (`https://confluence.sakaiproject.org/display/LAI/Learning+Analytics+Initiative`).

In previous incarnations, Alan was a QA director, a technical writer, an Internet/Linux course writer, a product line development officer, and a teacher. He likes to get his hands dirty with building, gluing systems, exploring data, and turning it into actionable information. He remains agile by ruining various development and acceptance environments and generally rampaging through the green fields of technological opportunity

About the Reviewers

Juan Vicente Herrera Ruiz de Alejo has a degree in computer science. He is the leader of the Madrid DevOps meetup. He is the teacher of DevOps master's program at Alcala de Henares University in Madrid and has been working in IT companies for the past 12 years.

He also works as a volunteer at an NGO dedicated to fighting breast cancer.

He is currently working for Logtrust.com and has worked for companies such as Colt telecom, Everis, and BBVA.

I would like to thank my wife, Emma, and my entire family for all their support.

Javier Delgado is an automation fanatic, continuous tasks (inspection, testing, and delivery) evangelist, and perpetual new-knowledge addict.

He works as a continuous delivery expert at ING Bank NV.

www.PacktPub.com

For support files and downloads related to your book, please visit www.PacktPub.com.

Did you know that Packt offers eBook versions of every book published, with PDF and ePub files available? You can upgrade to the eBook version at www.PacktPub.com and as a print book customer, you are entitled to a discount on the eBook copy. Get in touch with us at service@packtpub.com for more details.

At www.PacktPub.com, you can also read a collection of free technical articles, sign up for a range of free newsletters and receive exclusive discounts and offers on Packt books and eBooks.

https://www.packtpub.com/mapt

Get the most in-demand software skills with Mapt. Mapt gives you full access to all Packt books and video courses, as well as industry-leading tools to help you plan your personal development and advance your career.

Why subscribe?

- Fully searchable across every book published by Packt
- Copy and paste, print, and bookmark content
- On demand and accessible via a web browser

Customer Feedback

Thanks for purchasing this Packt book. At Packt, quality is at the heart of our editorial process. To help us improve, please leave us an honest review on this book's Amazon page at https://www.amazon.com/dp/1788297946.

If you'd like to join our team of regular reviewers, you can e-mail us at customerreviews@packtpub.com. We award our regular reviewers with free eBooks and videos in exchange for their valuable feedback. Help us be relentless in improving our products!

I would like to dedicate this book to all those empty bus stands, benches, cycles, cameras, roads, and trees who have witnessed my anger, emotions, love, and hostility. Without them, people would have come across real me (Pun Intended).

I apologize in advance if I have missed any name. I have tried to recollect every name with whom I have shared good memories. I don't have a good 'memory' and that is blessing as well as curse at times.

On a serious note, I would like to dedicate this book to Shreyansh (Shreyu-My sister (Jigisha)'s baby boy) showed me the power of innocence and smile, Vinay Kher for teaching me how to improve always and keeping my text messages in his mobile, my parents who are always there silently and pray for me, Simba (Priyanka Agashe) for supporting and encouraging me all the time and forced me to believe in myself, Indian Army, and all brave soldiers in uniform for protecting us.

Ashita A, Sourabh Mishra and Gowri, thanks for showing me mirror whenever it was required. I value your presence in my life. It was fun to learn about life from you. I might have forgotten everything you taught me the next day. Sorry for being childish but I can't change it.

I am grateful to Rinka, Bhagyashri, Avanti, Aishwarya P, Vijay, Priya, Harshal, Tejas, Sharvil P, Apoorva S, Nandan, Bhavna, Vishakha S, Pradnya B, Viral I, Chaitali, Sudeep, Amit R, Manisha Y, Vaishnavi, Parinda, Arpita, Jinesh, Vihan, Saurabh S, and Raghav H, who have always helped me, made me smile, and made my life easier in last few years or so.

I want to say thanks... and share my gratitude for everything I've been blessed with. I would like to thank Jigisha-Nitesh, Dada-Dadi, Priyanka-Hemant, Anupama-Mihir, Nalini and family, Kim and Yaashi, Kirti, Bindiya, Jai Jamba, Nitesh, Munal, Ashish B, Mayur Mothliya, Rohini, Aakanksha, Yohan Wadia, Rohan C, Chintan Solanki, Vijay Patel, Nikul, Paresh, Raju, Yogendra, Ajay, Ruchi, Navrang O, Dharmesh R, my village friends, Prakash, Mitul, Kanak, Bapu, Ravi, Vimal, Chitrang, Krimali, Saputara Group, Subhash, Ranjit, Rangusinh, Setan, Jayesh and his family, Ramesh and his family, Vijay Prajapati, Munni Bhabhi and her family and teachers.

Divya, Deepti, and Sneha... this wouldn't have possible without you guys. Thank you for inspiring me and keeping me on my toes.

Table of Contents

Preface

Jenkins is a Java-based automation server that supports the discovery of defects early in the software cycle and the deployment of application packages in an automated manner. Thanks to a rapidly growing number of plugins, Jenkins communicates with many types of systems, building and triggering a wide variety of tests and integrations with various release management services.

CI involves making small changes to software and then building and applying quality assurance processes. Defects not only occur in the code, but also appear in naming conventions, documentation, how the software is designed, build scripts, the process of deploying the software to servers, and so on. CI forces the defects to emerge early, rather than waiting for the software to be fully produced. If defects are caught in the later stages of the software development life cycle, the process will be more expensive. The cost of repair radically increases as soon as the bugs escape into production. Estimates suggest it is 100 to 1,000 times cheaper to capture defects early. Effective use of a CI server, such as Jenkins, could be the difference between enjoying a holiday and working unplanned hours to heroically save the day. And as you can imagine, in my day job as a senior developer with aspirations for quality assurance, I like long boring days, at least for mission-critical production environments.

Continuous Delivery (CD) involves the deployment of applications in web servers or application servers located on-premise or in cloud environments. Jenkins supports integration with many cloud service providers and also supports integration with Platform as a Service offerings too. With shell script and command execution support, many deployment and configuration scenarios can be achieved too.

Jenkins can automate the building of software regularly and trigger tests, pulling in the results and failing based on defined criteria. Failing early via build failure lowers the costs, increases confidence in the software produced, and has the potential to morph subjective processes into an aggressive metrics-based process that the development team feels is unbiased.

Jenkins is not just an automation server, it is also a vibrant and highly active community. Enlightened self-interest dictates participation.

What this book covers

Chapter 1, *Getting Started with Jenkins*, covers how to install Jenkins 2.x on Windows, CentOs, Microsoft Azure, and AWS. There are important recipes that show how to install or upload plugins, how to configure Proxy, how to configure JENKINS_HOME and tools in Manage Jenkins. This chapter will also cover how to create freestyle jobs for Ant and Maven projects

Chapter 2, *Management and Monitoring of Jenkins*, helps us understand master/agent architecture, how to manage Jenkins Build jobs using Eclipse, backing up and restoring Jenkins, command-line options in Jenkins using Jenkins CLI, managing disk usage, shutting down Jenkins safely, monitoring Jenkins, and configuring email notifications.

Chapter 3, *Managing Security*, covers how to improve security with Jenkins configuration, configure Matrix-based Security and handle a Project-based Matrix Authorization Strategy. It will also cover Jenkins and its integration with OpenLDAP and Active Directory. Later in the chapter, we will cover Jenkins and OWASP Zed Attack Proxy Integration, finding 500 errors and XSS attacks in Jenkins through fuzzing, exploring the OWASP Dependency-Check plugin, and working with the Audit Trail plugin.

Chapter 4, *Improve Code Quality*, explores the use of source code metrics. To save money and improve quality, you need to remove defects in the software life cycle as early as possible. This chapter covers details on how to integrate Jenkins with SonarQube, how to update center in SonarQube, quality gates, quality profiles and rules, verifying HTML, CSS, and JavaScript validity using SonarQube, verifying Java code using SonarQube, and configuring SonarQube as a Windows service.

Chapter 5, *Building Applications in Jenkins*, details approaches to configuring Ant, Maven, and Android projects for execution, how to configure environment variables, running Groovy scripts through Maven, running Ant through Groovy in Maven, and remotely triggering jobs through the Jenkins API.

Chapter 6, *Continuous Delivery*, discusses Continuous Delivery, how to archive artifacts, copying artifact from other build jobs, integrating Jenkins with Artifactory, deploying a WAR file from Jenkins to Tomcat, AWS Beanstalk, Azure App Services, and how to promote builds.

Chapter 7, *Continuous Testing*, details Continuous Testing, how to publish unit testing reports from Jenkins, creating Selenium test cases using Eclipse, integrating Jenkins and Selenium for functional testing, Jenkins and Cucumber Test reports, creating load tests in Apache JMeter, executing load tests from Jenkins, reporting JMeter performance metrics, and testing with FitNesse.

Chapter 8, *Orchestration*, explores orchestration of a pipeline, understanding upstream and downstream jobs, configuring upstream and downstream jobs, configuring a build pipeline, creating a pipeline job, using a sample pipeline for execution, configuring a pipeline job for end-to-end automation, and getting started with the Blue Ocean dashboard.

Chapter 9 , *Jenkins UI Customization*, details skinning Jenkins with the simple themes plugin, skinning and provisioning Jenkins using a WAR overlay, generating a home page, creating HTML reports, efficient use of views, saving screen space with the Dashboard View plugin, making noise with HTML5 browsers, and an extreme view for reception areas.

What you need for this book

This book is for beginners. It assumes that you are familiar with at least the Java programming language. Knowledge of core Java and JEE is essential in order to use this book to gain better insight. A strong understanding of program logic will provide you with the background to be productive with Jenkins while using plugins to write commands for the shell.

As the application development life cycle covers lot of tools in general, it is essential to have some knowledge of repositories such as SVN and Git, IDE tools such as Eclipse, and build tools such as Ant and Maven.

Knowledge of code analysis tools will make the job easier in terms of configuration and integration; however, it is not vital to perform the exercises given in this book. Most of the configuration steps are clearly mentioned. SonarQuve 6.3 version is used for code analysis.

You will be walked through the steps required to install Jenkins on a Windows and Linux-based host. In order to be immediately successful, you will need administrative access to a host that runs a modern version of Windows and Linux; Windows 10 is what will be used for demonstration purposes. If you are a more experienced reader, then a recent release of almost any distribution will work just as well (but you may be required to do a little bit of extra work that is not outlined in the book).

You can use a free trial of Microsoft Azure to work on some recipes.

Additionally, you will need access to the internet to download plugins that you do not already have, as well as an installation of Jenkins. Any normal hardware configuration is good enough, such as 4 GB RAM and 500 GB hard disk.

Who this book is for

Jenkins Continous Integration Cookbook is for beginners and advanced users both. This book targets developers and system administrators who are involved in the application development life cycle and are looking to automate it. Developers, technical leads, testers, and operational professionals are the target readers to jumpstart Jenkins. Readers should be aware of the issues faced by development and operations team as they are stakeholders in the application life cycle management process. The reasons to jumpstart Jenkins are to understand the importance of the contributions Continuous Integration (CI), Continuous Testing, and Continuous Delivery (CD) make to effective application life cycle management.

Conventions

In this book, you will find a number of styles of text that distinguish between different kinds of information. Here are some examples of these styles, and an explanation of their meaning.

Code words in text, database table names, folder names, filenames, file extensions, pathnames, dummy URLs, user input, and Twitter handles are shown as follows: "We can include other contexts through the use of the `include` directive."

A block of code is set as follows:

```
@charset "utf-8";
#test {
background-image: url(/userContent/camera.png);
}
#main-table{
background-image: url(/userContent/camera.png)
!important;
```

When we wish to draw your attention to a particular part of a code block, the relevant lines or items are set in bold:

```
<project xmlns="http://maven.apache.org/POM/4.0.0"
xmlns:xsi="http://www.w3.org/2001/XMLSchema-instance"
xsi:schemaLocation="http://maven.apache.org/POM/4.0.0
http://maven.apache.org/maven-v4_0_0.xsd">
```

```
<modelVersion>4.0.0</modelVersion>
<groupId>nl.uva.berg</groupId>
```

Any command-line input or output is written as follows:

```
----Project and session
Project: class org.apache.Maven.model.Model
Session: class org.apache.Maven.execution.MavenSession
longname: SuperGood
```

New terms and **important words** are shown in bold. Words that you see on the screen, in menus or dialog boxes for example, appear in the text like this: "Clicking the **Next** button moves you to the next screen."

Warnings or important notes appear in a box like this.

Tips and tricks appear like this.

Reader feedback

Feedback from our readers is always welcome. Let us know what you think about this book—what you liked or may have disliked. Reader feedback is important for us to develop titles that you really get the most out of.

To send us general feedback, simply send an e-mail to feedback@packtpub.com, and mention the book title via the subject of your message.

Customer support

Now that you are the proud owner of a Packt book, we have a number of things to help you to get the most from your purchase.

Downloading the example code

You can download the example code files for this book from your account at http://www.packtpub.com. If you purchased this book elsewhere, you can visit http://www.packtpub.com/support and register to have the files emailed directly to you.

You can download the code files by following these steps:

1. Log in or register to our website using your email address and password.
2. Hover the mouse pointer on the **SUPPORT** tab at the top.
3. Click on **Code Downloads & Errata**.
4. Enter the name of the book in the **Search** box.
5. Select the book for which you're looking to download the code files.
6. Choose from the drop-down menu where you purchased this book from.
7. Click on **Code Download**.

Once the file is downloaded, please make sure that you unzip or extract the folder using the latest version of:

- WinRAR / 7-Zip for Windows
- Zipeg / iZip / UnRarX for Mac
- 7-Zip / PeaZip for Linux

The code bundle for the book is also hosted on GitHub at https://github.com/PacktPublishing/Jenkins-Continuous-Integration-Cookbook-Third-Edition. We also have other code bundles from our rich catalog of books and videos available at https://github.com/PacktPublishing/. Check them out!

Downloading the color images of this book

We also provide you with a PDF file that has color images of the screenshots/diagrams used in this book. The color images will help you better understand the changes in the output. You can download this file from https://www.packtpub.com/sites/default/files/downloads/JenkinsContinuousIntegrationCookbookThirdEdition_ColorImages.pdf.

Errata

Although we have taken every care to ensure the accuracy of our content, mistakes do happen. If you find a mistake in one of our books-maybe a mistake in the text or the code-we would be grateful if you could report this to us. By doing so, you can save other readers from frustration and help us improve subsequent versions of this book. If you find any errata, please report them by visiting `http://www.packtpub.com/submit-errata`, selecting your book, clicking on the **Errata Submission Form** link, and entering the details of your errata. Once your errata are verified, your submission will be accepted and the errata will be uploaded to our website or added to any list of existing errata under the Errata section of that title.

To view the previously submitted errata, go
to `https://www.packtpub.com/books/content/support` and enter the name of the book in
the search field. The required information will appear under the **Errata** section.

Piracy

Piracy of copyrighted material on the internet is an ongoing problem across all media. At
Packt, we take the protection of our copyright and licenses very seriously. If you come
across any illegal copies of our works in any form on the internet, please provide us with
the location address or website name immediately so that we can pursue a remedy.

Please contact us at `copyright@packtpub.com` with a link to the suspected pirated
material.

We appreciate your help in protecting our authors and our ability to bring you valuable
content.

Questions

If you have a problem with any aspect of this book, you can contact us
at `questions@packtpub.com`, and we will do our best to address the problem.

1
Getting Started with Jenkins

In this chapter, we will discuss how to install and configure Jenkins, and what new features or UI improvements are available from Jenkins 2 and later. We will cover the following recipes:

- Installing Jenkins 2 on Windows
- Installing Jenkins 2 on CentOS
- Installing Jenkins 2 on Azure
- Installing Jenkins as a service in Windows
- Installing plugins in Jenkins
- Uploading plugins in Jenkins
- Configuring proxy in Jenkins
- Configuring global settings in Jenkins
- Configuring JENKINS_HOME
- Understanding JENKINS_HOME directory
- Using different ports for Jenkins
- Configuring JAVA_HOME in Jenkins
- Configuring Git in Jenkins
- Configuring ANT_HOME in Jenkins
- Configuring MAVEN_HOME in Jenkins
- Configuring GRADLE_HOME in Jenkins
- Creating a Freestyle job for an Ant project
- Creating a Maven job for a Maven project

Introduction

Jenkins is an open source automation server that is widely used by many organizations to implement popular DevOps practices, such as Continuous Integration and Continuous Delivery. Jenkins is feature-rich and is vastly extendable through plugins. Further, Jenkins and its plugins improve rapidly. There is a new minor version of Jenkins released weekly, mostly with improvements, occasionally with bugs. The community manages core stability via the use of a long-term support release of Jenkins, which is mature and less feature-rich when compared to the latest version. For a stable system in a complex environment, you need to monitor, clean up storage, back up, keep control of your Jenkins scripts, and consistently clean and polish. This chapter has recipes for the most common tasks. Proper maintenance lowers the risk of failures, such as:

- **New plugins causing exceptions**: There are a lot of good plugins being written with rapid version changes. In this situation, it is easy for you to accidentally add new versions of plugins with new defects. There have been a number of occasions during upgrades when suddenly the plugin does not work. To combat the risk of plugin exceptions, consider using a test Jenkins instance before releasing to a critical system.

- **Storage overflowing with artifacts**: If you keep a build history that includes artifacts such as WAR files, large sets of JAR files, or other types of binaries and source code, then your storage space will be consumed at a surprising rate. Storage costs have decreased tremendously, but storage usage equates to longer backup times and more communication from slave to master. To minimize the risk of disk overflowing, you will need to consider your backup and restore policy and the associated build retention policy expressed in the advanced options of jobs.

- **Script spaghetti**: As jobs are written by various development teams, the location and style of the included scripts vary. This makes it difficult for you to keep track. Consider using well-defined locations for your scripts and a scripts repository managed through a plugin.

- **Resource depletion**: As memory is consumed, or the number of intense jobs increases, then Jenkins slows down. Proper monitoring and quick reactions reduce impact.

- **A general lack of consistency between jobs due to organic growth**: Jenkins is easy to install and use. The ability to seamlessly turn on plugins is addictive. The pace of adoption of Jenkins within an organization can be breathtaking. Without a consistent policy, your teams will introduce lots of plugins and also lots of ways of performing the same work. Conventions improve consistency and readability of jobs and thus decrease maintenance.

The Jenkins community is working hard on your behalf. If you see an issue, please report it back.

Signing up to the community:

To add community bug reports or modify wiki pages, you will need to create an account at:
`https://wiki.jenkins-ci.org/display/JENKINS/Issue+Tracking`.

Installing Jenkins 2 on Windows

Let's install Jenkins 2 on a Windows operating system. It can be a physical machine, virtual machine available on Cloud.

Getting ready

To carry out this recipe, you need to download Jenkins.

For a business unit, it is advisable to have the following requirements:

- Java 8
- 4 GB + RAM
- 500 GB+ free disk space

How to do it...

Let's install Jenkins now by following these steps:

1. Go to `https://jenkins.io`.

2. Click on **Download**, as shown in the following screenshot:

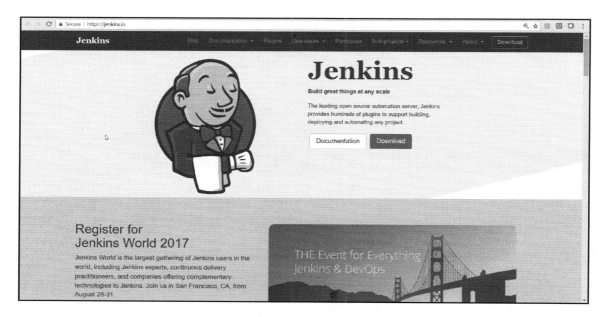

2. Download the latest Windows package from Jenkins, available at:
    `http://mirrors.jenkins.io/windows/latest`.
3. Click on the package and follow the step-by-step instructions to install it.

Installing Jenkins 2 on CentOS

Let's look at the steps required to install Jenkins on CentOS.

Getting ready

For a business unit, it is advisable to have the following requirements:

*   Java 8
*   4 GB+ RAM
*   500 GB+ free disk space

Jenkins requires Java. To install Java, execute:

```
sudo yum install java
```

How to do it...

1. Jenkins' stable and recent versions are available in a YUM repository.
2. Add the Jenkins repository to the yum repos:

   ```
   sudo wget -O /etc/yum.repos.d/jenkins.repo
   http://pkg.jenkins-ci.org/redhat/jenkins.repo
   ```

3. For the stable version, execute:

   ```
   sudo wget -O /etc/yum.repos.d/jenkins.repo
   http://pkg.jenkins-ci.org/redhat-stable/jenkins.repo
   ```

4. Import the following key:

   ```
   sudo rpm --import
   https://jenkins-ci.org/redhat/jenkins-ci.org.key
   ```

5. Install Jenkins by executing the following command:

   ```
   sudo yum install jenkins
   ```

There's more...

- To start the Jenkins service, execute:

  ```
  sudo service jenkins start
  ```

- To stop the Jenkins service, execute:

  ```
  sudo service jenkins stop
  ```

- To restart the Jenkins service, execute:

  ```
  sudo service jenkins restart
  ```

Installing Jenkins 2 on Azure

Microsoft Azure is one of the most popular cloud service providers in recent times. Let's try to install Jenkins on Azure.

Getting ready

You need to have a Microsoft Azure subscription for Jenkins installation on Azure. A free trial for one month is also available:

1. Go to `https://jenkins.io.</span>`
2. Click on **Download**.

How to do it...

Let's see how to install Jenkins on Azure:

1. Click on the **Deploy to Azure** link on the Jenkins download page:

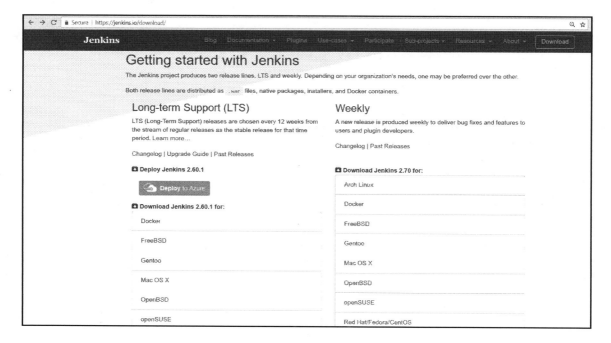

2. It will redirect you to **Azure Marketplace**.
3. Verify the **Pricing** plans and categories involved in it on the same page.
4. Click on **GET IT NOW**. These steps are demonstrated in the following screenshot:

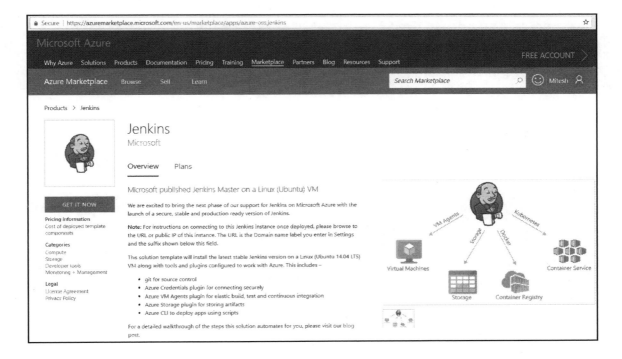

5. In the **Create this app in Azure** tab, click on **Continue**:

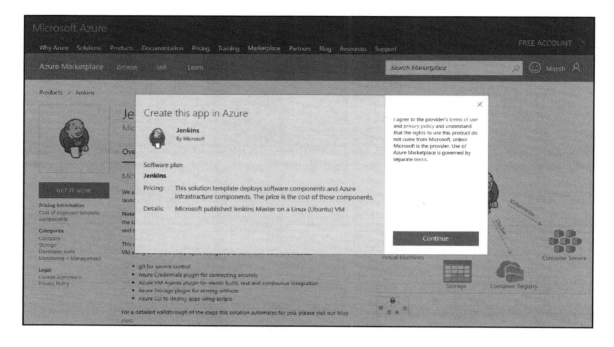

6. If you already have the Azure subscription, then login with the username and password.
7. **Deployment model** is already selected.
8. Click on **Create**:

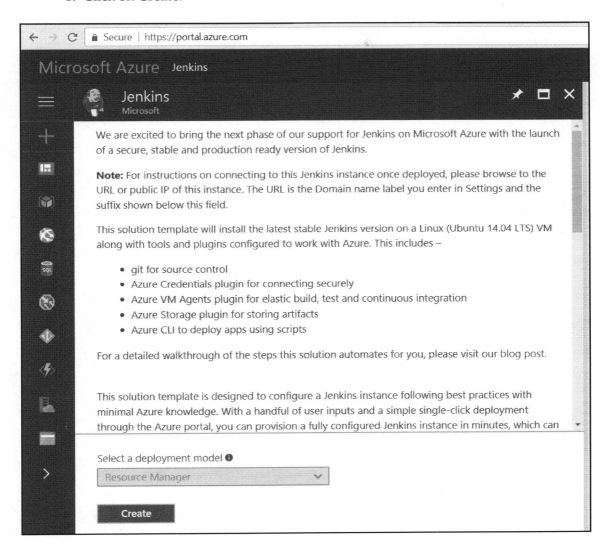

9. Provide **Password, Jenkins release type**, and **Subscription** details, as demonstrated in this next screenshot:

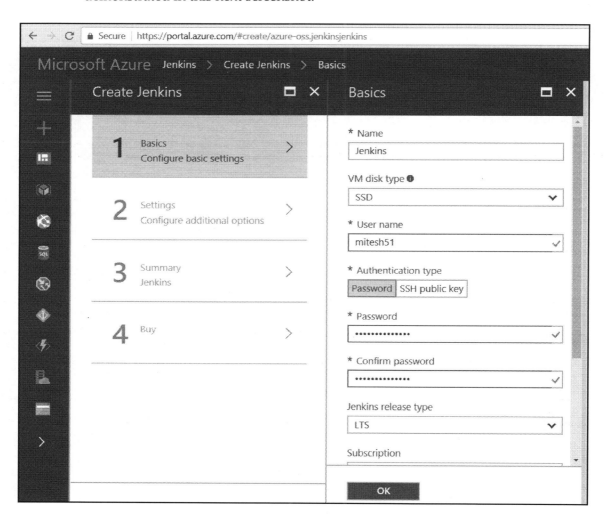

10. Select **Create new** and provide **Resource group** name.
11. Select the **Location** as per your preference.
12. Click on **OK**:

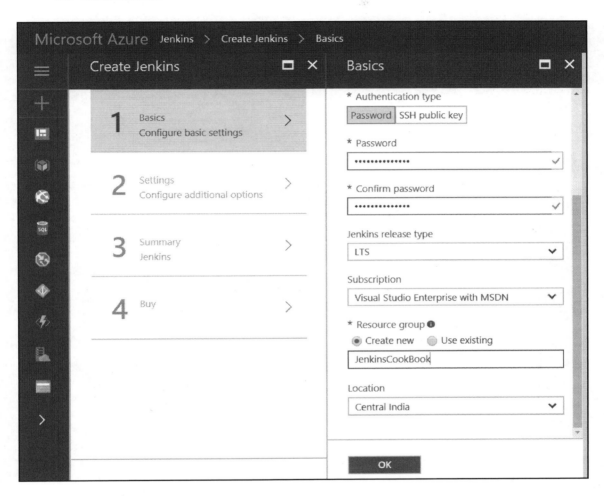

13. Select the **Size** based on the requirement.
14. Provide a unique **Domain name label**.
15. Click **OK**:

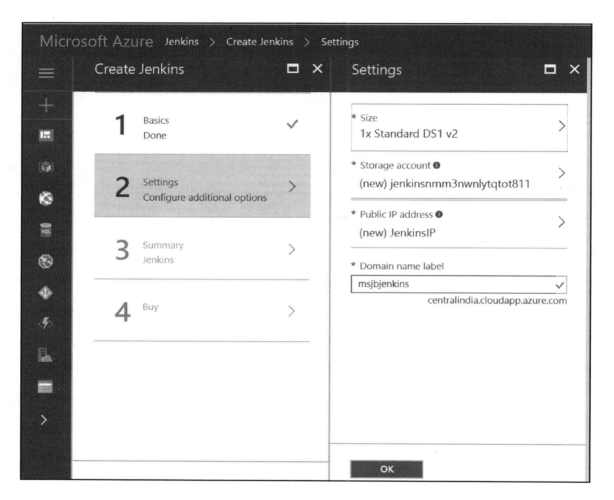

16. Review the selection.
17. Automated **validation** will be executed based on your selection.
18. Click on **OK**:

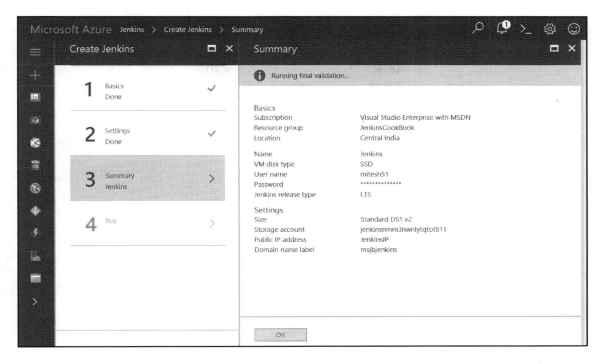

19. Review the **Template** link available before clicking on the **Purchase** button:

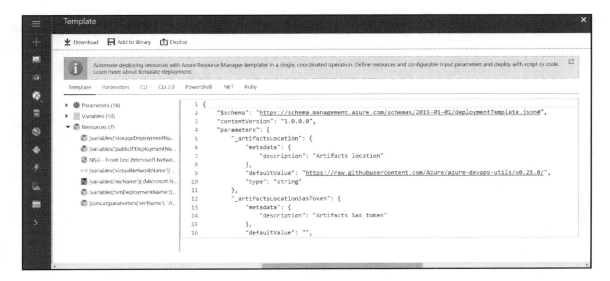

20. Once ready, click on **Purchase**:

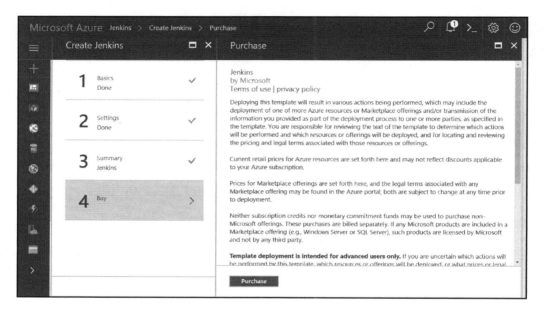

21. In the Azure portal, click on the **Resource groups** you have created. Review the resources that are being created one by one. Review the deployments in the **Overview** section.

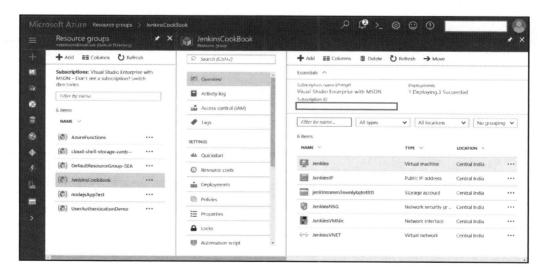

22. Click on the JenkinsIP and visit the domain name associated with it:

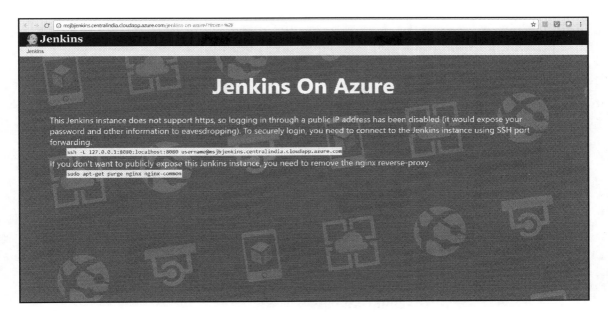

23. Download PuTTY or any other `ssh` client so we can connect to the URL mentioned in the Jenkins page.
24. Go to the location where `putty.exe` is available.
25. Execute the command given on the Jenkins page in command prompt.

26. Select **Yes** in **PuTTY Security Alert**:

27. Open the browser and navigate to the URL, `http://localhost:8080`.
28. It will ask for the **Administrator password**:

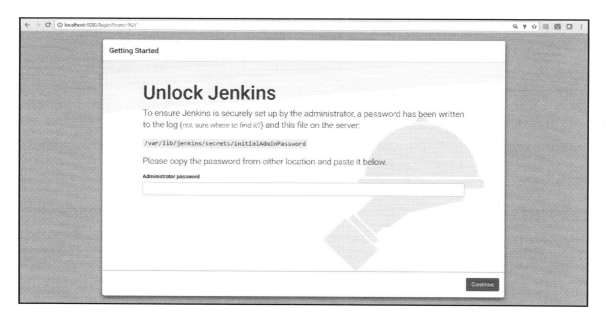

29. In the PuTTY window, execute the `cat` command to get details of the file mentioned for the **Administrator password**.

30. Replace that password in the **Administrator password** box and click on **Continue**:

```
mitesh51@Jenkins:~$ sudo cat /var/lib/jenkins/secrets/initialAdminPassword
e0a0e477a2234e7bb45061173512eeff
mitesh51@Jenkins:~$
```

31. Click on **Install suggested plugins**:

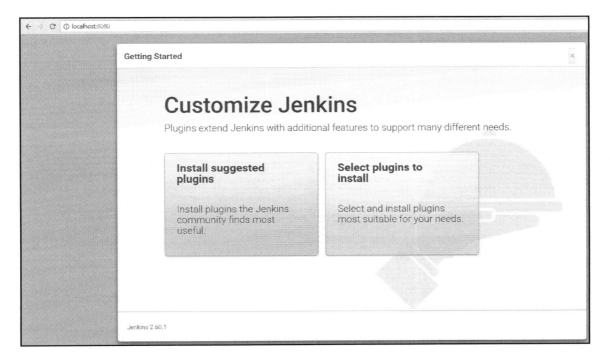

32. Once all plugins are installed successfully, **Create First Admin User**. Click **Save and Finish**, as demonstrated in this next screenshot:

33. Now, the Jenkins setup is completed. Click on **Start using Jenkins**:

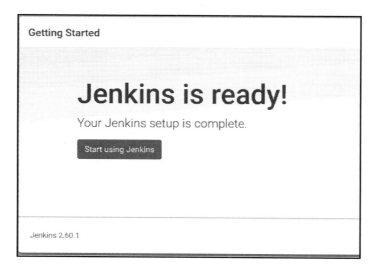

34. Finally, we are at the dashboard screen:

How it works...

Behind the scene, the template creates all the resources that are required to host Jenkins, including virtual network, network security group, virtual machine, and so on, based on the best practices; and then Jenkins is installed and configured in a secured environment in Microsoft Azure.

Installing Jenkins as a Service in Windows

Installing Jenkins as a Windows service allows you to start Jenkins as soon as the machine starts, and regardless of who is interactively using Jenkins.

Getting ready

Install and configure Jenkins on Windows.

How to do it...

Follow these steps to install Jenkins as a service in Windows:

1. Go to the Jenkins dashboard.
2. Click on **Manage Jenkins**.
3. Click on **Install as Windows Service**, as shown in the following diagram:

 Install as Windows Service
Installs Jenkins as a Windows service to this system, so that Jenkins starts automatically when the machine boots.

4. Keep **Installation Directory** as the default and click on **Install**:

 Install as Windows Service

Installing Jenkins as a Windows service allows you to start Jenkins as soon as the machine starts, and regardless of who is interactively using Jenkins.

Installation Directory F:\1.DevOps2016\#JenkinsEssentials\FirstDraft\jenkinsHome

Install

5. Once Windows as a Service installation is successfully completed, click on **Yes**:

 Installation Complete

Installation is successfully completed. Do you want to stop this Jenkins and start a newly installed Windows service?

 Yes

6. Now Jenkins will be available as a service in the Windows system.

How it works...

Go to **Control Panel** and search for **Services**.

Click on **Services (Local)** to view:

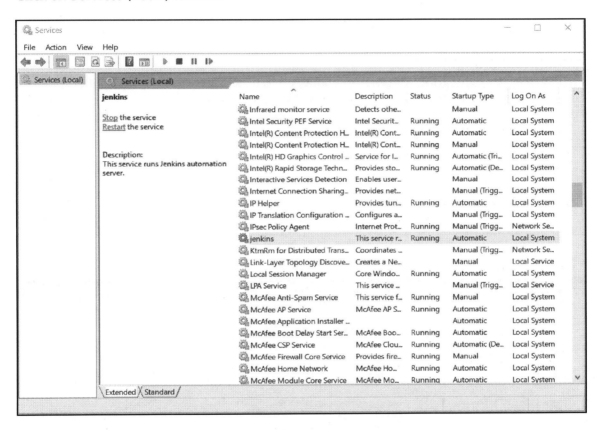

Once the Jenkins service is available, you can right-click on it and start, stop, or restart services based on your requirements.

Installing plugins in Jenkins

Jenkins is an open source automation server that is widely used and extensible due to more than 400+ plugins. Plugins make Jenkins' integration with other tools very easy. You can create your own plugins also.

Getting ready

There are various categories of plugins available, such as **Source Code Management**, **Slave launchers and controllers**, **Build triggers**, **Build tools**, **Build notifies**, **Build reports**, **Other Post-build Actions**, **External site/tool integrations**, **UI plugins**, **Authentication and user management**, **Android development**, **iOS development**, **.NET development**, **Ruby development**, **Library plugins**, and so on.

How to do it...

1. Go to the Jenkins dashboard. Click on **Manage Jenkins** and then **Manage Plugins**:

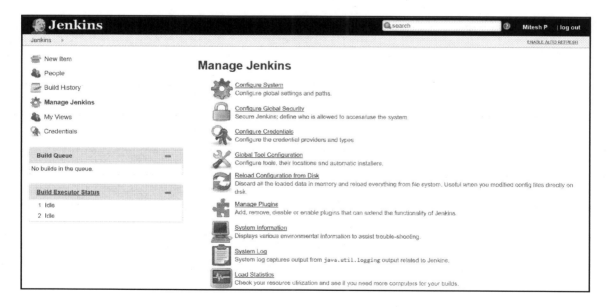

2. Go to **Available** tab and select any plugin to install. Click on **Install without restart**:

3. Verify the successful plugin installation, as demonstrated in this next screenshot:

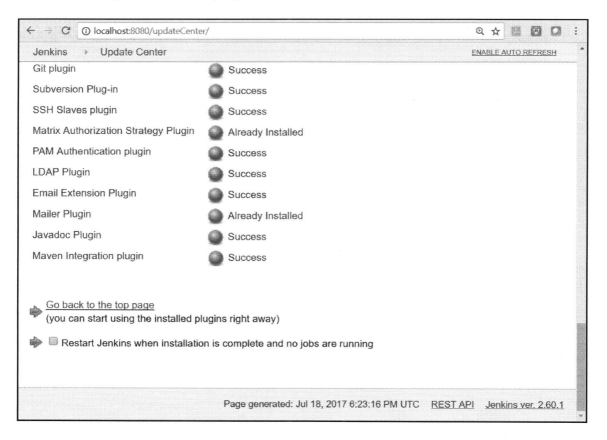

If installation is pending with restart, then restart Jenkins.

How it works...

Once the plugin is installed, a specific block is added in a build job or in the relevant section in **Manage Jenkins**.

You only need to provide some parameters and credentials for integration of external tools or services with Jenkins.

There's more...

Jenkins defines interfaces or abstract classes that model a facet of a build system. Interfaces or abstract classes define agreement on what needs to be implemented; and Jenkins uses plugins to extend those implementations.

See also

- Visit the Plugin tutorial, `https://wiki.jenkins.io/display/JENKINS/Plugin+tutorial` for more details.

Uploading plugins in Jenkins

There will be instances where you have all the plugins downloaded from `https://updates.jenkins-ci.org/download/plugins/`, or you may create your own plugin and you want to utilize that in Jenkins. This recipe will explain how to upload these plugins in Jenkins.

Getting ready

Download the required plugin `https://updates.jenkins-ci.org/download/plugins/` or create a plugin using the Plugin tutorial, `https://wiki.jenkins.io/display/JENKINS/Plugin+tutorial`.

How to do it...

For this recipe, we will download a plugin and upload it from the Jenkins dashboard:

1. Download the **copyartifact/** plugin (`.hpi`) file:

2. Download the latest version to your system:

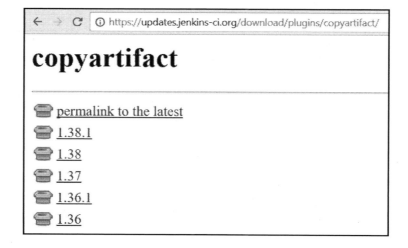

3. Go to the Jenkins dashboard.
4. Click on **Manage Jenkins**.
5. Click on **Manage plugins**.
6. Go to the **Advanced** tab. Click on **Choose File** in the **Upload Plugin** section:

7. Click on **Upload**.

How it works...

Once a plugin is uploaded successfully, we can utilize extensibility provided by the plugin that is uploaded into Jenkins.

Configuring proxy in Jenkins

Jenkins is often installed in organizations behind the proxy server. In such scenarios, it is important to configure a proxy in the Jenkins dashboard so plugin updates can be installed successfully.

Getting ready

Get all the details related to the server name, port number, and credentials that are allowed to access the proxy server.

How to do it...

1. Go to the Jenkins dashboard.
2. Click on **Manage Jenkins**.
3. Click on **Manage plugins**.
4. Go to the **Advanced** tab.
5. Provide **Server**, **Port**, **User name**, **Password**, and **No Proxy Host**:

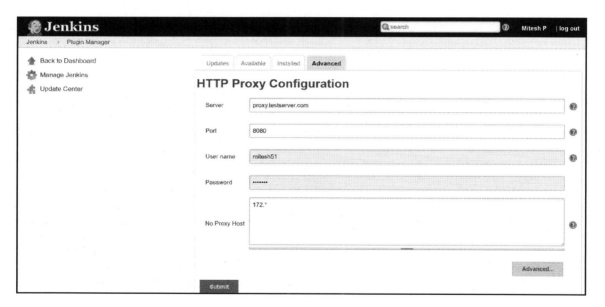

6. Click on **Submit**.

Configuring global settings in Jenkins

Configure system is the place where initial settings can be done, and it is useful. You can configure SMTP server details, SonarQube server details, environment variables, and so on.

Getting ready

To configure global settings and paths, we need to go to **Configure System** in the Jenkins dashboard.

How to do it...

1. Go to the Jenkins dashboard.
2. Click on **Manage Jenkins**.
3. Click on **Configure System**.
4. Verify the **Home directory** available:

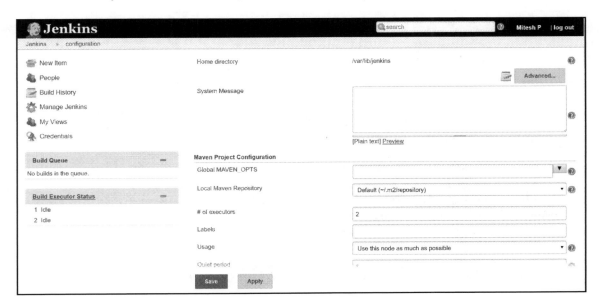

5. In the **Configure System** page, we can define **Environment variables** too so that it can be used during the execution of build jobs.

6. For example, we can configure the ANDROID SDK path in **Environment variables** in order to set Continuous Integration for Android Apps.

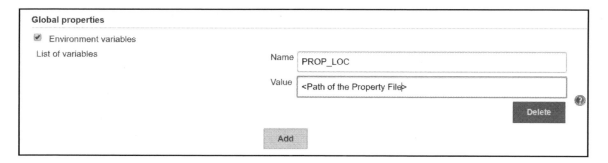

7. Another important configuration available on the same page is **Jenkins Location**. You can specify the HTTP address of the Jenkins installation, as Jenkins cannot reliably detect such a **Jenkins URL** from within itself:

There's more...

There are some important configurations that you need to do here in the **Configure System** section, such as **SCM Polling, E-mail Notification, Extended E-mail Notification, Git plugin, Disk usage, Quality Gates - SonarQube, Build Pipeline Plugin, Copyartifact: Upstream build that triggered this job, Audit Trail, SonarQube servers**, and so on.

Configuring JENKINS_HOME

The .jenkins is the main directory that contains all the details for Jenkins installation files, configurations, plugins, build job configuration, and so on.

Getting ready

It is important to keep the `.jenkins` directory at a location where a good amount of free space is available. By default, Jenkins creates `.jenkins` (or `JENKINS_HOME`) at a specific location considering the operating systems.

For example, in Windows it is available at `C:\Users\<USER_NAME>\.jenkins`.

How to do it...

1. In Windows, to change to `JENKINS_HOME`, go to the **Control Panel** | **All Control Panel Items** | **System**.
2. Click on **Advanced System Settings**.
3. Click on **Environment Variables**.
4. Create a new variable **JENKINS_HOME** and give the path:

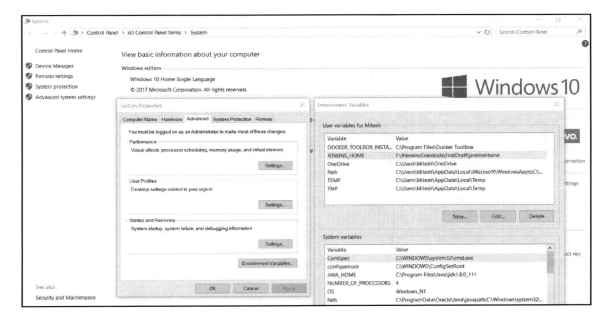

5. In Ubuntu, go to `/etc/default/Jenkins`.

6. Change the `JENKINS_HOME` location:

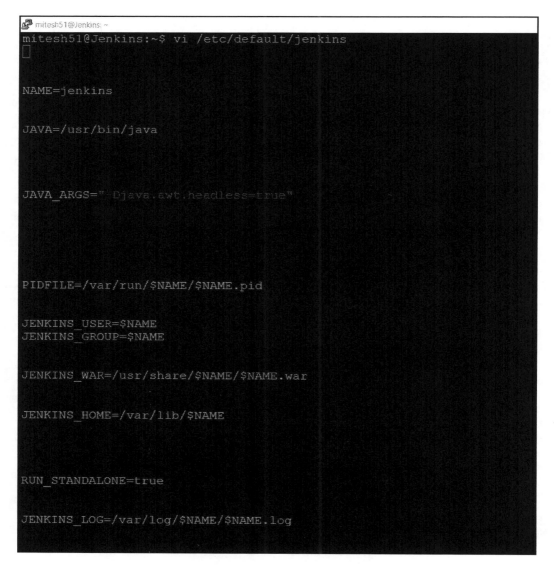

```
mitesh51@Jenkins: ~
mitesh51@Jenkins:~$ vi /etc/default/jenkins


NAME=jenkins

JAVA=/usr/bin/java



JAVA_ARGS=" Djava.awt.headless=true"




PIDFILE=/var/run/$NAME/$NAME.pid

JENKINS_USER=$NAME
JENKINS_GROUP=$NAME

JENKINS_WAR=/usr/share/$NAME/$NAME.war

JENKINS_HOME=/var/lib/$NAME


RUN_STANDALONE=true

JENKINS_LOG=/var/log/$NAME/$NAME.log
```

7. Once changes are done, save the changes.

How it works...

Once JENKINS_HOME is changed, you need to restart Jenkins. The next time Jenkins starts, it will take JENKINS_HOME as the location that you have configured.

There's more...

The following table describes the default location of JENKINS_HOME in different operating systems:

Operating system	$JENKINS_HOME location
Windows	C:\Program Files (x86)\jenkins or C:\Users\<USER>\.jenkins
Mac OSX	Macintosh HD/Users/Shared/Jenkins
Ubuntu/Debian	/var/lib/jenkins
Red Hat/CentOS/Fedora	/var/lib/jenkins
OpenSUSE	/var/lib/jenkins
FreeBSD	/usr/local/etc/jenkins
OpenBSD	/usr/local/etc/jenkins

Understanding JENKINS_HOME directory

In this recipe, we will discuss the directories available in the JENKINS_HOME directory.

Getting ready

Locate the JENKINS_HOME directory from the **Environment Variables,** or go to the default locations where JENKINS_HOME is available in different operating systems.

How to do it...

1. You have many files and directories in the JENKINS_HOME directory. We will give brief information on some important files and directories:

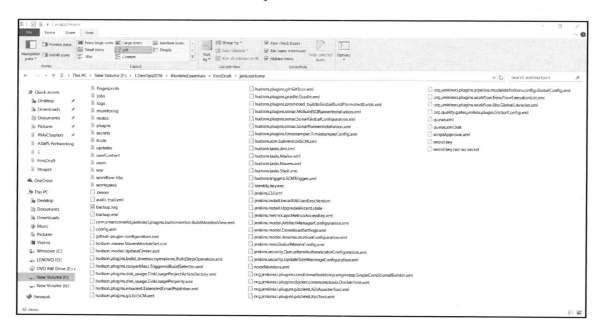

2. The following are some important files and directories in the JENKINS_HOME directory:

config.xml	Jenkins root configuration file
fingerprints	It stores fingerprint records, if any
plugins	It is a root directory for all Jenkins plugins
jobs	It is a root directory for all Jenkins jobs
logs	It stores all log files
secrets	It is a root directory for the secret + key for credential decryption
users	It stores all user-related details in Jenkins
war	It stores all details related to the JENKINS_WAR file

workspace	It stores all the files and artifacts related to different build jobs, and it moves content to jobs directory when archiving elements.

See also

In the JENKINS_HOME directory, open config.xml in any of the text editors and review the options available in the file.

Using different ports for Jenkins

By default, Jenkins runs on port number 8080.

Getting ready

There are scenarios where Tomcat is running on 8080, or any other application is running on 8080 port. In such cases, to avoid port conflicts you need to change the Jenkins port.

How to do it...

Let's change a port on which Jenkins runs:

1. If you run Jenkins using the command line, then you can execute a command such as java -jar -httpPort=9999 jenkins.war to change the existing port from 8080 to 9999.

2. Another way to change the port while Jenkins is installed using the Windows package is as follows:

   - Go to the Program Files/Jenkins directory where you installed Jenkins
   - Open the Jenkins.xml in the editor
   - Find "--httpPort=8080" and replace the port 8080 with the new port number

How it works...

First, you installed a virtual image of Ubuntu, changed the password so that it is harder for others to log in, and updated the guest OS for security patches.

Configuring JAVA_HOME in Jenkins

Jenkins is an open source automation server that can be used to configure Continuous Integration for projects written in many programming languages. Let's consider the case of an application that is Java-based.

We need to tell Jenkins where Java is installed.

Getting ready

Download the required Java version based on the requirements of an application, or install automatically.

How to do it...

1. Open the Jenkins dashboard.
2. Go to **Manage Jenkins**.
3. Go to **Global Tool Configuration** to configure tools, their locations, and automatic installers.
4. Go to the **JDK** section.
5. Give the **Name** and tick the **Install automatically** option; provide details for the Oracle account to download JDK successfully.
6. You can give a logical name such as JDK 1.7 or JDK 1.8 to identify the correct version while configuring a build job.
7. You can add multiple JDKs based on the version, so if different applications require different JDKs then the scenario can be managed easily by adding JDK in Jenkins:

How it works...

When you create a build job in Jenkins and configure it, you need to specify the Java version that will be used by the build execution. You can use existing Java available on the system as well if you don't want to install automatically.

In the general section of the build job, we can select a JDK from the list. This list contains all the JDKs that we have configured in the **Global Tool Configuration**.

Configuring Git in Jenkins

Jenkins can be integrated with many source code repositories, and Git is one of them. Let's consider the case of an application that is Java-based and the source code is stored in Git, Gitlab, and/or GitHub.

We need to tell Jenkins where Git is installed in the local system.

Getting ready

Download the required Git version based on the operating system, or install automatically.

How to do it...

1. Open the Jenkins dashboard.
2. Go to **Manage Jenkins**.
3. Go to **Global Tool Configuration** to configure the tools, their locations, and automatic installers.
4. Go to the **Git** section.
5. Give the **Name** and click on **Install Automatically**, or provide a path to Git.
6. You can add multiple Gits based on the version or for the specific agent. You need to give a meaningful name so it can be identified easily while configuring the build job:

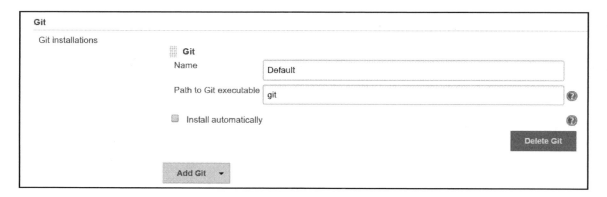

How it works...

When you create a build job in Jenkins and configure it, you need to specify the Git version that will be used by the build execution. You can use existing Git installation available on the system as well if you don't want to install automatically.

In the **Source Code Management** section, select the appropriate Git that is configured in **Global Tool Configuration** from the list.

Go to the Git executable configuration to change the Git installable.

Configuring ANT_HOME in Jenkins

Jenkins is an open source automation server that can be using to configure Continuous Integration for projects written in many programming languages. Let's consider the case of an application that is Java-based, and which has Ant as a build tool.

We need to tell Jenkins where the Ant installable directory is available.

Getting ready

Download the required Ant version or install automatically.

How to do it...

1. Open the Jenkins dashboard.
2. Go to **Manage Jenkins**.
3. Go to **Global Tool Configuration** to configure the tools, their locations, and automatic installers.
4. Go to the **Ant** section.
5. Give the **Name** and click on **Install Automatically**, or give the path to an existing location where the Ant installation is available.
6. You can give a logical name such as ANT 1.10.1 or ANT 1.9.1 to identify the correct version while configuring a build job.
7. You can add multiple Ants based on the version in Jenkins:

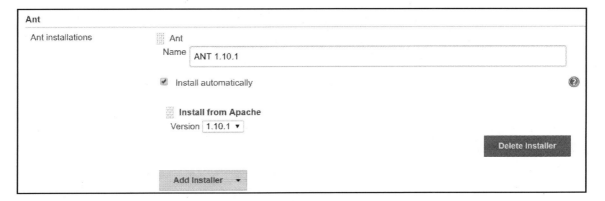

How it works...

When you create a build job in Jenkins and configure it, you need to specify the Ant version that will be used by the build execution. You can use existing Ant installation available on the system as well if you don't want to install automatically.

Configuring MAVEN_HOME in Jenkins

Jenkins is an open source automation server that can be using to configure Continuous Integration for rojects written in many programming languages. Let's consider the case of an application that is Java-based and, which has Maven as a build tool.

We need to tell Jenkins where the Maven installable directory is available.

Getting ready

Download the required Maven version or install automatically.

How to do it...

1. Open the Jenkins dashboard.
2. Go to **Manage Jenkins**.
3. Go to **Global Tool Configuration** to configure the tools, their locations, and automatic installers.
4. Go to the Maven section.
5. Give the **Name** and click on **Install Automatically**, or give the path to the existing location where the Maven installation is available.
6. You can give a logical name such as `Maven 3.5.0` or `Maven 3.4.0` to identify the correct version while configuring a build job:

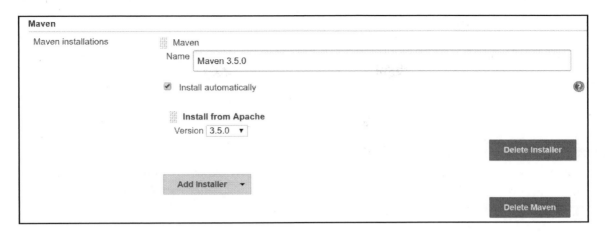

7. You can add multiple Mavens based on the version in Jenkins.

How it works...

When you create a build job in Jenkins and configure it, you need to specify the Maven version that will be used by the build execution. You can use existing Maven installation available on the system as well if you don't want to install automatically.

Configuring GRADLE_HOME in Jenkins

Jenkins is an open source automation server that can be using to configure Continuous Integration for projects written in many programming languages. Let's consider the case of an application that is Android-based, and which has Gradle as a build tool.

We need to tell Jenkins where the Gradle installable directory is available.

Getting ready

Download the required Gradle version or install automatically.

How to do it...

1. Open the Jenkins dashboard.
2. Go to **Manage Jenkins**.
3. Go to **Global Tool Configuration** to configure the tools, their locations, and automatic installers.
4. Go to the **Gradle** section.
5. Give the **Name** and click on **Install Automatically**,
   or give the path to the existing location where the Gradle installation is available.
6. You can give a logical name such as `Gradle 4.0.1` or `Gradle 4.0.0` to identify the correct version while configuring a build job:

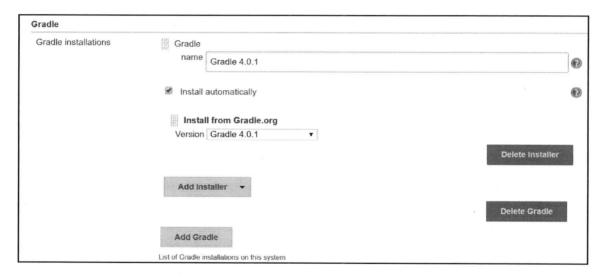

7. You can add multiple Gradles based on the version in Jenkins.

How it works...

When you create a build job in Jenkins and configure it, you need to specify the Gradle version that will be used by the build execution. You can use existing Gradle installation available on the system as well if you don't want to install automatically.

Creating a Freestyle job for Ant Project

A build job is a basic execution unit in Jenkins. We can perform many actions using build jobs. We can execute commands, send notifications, configure Continuous Integration, and so on.

Getting ready

You will need to configure tools based on the application, such as Ant, Gradle, Java, Git, and so on.

How to do it...

1. Open the Jenkins dashboard.
2. Click on **New Item**.
3. **Enter an item name**.
4. Select a template **Freestyle project**.
5. Click on **OK**:

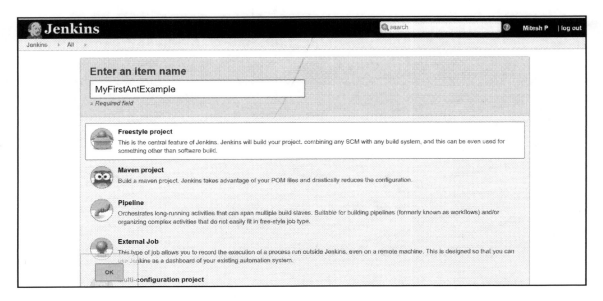

6. Go to the **Source Code Management** section and select **Git**.
7. Provide the **Repository URL**.
8. Provide **Credentials**, as demonstrated in the next screenshot:

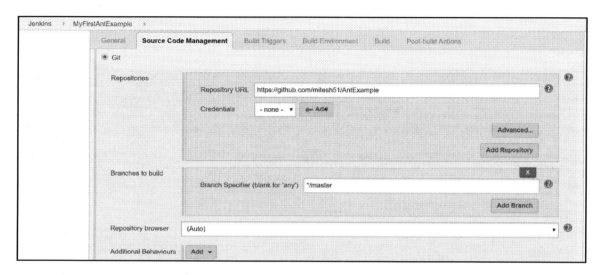

9. In the **Build** section, click on the **Add build step** and select **Invoke Ant**.
10. Select the Ant name based on our **Global Tool Configuration**.
11. Provide **Targets**. In Ant, we can give a target based on the targets defined in the `build.xml` file:

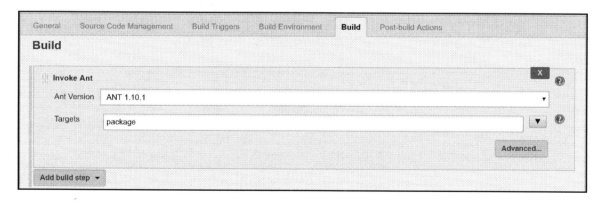

12. Click on **Save**.

How it works...

When you go to the Build Job page and click on **Build now**, it will execute the build based on the configuration.

Creating a Maven Job for Maven Project

A build job is a basic execution unit in Jenkins. We can perform many actions using build jobs. We can execute commands, send notifications, configure Continuous Integration, and so on.

Getting ready

You will need to configure the tools based on the application, such as Maven, Java, Git, and so on.

How to do it...

1. Open the Jenkins dashboard.
2. Click on **New Item**.
3. **Enter an item name**.
4. Select a template **Maven project**.

5. Click on **OK**:

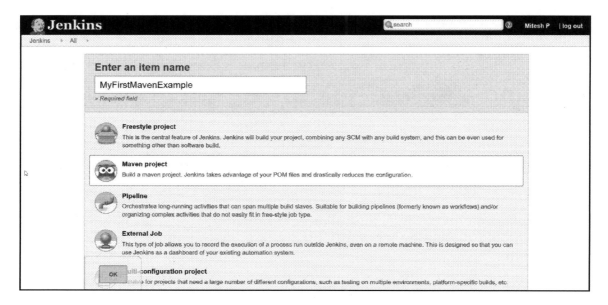

6. Go to the **Source Code Management** section and select **Git**.
7. Provide the **Repository URL**.
8. Provide **Credentials**.
9. In the **Build** section, the **Root POM** name will be already available.
10. Maven has its own set of goals and we can execute any one of those goals based on requirements. These steps are demonstrated in this next screenshot:

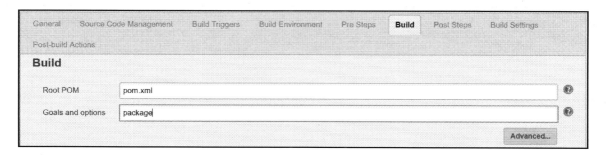

11. Click on **Save**.

How it works...

When you go to the Build Job page and click on **Build now**, it will execute the build based on the configuration.

2
Management and Monitoring of Jenkins

In this chapter, we will cover the following recipes:

- Understanding master/agent architecture
- Managing Jenkins Build jobs using Eclipse
- Backing up and restoring Jenkins
- Command line options in Jenkins using Jenkins CLI
- Modifying the Jenkins configuration from the command line
- Managing disk usage
- Shutting down Jenkins safely
- Monitoring Jenkins with JavaMelody
- Monitoring Jenkins job using Build Monitor View
- Configuring mail notifications
- Signaling the need to archive

Understanding master/agent architecture

Jenkins supports the master/agent architecture. In master/agent architecture, we can install Jenkins on master and then utilize other agents for distributing the load.

We shoulddelegate Jenkins jobs to agents for execution. This way, we can support multiple executions using different resources.

There are specific scenarios where master/agent architecture is extremely useful, such as following:

- The Jenkins machine has limited capacity; even with the higher capacity, there will be a time where it can't fulfil all requests. By distributing the load on agent nodes, we can free resources available on the system where Jenkins is installed.
- Different jobs require different kinds of resources, and they are restricted to specific machines only. In such a case, we can only utilize that machine and it is not possible to configure it on a system where Jenkins is installed, so it's often better to utilize that machine as an agent.
- Different operating systems are required or some tools work only in specific OS, so we can utilize those tools by making a system agent on which they are installed.
- To avoid a single point of failure by installing each and every tool on the Jenkins machine.

Murphy as a friend:

You should assume the worst for all of the recipes in this book: aliens attacking, coffee on the motherboard, cats eating your cable, the cable eating the cat, and so on. Make sure that you are using a test Jenkins instance.

Getting ready

The important thing here is we don't install Jenkins on any agent nodes at all. We only install Jenkins on master and utilize that Jenkins for orchestrating master/agent architecture.

Just to note: on whichever system we install Jenkins, it becomes the master. Just verify that by navigating to **Manage Jenkins** | **Manage Nodes**.

1. Navigate to **Manage Jenkins | Manage Nodes** and click on **New Node**:

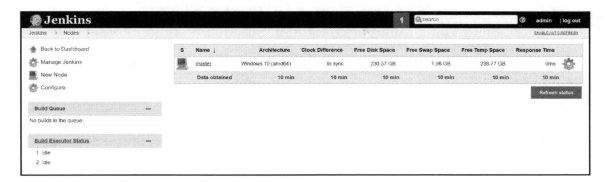

2. Give the **Node name** and select **Permanent Agent**; click **OK**:

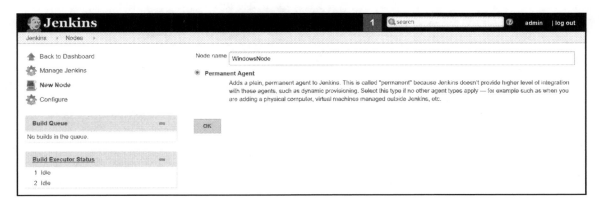

How to do it...

1. Jenkins stable and more recent versions are available in a YUM repository. Following is a table that provides details for configuration of Agents:

# of executors	• Here, we can specify the number of concurrent builds that Jenkins may execute on this agent node. • Agents must have at least one executor, and in case we don't want any execution, then we can configure this setting as 0.

Remote root directory	• An agent node requires us to have a directory dedicated to Jenkins. Specify the path to this directory on the agent. • Use an absolute path only. All job configurations, build logs, and artifacts are stored on the master. • Workspace is available on the agent node.
Labels	• Labels or tags can be utilized to group multiple agent nodes into a logical collection. • The best thing is that we can use this mechanism as a pool of resources to execute build jobs in Jenkins. • For example, we have multiple agents where a test infrastructure is set up. We have two or three projects whose automated testing is done by the QA team. • In such a scenario, we can provide the same `Test` label or tag it to all agent nodes where the test infrastructure is available and then assign the same `Test` label to those projects. • What this does is execute the build jobs on any one of the Test agents with the `Test` label and not without it.
Usage	• This setting controls how Jenkins schedules builds on specific agent nodes. • Use this node as much as possible: This is the default setting where, most of the time, the `Agent` node will be utilized for job execution. • `Only build jobs with label expressions matching this node`: with this setting, Jenkins will execute a build on this agent node when the project is configured to execute on this node with a label expression.
Launch method	• This setting controls how Jenkins starts a specific agent node. • **Launch agent via Java Web Start**: Allows an agent to be launched using Java Web Start. • Launch agent via execution of command on the master by remotely executing a process on another machine, for example, via SSH or RSH. • Launch slave agents via SSH by sending commands over a secure SSH connection. • Let Jenkins control this Windows slave as a Windows service, as it starts a Windows slave with a remote management facility built into Windows.

Availability	• This setting controls when Jenkins starts and stops this agent. • Keep this agent online as much as possible. • Take this agent online and offline at specific times. • Take this agent online when in demand, and offline when idle.
Environment variables	• We can define agent node-specific environment variables here.
Tool locations	• We can define agent node-specific tool locations here.

2. Configure the settings and click on **Save**:

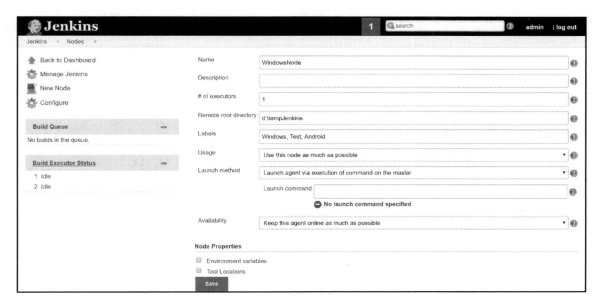

3. We can see the newly created agent in the node list as disconnected. Click on it:

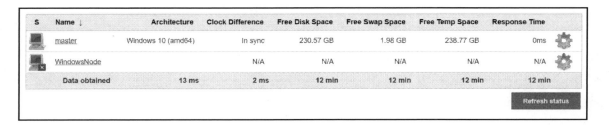

4. See the details available on the agent page. We are not able to start it:

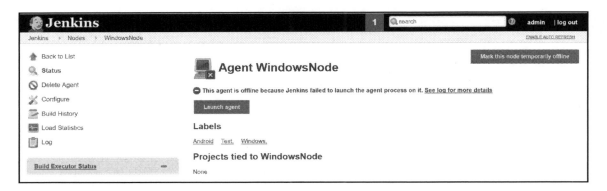

5. Go to **Manage Jenkins** | **Configure Global Security** | **Enable security**. In the **TCP port for the JNLP agents** setting, select **Random**:

6. Click on **Save**:

7. Go to the agent node again and execute the given command from the agent node's terminal or command line and then it should be connected:

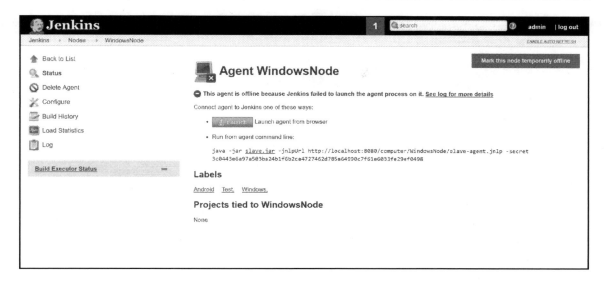

8. To configure a job to a specific node, go to the build job and click on **Configure**.
9. In the **General** section, select **Restrict where this project can be run** and provide the label of the agent node that we have created:

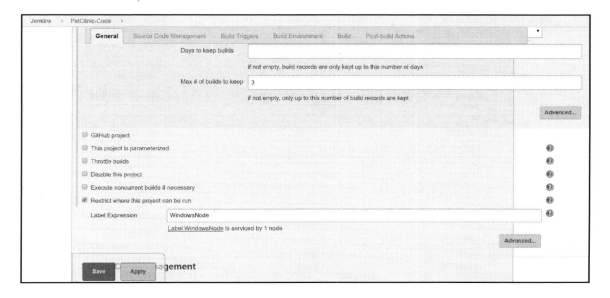

10. Go to **Manage Nodes** and select the agent node to verify the build job associated with it:

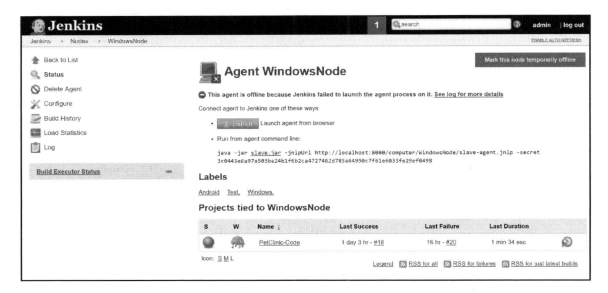

11. This is how we can create a master/agent architecture and distribute the load across agents with only one master available.

Managing Jenkins build jobs using Eclipse

Can we execute a Jenkins job from Eclipse? Yes we can! So, let's see how to do that.

Getting ready

1. Go to **Help** | **Install New Software...**:

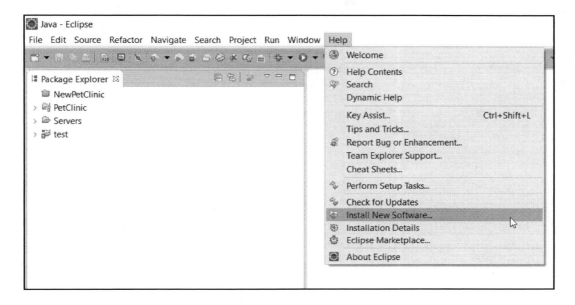

2. Add a site for **Mylyn** and click on **Next >**:

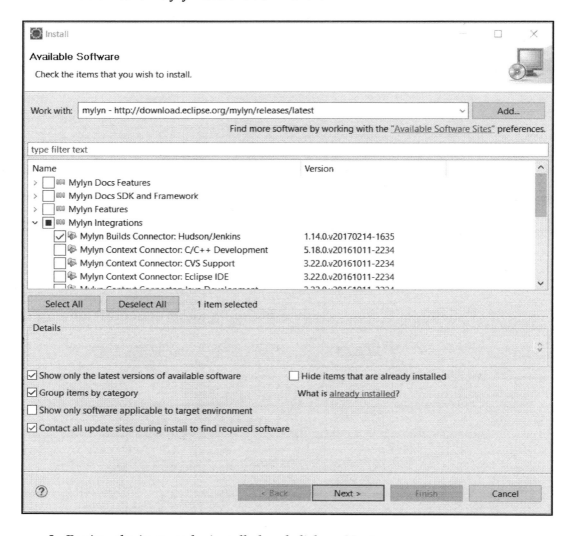

3. Review the items to be installed and click on **Next >**.
4. Accept the terms of the license agreement and then click on **Finish**. It will start installing the Mylyn package.
5. Once it is finished, **Restart Eclipse**.

How to do it...

Let's see how to trigger a Jenkins build from Eclipse.

1. In the Windows menu, click on **Views**.
2. Select **Mylyn** and click on **Builds**. Then, click **OK**:

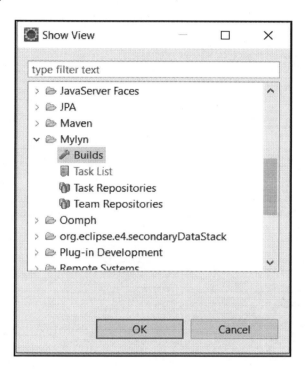

3. In the **Builds** section, click on the build server link:

Eclipse in Java View

4. Select **Hudson (supports Jenkins)** and click on **Next >**:

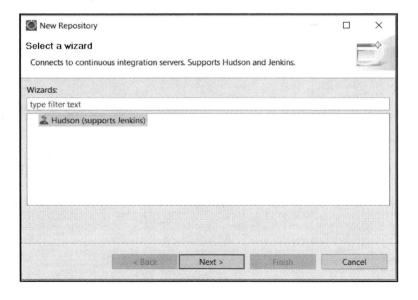

5. Provide the **Server** details. Provide the **User** and **Password**. Then, click **Finish**:

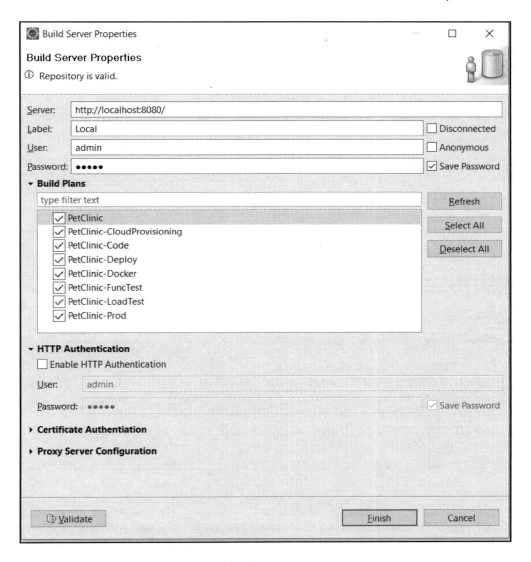

6. Find the list of jobs in the **Build** section, shown as follows. Select any job and click on **Run Build** to execute it from Eclipse:

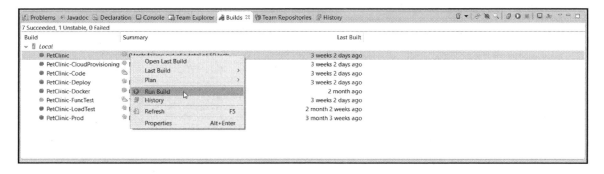

7. Try other options as an exercise.

Backing up and restoring Jenkins

A core task for the smooth running of Jenkins is the scheduled backing up of its home directory. This is not necessarily all the artifacts, but is at least its configuration and the history of testing, which plugins will need to make reports.

Backups are not interesting unless you can also restore. There is a wide range of stories on this subject. My favorite (and I won't name the well-known company involved) is that, sometime in the early 70's, a company bought a very expensive piece of software and a tape backup facility to back up all the marketing results being harvested through their mainframes. However, not everything was automated. Every night, a tape needed to be moved into a specific slot. A poorly paid worker was allocated the task. For a year, the worker would professionally fulfill the task. One day, a failure occurred and a backup was required. The backup failed to restore. The reason was that the worker also needed to press the record button every night, but this was not mentioned in the tasks assigned to him. There was a failure to regularly test the restore process. The process failed, not the poorly paid person. Hence, through learning lessons from history, this recipe describes both backup and restore.

The rapid evolution of plugins and the validity of recipes:

Plugins improve aggressively and you may need to update them weekly. Although it is unlikely that the core configuration will change, it is quite likely that extra options will be added, increasing the variables that you input in the GUI. Therefore, the screenshots shown in this book may be slightly different from the most modern version, but the recipes should remain intact.

Getting ready

Let's now install the all-important plugins required for the following sections at once:

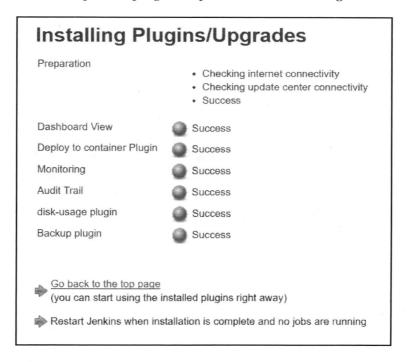

The backup plugin allows us to back up **JENKINS_HOME** and restore it.

How to do it...

1. Go to **Manage Jenkins** and click on **Backup Manager**:

 Disk Usage
Displays per-project disk usage

 Manage Users
Create/delete/modify users that can log in to this Jenkins

 In-process Script Approval
Allows a Jenkins administrator to review proposed scripts (written e.g. in Groovy) which run inside the Jenkins process and so could bypass security restrictions.

 Backup manager
Backup or Restore Jenkins configuration files

 Monitoring of Jenkins master
Monitoring of memory, cpu, http requests and more in Jenkins master.
You can also view the monitoring of Jenkins nodes.

 Prepare for Shutdown
Stops executing new builds, so that the system can be eventually shut down safely.

2. Click on **Setup**:

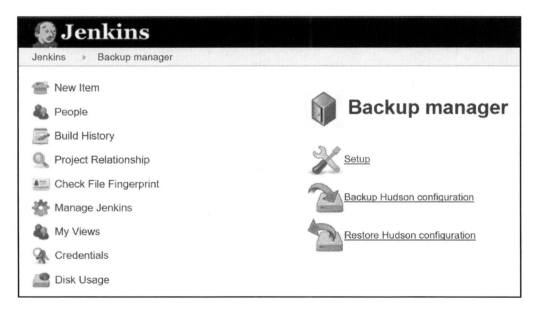

3. Configure the **Backup directory, Format, File name template,** and so on:

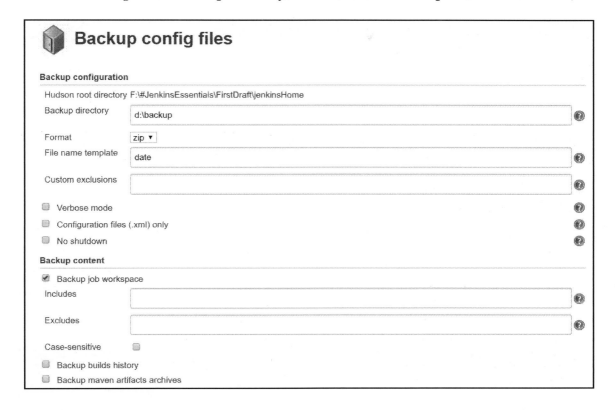

4. Click on the **Backup Hudson configuration**:

5. Once the backup is completed successfully, verify the logs:

```
                          Jenkins is going to shut down

[ INFO] Backup started at [05/27/17 15:01:27]
[ INFO] Setting hudson in shutdown mode to avoid files corruptions.
[ INFO] Waiting all jobs end...
[ INFO] Number of running jobs detected : 0
[ INFO] All jobs finished.
[ INFO] Full backup file name : d:\backup\YYYYDDMM_hhmm
[ INFO] Saved files : 12482
[ INFO] Number of errors : 0
[ INFO] Cancel hudson shutdown mode
[ INFO] Backup end at [05/27/17 15:03:51]
[ INFO] [143.935s]
```

6. Go to **Backup Manager** and click on **Restore Hudson configuration**:

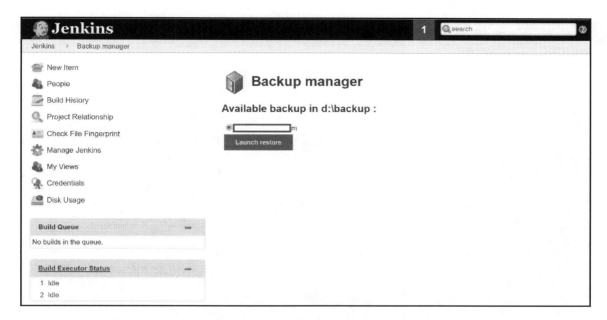

See also

Currently, there is more than one plugin for backups. I have chosen the `thinBackup` plugin (`https://wiki.jenkins-ci.org/display/JENKINS/thinBackup`), as it allows scheduling.

Command-line options in Jenkins using Jenkins CLI

You can access various features in Jenkins through a command-line tool.

Getting ready

Download the `Jenkins-cli.jar` file from the link available on the Jenkins dashboard.

How to do it...

1. Go to the location where `Jenkins-cli.jar` is downloaded and execute the `java -jar jenkins-cli.jar -s http://localhost:8080/ help` command to see the help of CLI commands:

```
Command Prompt                                              —    □    ×
C:\Users\Mitesh\Downloads>java -jar jenkins-cli.jar -s http://localhost:8080/ help
 add-job-to-view
   Adds jobs to view.
 build
   Builds a job, and optionally waits until its completion.
 cancel-quiet-down
   Cancel the effect of the "quiet-down" command.
 clear-queue
   Clears the build queue.
 connect-node
   Reconnect to a node(s)
 console
   Retrieves console output of a build.
 copy-job
   Copies a job.
 create-credentials-by-xml
   Create Credential by XML
 create-credentials-domain-by-xml
   Create Credentials Domain by XML
 create-job
   Creates a new job by reading stdin as a configuration XML file.
 create-node
   Creates a new node by reading stdin as a XML configuration.
 create-view
   Creates a new view by reading stdin as a XML configuration.
 declarative-linter
   Validate a Jenkinsfile containing a Declarative Pipeline
 delete-builds
   Deletes build record(s).
 delete-credentials
   Delete a Credential
 delete-credentials-domain
   Delete a Credentials Domain
 delete-job
   Deletes job(s).
 delete-node
   Deletes node(s)
 delete-view
   Deletes view(s).
```

2. Execute the following commands:

```
java -jar jenkins-cli.jar -s http://localhost:8080/ version
java -jar jenkins-cli.jar -s http://localhost:8080/ who-am-i
java -jar jenkins-cli.jar -s http://localhost:8080/ list-jobs
```

3. Verify the output, shown as follows:

```
Command Prompt                                          —   □   ×

C:\Users\Mitesh\Downloads>java -jar jenkins-cli.jar -s http://localhost:8080/ version
2.73

C:\Users\Mitesh\Downloads>java -jar jenkins-cli.jar -s http://localhost:8080/ who-am-i
Authenticated as: anonymous
Authorities:
  anonymous

C:\Users\Mitesh\Downloads>java -jar jenkins-cli.jar -s http://localhost:8080/ list-jobs

AzureAppDeploy
CucumberProject
CucumberProject2
FirstAndroidProject
FirstAntExample
FirstJob
FirstPipeline
Main-PetClinic
Maven-Sample
mitesh51
PetClinic-Code
PetClinic-Deploy
PetClinic-FuncTest
PetClinic-LoadTest
PetClinic-Package
PetClinic-Prod
PetClinicWebHook
SonarHTMLCSSJS
SpringBoot
Test
TestPipeline
ZapTest
ZapTestBackup

C:\Users\Mitesh\Downloads>
```

4. Try other commands yourself.

Modifying the Jenkins configuration from the command line

You may well be wondering about the XML files at the top level of the Jenkins workspace. These are configuration files. The `config.xml` file is the main one that deals with the default server values, but there are also specific ones for any plugins that have values set through the GUI.

There is also a `jobs` subdirectory underneath the workspace. Each individual job configuration is contained in a subdirectory with the same name as the job. The job-specific configuration is then stored in `config.xml` within the subdirectory. It's a similar situation for the `users` directory: there is one subdirectory per user, with the personal information stored in `config.xml`.

Under a controlled situation where all the Jenkins servers in your infrastructure have the same plugins and version levels, it is possible for you to test on one test machine and then push the configuration files to all the other machines. You can then restart the Jenkins servers with the **command-line interface (CLI)**.

This recipe familiarizes you with the main XML configuration structure and then provides hints about the plugin API based on the details of the XML.

Getting ready

You will need a Jenkins server with security enabled and the ability to edit files, either by logging in and working from the command line or through editing with a text editor.

How to do it...

Let's see how to modify the Jenkins configuration.

1. In the top-level directory of Jenkins, look for the `config.xml` file. Edit the line with `numExecutors`, changing the number 2 to 3:

   ```
   <numExecutors>3</numExecutors>
   ```

2. Restart the server. You will see that the number of executors has increased from the default two to three.

3. Plugins persist their configuration through XML files. To prove this point, look for the `thinBackup.xml` file. You will not find it unless you have installed the `thinBackup` plugin.

How it works...

Jenkins uses **XStream** (`http://xstream.codehaus.org/`) to persist its configuration into a readable XML format. The XML files in the workspace are configuration files for plugins, tasks, and an assortment of other persisted information. The `config.xml` file is the main configuration file. Security settings and global configuration are set here and reflect changes made through the GUI. Plugins use the same structure and the XML values correspond to member values in the underlying plugin classes. The GUI itself is created from XML via the Jelly framework (`http://commons.apache.org/jelly/`).

By restarting the server, you are certain that any configuration changes are picked up during the initialization phase.

 It is also possible to use **Reload configuration** from a storage feature from the **Manage Jenkins** page, and to load an updated configuration without restarting.

Managing disk usage

Jenkins stores multiple jobs and the multiple builds created are stored on the machine. It is important to keep track of disk usage, as, over time, builds from multiple projects will take up a lot of space.

Getting ready

Go to **Dashboard | Manage Jenkins | Manage Plugins | Available | Install Disk Usage plugin**.

How to do it...

This plugin gives details on disk usage on the system where Jenkins is installed.

1. Go to **Dashboard** | **Manage Jenkins** | **Disk Usage**:

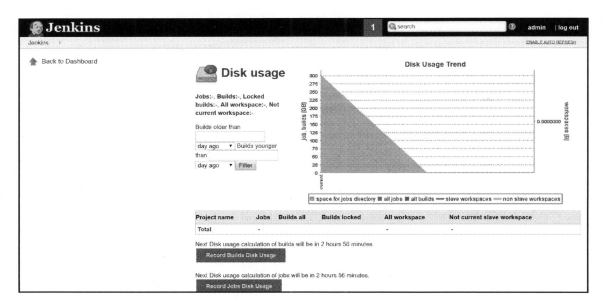

2. Go to **Manage Jenkins** and click on **Configure System**. Go to the **Disk usage** section and click on **Show disk usage trend graph on the project page**:

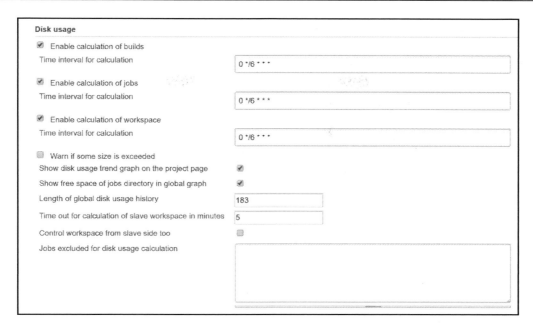

3. Go to a specific project and verify whether the **Disk Usage Trend** chart is available or not:

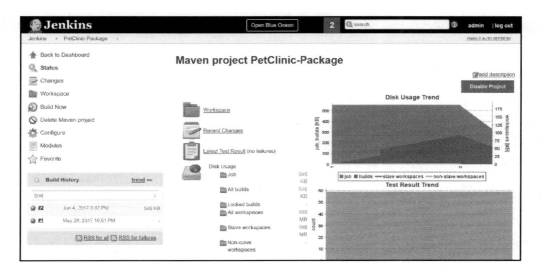

4. In the next recipe, we will try to modify the build status using log parsing.

See also

To start the Jenkins service, execute:

```
sudo service jenkins start
```

Shutdown Jenkins safely

Is it possible to stop executing new builds so that the system can eventually be shut down safely? Let's find out in the following recipe.

Getting ready

You need to have administrative access to Jenkins.

How to do it...

1. Go to the Jenkins dashboard, then **Manage Jenkins Prepare for Shutdown**:

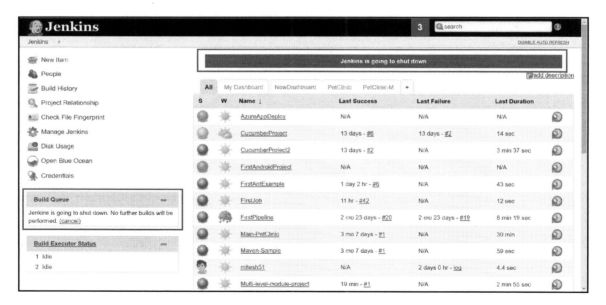

2. Go to the Jenkins dashboard again, then **Manage Jenkins** to **Cancel Shutdown**:

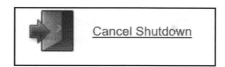

Monitoring Jenkins with JavaMelody

JavaMelody (`http://code.google.com/p/javamelody/`) is an open source project that provides comprehensive monitoring. The Jenkins plugin monitors both the master instance of Jenkins and also its nodes. The plugin provides a detailed wealth of important information. You can view evolution charts ranging from 1 day or 1 week to months for the main quantities, such as CPU or memory. Evolution charts are very good at pinpointing scheduled jobs that are resource-hungry.

The `Monitoring` plugin provides the monitoring of Jenkins with JavaMelody. It provides charts for CPU, memory, system load average, HTTP response time, and so on. It also provides details of HTTP sessions, errors and logs, actions for garbage collection, heap dumps, invalid session(s), and so on.

Getting ready

Install the **Monitoring** plugin from the Jenkins dashboard:

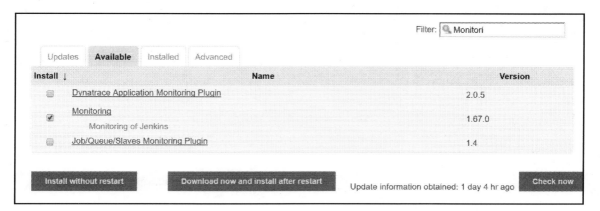

How to do it...

1. On the Jenkins dashboard, click on **Manage Jenkins**. Click on **Monitoring of Jenkins master,** as shown in the following screenshot:

Jenkins CLI
Access/manage Jenkins from your shell, or from your script.

Script Console
Executes arbitrary script for administration/trouble-shooting/diagnostics.

Manage Nodes
Add, remove, control and monitor the various nodes that Jenkins runs jobs on.

About Jenkins
See the version and license information.

Manage Old Data
Scrub configuration files to remove remnants from old plugins and earlier versions.

Install as Windows Service
Installs Jenkins as a Windows service to this system, so that Jenkins starts automatically when the machine boots.

Manage Users
Create/delete/modify users that can log in to this Jenkins

In-process Script Approval
Allows a Jenkins administrator to review proposed scripts (written e.g. in Groovy) which run inside the Jenkins process and so could bypass security restrictions.

Monitoring of Jenkins master
Monitoring of memory, cpu, http requests and more in Jenkins master.
You can also view the monitoring of Jenkins nodes.

Prepare for Shutdown
Stops executing new builds, so that the system can be eventually shut down safely.

2. It will open the statistics of JavaMelody monitoring, as shown in the following screenshot. Observe all of the statistics:

---
[84]

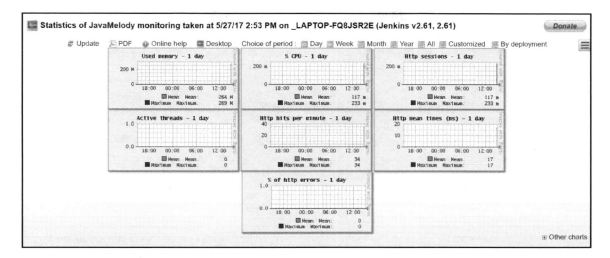

3. Click on **Other charts** and observe the other details related to **Garbage Collector time**, **Threads count**, and so on:

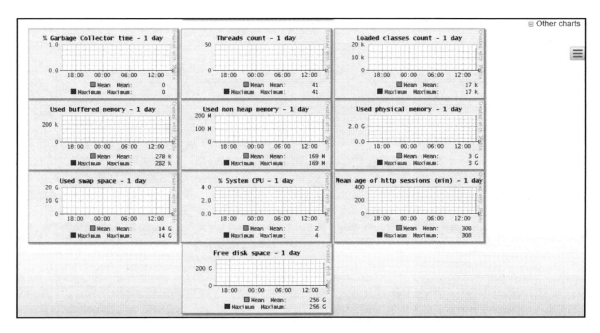

Java Melody with Garbage Collector and Thread Count

4. Scroll down the page and find **Statistics system error logs**. To get more information, click on the **Details** link of any section. The statistics for HTTP are as shown in the following figure:

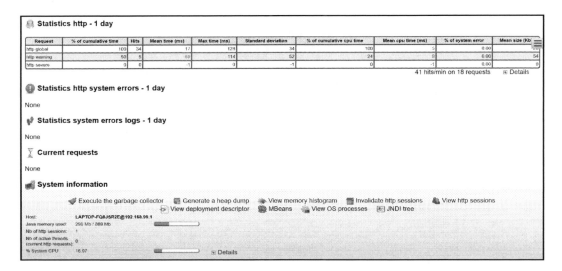

5. Verify that the details are available on the **Threads** as well:

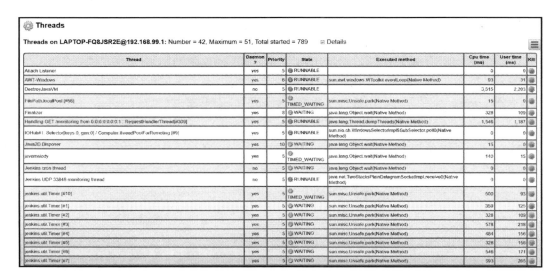

Java Melody - Threads

There's more...

Monitoring is the foundation of comprehensive testing and troubleshooting. This section explores the relationship between these issues and the measurements exposed in the plugin.

Troubleshooting with JavaMelody - memory

Your Jenkins server can at times have memory issues due to greedy builds, leaky plugins, or some hidden complexity in the infrastructure. JavaMelody has a comprehensive range of memory measurements, including a heap dump and a memory histogram.

The Java virtual machine divides memory into various areas and, to clean up, it removes objects that have no references to other objects. Garbage collection can be CPU-intensive when it is busy, and the nearer to consumption of full memory, the busier garbage collection becomes. To an external monitoring agent, this looks like a CPU spike that is often difficult to track down. Just because the garbage collector manages memory, it is also a fallacy to believe that there is no potential for memory leakage in Java. Memory can be held for too long by many common practices such as custom caches or calls to native libraries.

Slow burning memory leaks will show up as gentle slopes on memory-related evolution graphs. If you suspect that you have a memory leak, then you can get the plugin to force a full garbage collection through the **Execute the garbage collector** link. If it is not a memory leak, the gentle slope will abruptly fall.

Memory issues can also express themselves as large CPU spikes as the garbage collector franticly tries to clean up, but can barely clean enough space. The garbage collector can also pause the application while comprehensively looking for-no-longer referenced objects ("Stop the world garbage collection"), thus causing long response times for web browser requests. This can be seen through the **mean** and **max** times in **Statistics http - 1 day**.

Troubleshooting with JavaMelody - painful jobs

You should consider the following points:

- **Offload work**: For a stable infrastructure, offload as much work from the master instance as possible. If you have scheduled tasks, keep the heaviest ones separate in time. Time separation not only evens out load, but also makes finding the problematic build easier through the observation of the evolution charts of JavaMelody. Also consider spatial separation; if a given node or a labeled set of nodes shows problematic issues, then start switching around the machine location of jobs and view their individual performance characteristics through `http://host:port/monitoring/nodes`.

- **Hardware is cheap**: Compared to paying for human hours, buying an extra 8 GB is roughly equivalent to one man hour's effort.

 A common gotcha is to add memory to the server, while forgetting to update the init scripts to allow Jenkins to use more memory.

- **Review the build scripts**: Javadoc generation and custom Ant scripts can fork JVMs and reserve memory defined within their own configuration. Programming errors can also be the cause of frustration. Don't forget to review JavaMelody's report on **Statistic system error log** and **Statistic http system errors**.

- **Don't forget external factors**: Factors include backups, cron jobs, updating the locate database, and network maintenance. These will show up as periodic patterns in the evolution charts.

- **Strength in numbers**: Use JavaMelody in combination with the disk usage plugin and others to keep a comprehensive overview of the vital statistics. Each plugin is simple to configure, but their usefulness to you will grow more quickly than the maintenance costs of adding extra plugins.

Monitoring a Jenkins Job using a Build Monitor View

The `Build Monitor` plugin provides a visualization of the status and progress of selected Jenkins jobs. It displays an updated view automatically every couple of seconds using AJAX. It can easily accommodate different computer screen sizes too.

Getting ready

Go to **Manage Jenkins** | **Manage Plugins** | **Available** tab. Install the **Build Monitor View** plugin:

Go to the Jenkins dashboard.

How to do it...

1. Click on **New View**:

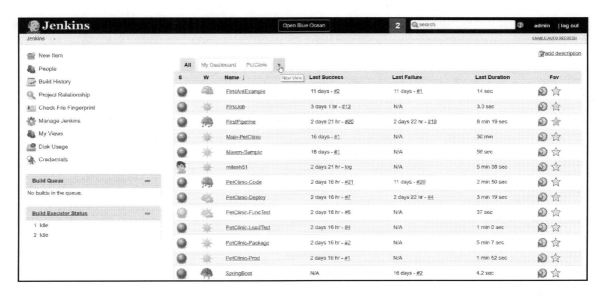

Jenkins Dashboard - Create New View

2. Provide **View name** and select **Build Monitor View**. Click **OK**:

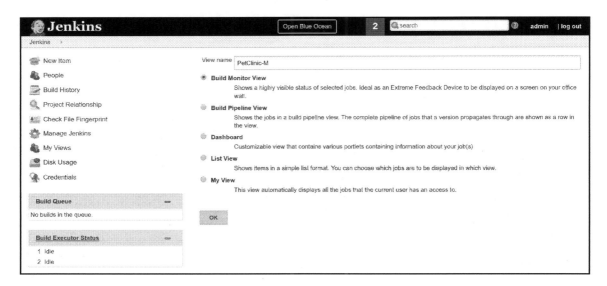

3. Select the jobs to be displayed in the newly created Build Monitor View. Click **Save**:

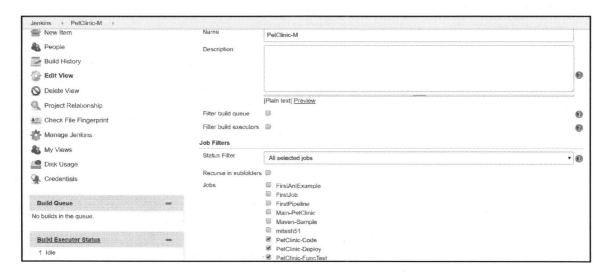

4. Verify the status of the Build Monitor View on the Jenkins dashboard:

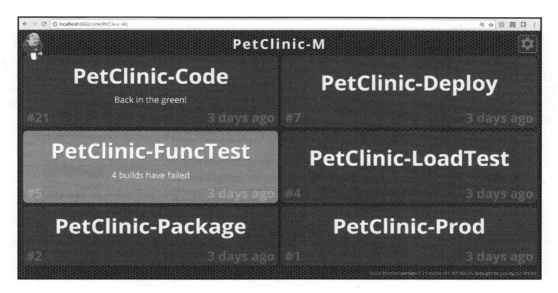

In a single window, we can get the status of multiple jobs.

Configuring mail notifications

How about sending a mail notification when a build is successful or fails?

Getting ready

It is essential to know when something fails so that we can take corrective measures at the right time. You need to have an email account to configure email notifications in Jenkins and SMTP details.

How to do it...

1. Go to **Manage Jenkins** and go to the **E-mail Notification** section. Provide all the necessary details based on the email account:

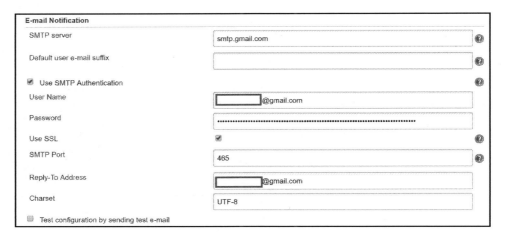

2. In the build job where you want to configure mail notifications, go to **Post-build Actions** and select **E-mail Notification**. Provide a recipients list with one of the checkbox selected:

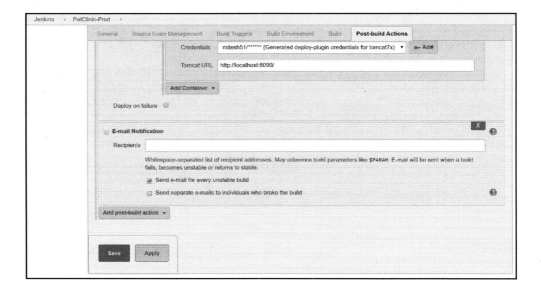

3. Go to **Post-build Actions** of the Jenkins build job and select **Editable Email notification** to send more customized emails to recipients:

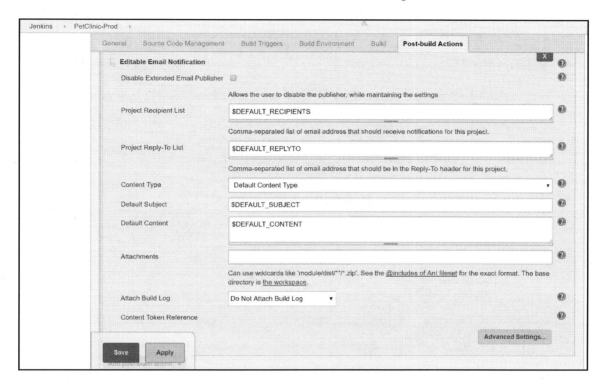

4. This is how email notifications can be configured.

Signaling the need to archive

Each development team is unique. Teams have their own way of doing business. In many organizations, there are one-off tasks that need to be done periodically. For example, at the end of each year, making a full backup of the entire filesystem.

This recipe details a script that checks for the last successful run of any job; if the year is different to the current year, then a warning is set at the beginning of the job's description. Thus, it is hinting to you that it's time to perform an action, such as archiving and then deleting. You can of course programmatically do the archiving. However, for high-value actions, it is worth forcing interceding, letting the Groovy scripts focus your attention.

Getting ready

Log in to Jenkins with an administrative account.

How to do it...

1. Within the **Manage Jenkins** page, click on the **Script Console** link and run the following script:

```
def warning='[You can ARCHIVE this Job]'
def now=new Date()

for (job in hudson.model.Hudson.instance.items) {
println "\nName: ${job.name}"
    Run lastSuccessfulBuild = job.getLastSuccessfulBuild()
if (lastSuccessfulBuild != null) {
def time = lastSuccessfulBuild.getTimestamp().getTime()
if (now.month.equals(time.month)){
println("Project has same month as build");
}else {
if (job.description.startsWith(warning)){
println("Description has already been changed");
}else{
job.setDescription("${warning}")
        }
    }
  }
}
```

2. Provide the script in **Script Console** and click on **Run**:

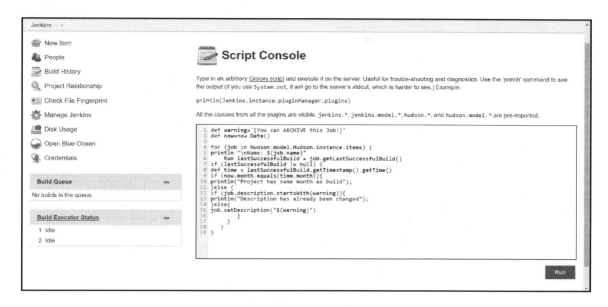

3. Successful execution of the script will give output based on the build jobs available in your Jenkins. The following is the sample output:

```
Jenkins ▸

                                    Result

                    Name: AzureAppDeploy

                    Name: CucumberProject
                    Project has same month as build

                    Name: CucumberProject2
                    Project has same month as build

                    Name: FirstAndroidProject

                    Name: FirstAntExample
                    Project has same month as build

                    Name: FirstJob
                    Project has same month as build

                    Name: FirstPipeline

                    Name: Main-PetClinic

                    Name: Maven-Sample

                    Name: mitesh51

                    Name: PetClinic-Code

                    Name: PetClinic-Deploy

                    Name: PetClinic-FuncTest
```

4. Any project that had its last successful build in another month than this will have the description **You can archive this job** added to its description, as shown in the following screenshot:

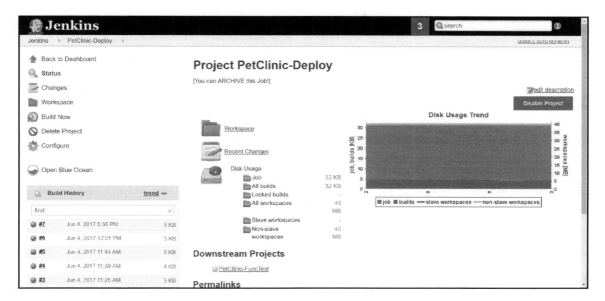

5. Click on **Configure** to check the description as well:

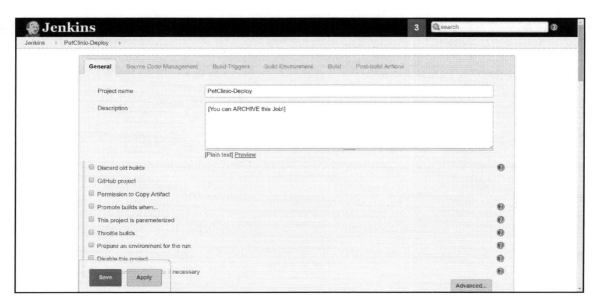

How it works...

Let's see how the script will be executed:

- A warning string is defined and the current date is now stored. Each job in Jenkins is programmatically iterated via the `for` statement.
- Jenkins has a class to store build run information. The runtime information is retrieved via `job.getLastSuccessfulBuild()` and is stored in the `lastSuccessfulBuild` instance. If no successful build has occurred, then `lastSuccessfulBuild` is set to null; otherwise, it has the runtime information.
- The time of the last successful build is retrieved and then stored in the `time` instance via `lastSuccessfulBuild.getTimestamp().getTime()`.

The current year is compared with the year of the last successful build and, if they are different and the warning string has not already been added to the front of the job description, then the description is updated.

Javadoc:

You will find the job API mentioned at `http://javadoc.jenkins-ci.org/hudson/model/Job.html` and the run information at `http://javadoc.jenkins-ci.org/hudson/model/Run.html`.

There's more...

Before writing your own code, you should review what already exists. With 1,000 plugins and expanding, Jenkins has a large, freely available, and openly licensed example code base. Although in this case, the standard API was used, it is well worth reviewing the plugin code base. In this example, you will find part of the code reused from the `lastsuccessversioncolumn` plugin. (`http://tinyurl.com/pack-jenkins-1`).

If you find any defects while reviewing the plugin code base, please contribute to the community via patches and bug reports.

3
Managing Security

In this chapter, we will cover the following recipes:

- Improving security with Jenkins configuration
- Configuring Authorization - Matrix-based security
- Configuring a Project-based Matrix Authorization Strategy
- Jenkins and OpenLDAP integration
- Jenkins and Active Directory integration
- Jenkins and OWASP Zed attack proxy integration
- Testing for OWASP's top 10 security issues
- Finding 500 errors and XSS attacks in Jenkins through fuzzing
- Avoiding sign-up bots with JCaptcha

Introduction

In this chapter, we'll discuss the security of Jenkins, taking into account that Jenkins can live in a rich variety of infrastructures. We will also look at how to scan for known security issues in the libraries used by Java code that Jenkins compiles.

The only perfectly secure system is a system that does not exist. For real services, you will need to pay attention to the different surfaces open to attack. Jenkins' primary surfaces are its web-based graphical user interface and its trust relationships with its slave nodes and the native OS. Online services need vigorous attention to their security surface. For Jenkins, there are three main reasons why:

- Jenkins has the ability to communicate with a wide range of infrastructures through either its plugins or the master-slave topology
- The rate of code change around the plugins is high and open to the accidental inclusion of security-related defects
- You need to harden the default install

Another positive thing is that Jenkins code is freely available for review and the core community keeps a vigilant eye.

Improving security with Jenkins configuration

In this section, we will cover how to manage multiple users.

Getting ready

Through user management, we can provide access to Jenkins to multiple users and provide them with roles based on project-based access when it is required. The **Manage Users** will only appear if the selected security realm is Jenkins' own user database.

1. Go to **Manage Jenkins** and click on **Manage Users**:

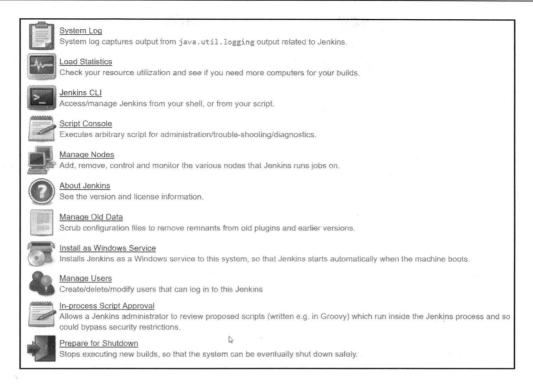

2. Verify the existing **admin** user available in Jenkins:

3. Click on the **Create User** link and provide details:

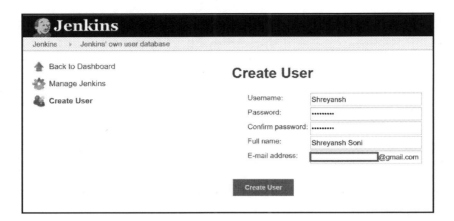

4. Verify the list of users in **Manage Jenkins | Manage Users**:

You can change or delete users from **Manage Jenkins | Manage Users**.

How to do it...

1. To allow sign up and access to only logged in users, go to **Manage Jenkins | Configure Global Security**.
2. In the **Access Control** section, click on **Jenkins' own user database** and select **Allow users to sign up**:

3. So, this is how we can create users and allow users to sign up, as well as to access Jenkins.

Configuring Authorization - Matrix-based security

In the **Authorization** section, we can configure **Matrix-based security** so that we can configure who can do what. We can configure predefined roles available in Jenkins.

Getting ready

Select **Matrix-based security** and add a name in the **User/group to add** box. Make sure that you give access to **admin** before saving it; otherwise, the Jenkins account will be locked out:

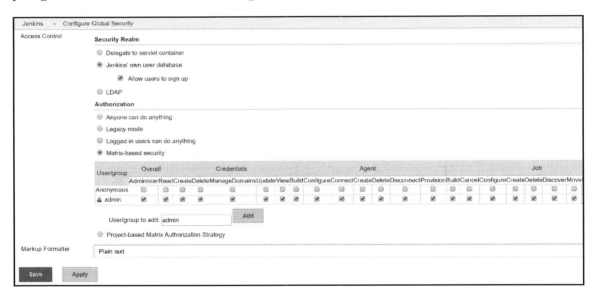

How to do it...

1. Give the name of our newly created user, click on **Add**, and provide all the required rights. We can do the same thing for different users.
2. Click on **Save**:

3. To verify the access, open a new incognito window in the browser and log in with the **User** and **Password** of the newly created user:

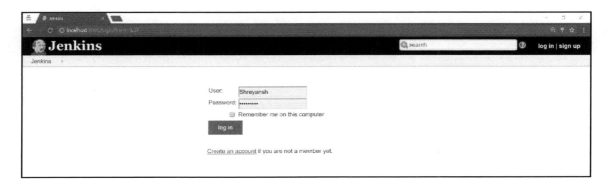

4. Verify that the limited access is available to the new user. The **New Item** and **Manage Jenkins** links are not available:

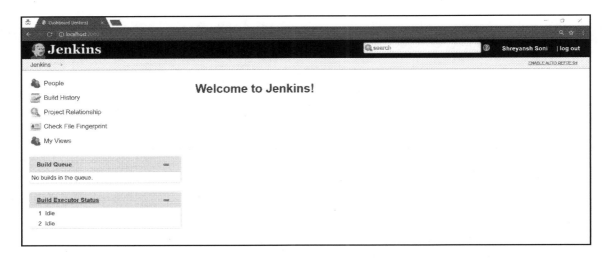

5. Now go to **Manage Jenkins | Global Security Configuration**. Allow **Read** rights in the **Job** category for the user **Shreyansh**.

6. Click on **Save**:

7. Go to the incognito window that we opened before and refresh the page. Now we have read access to the jobs available in Jenkins:

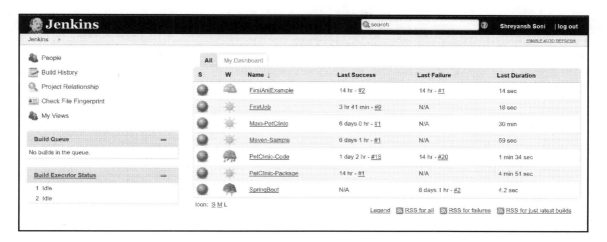

8. We can see the jobs, but we can't execute them, as rights are not available:

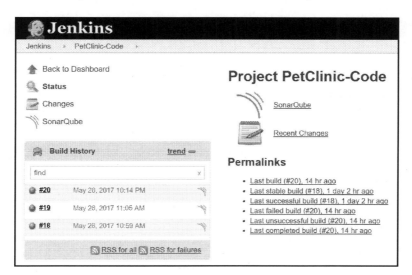

9. This is how we can manage users and authorization in Jenkins. In the next section, we will learn how to give project-based access.

Configuring a Project-based Matrix Authorization Strategy

Project-based Matrix Authorization Strategy is an extension of **Matrix-based security**. It allows an access control list matrix to be defined for each project. This feature is very useful when we want to give access to specific jobs to specific users so that the security of Jenkins is not compromised.

Getting ready

Go to **Manage Jenkins | Global Security Configuration**.

How to do it...

1. In the **Authorization** section, select **Project-based Matrix Authorization Strategy**.
2. Give **admin** all rights and **Save**:

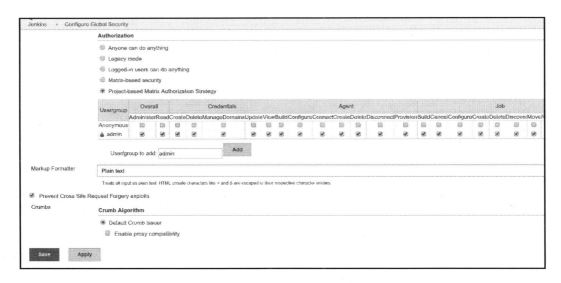

3. Go to the incognito window where we logged in using the credentials of **Shreyansh**.

4. Refresh the page and we will get **Access Denied**. The reason is that we haven't given any rights to **Shreyansh** in **Project-based Matrix Authorization Strategy**:

5. We need to provide overall **Read** rights so **Shreyansh** can access the Jenkins dashboard:

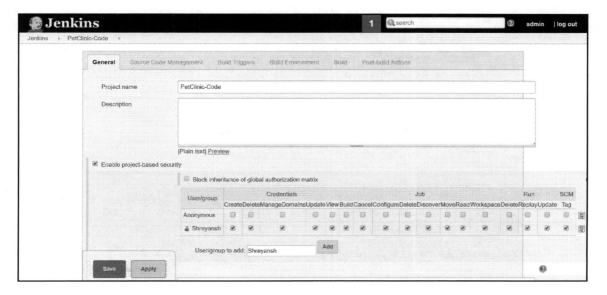

6. Now, go to the individual build job as an admin and select **Enable project-based security** in the job configuration page.

7. Add **Shreyansh** as a user and click on **Save**:

8. Now, go to the incognito window where **Shreyansh** is logged in and refresh the page.
9. We can see one job, which we have configured to give access to **Shreyansh**:

10. Click on the build and verify that all the rights are available to the user **Shreyansh**:

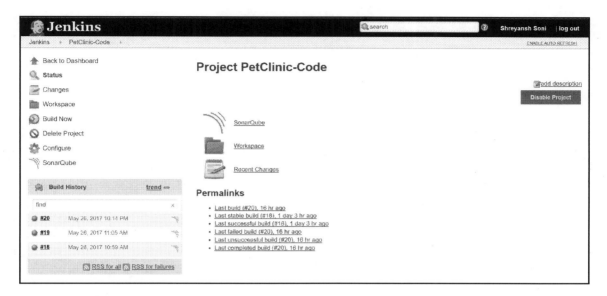

Now we have finished user management, role-based access, and project-based access in Jenkins as a part of securing Jenkins.

Jenkins and OpenLDAP integration

The **Lightweight Directory Access Protocol (LDAP)** provides a highly popular open standards directory service. It is used in many organizations to display user information to the world. LDAP is also used as a central service to hold user passwords for authentication and can contain information necessary for routing mail, POSIX account administration, and various other pieces of information that external systems may require. Jenkins can directly connect to LDAP for authentication or indirectly through the CAS SSO server (http://www.jasig.org/cas), which then uses LDAP as its password container. Jenkins also has an email plugin (https://wiki.jenkins-ci.org/display/JENKINS/LDAP+Email+Plugin) that pulls its routing information out of LDAP.

Because LDAP is a common enterprise service, Jenkins may also encounter LDAP while running integration tests as part of the build application's testing infrastructure.

This recipe shows you how to quickly install an OpenLDAP server named `slapd` and then add organizations, users, and groups via **LDAPData Interchange Format (LDIF)**, a simple text format for storing LDAP records (`http://en.wikipedia.org/wiki/LDAP_Data_Interchange_Format`).

 Active Directory is also popular in corporate environments. Jenkins has a plugin for Active Directory (`https://wiki.jenkins-ci.org/display/JENKINS/Active+Directory+plugin`).

Getting ready

For this recipe, you will install OpenLDAP on Ubuntu 14.04 LTS or newer. You can create a virtual machine using VirtualBox or the VMware Workstation too.

Here, the Ubuntu virtual machine is created in Microsoft Azure. You can set up a free trial account for Microsoft Azure and try this out:

1. On the left sidebar, click on **Virtual Machines** and click on **Add**. Select **Ubuntu Server 14.04 LTS** and click on **Create**:

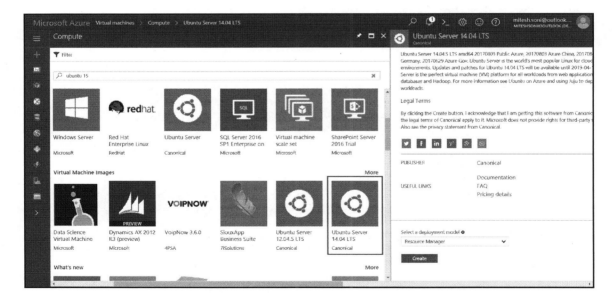

2. Provide the virtual machine's **Name, User name, Password, Subscription,** and **Resource group** name.
3. Select **Location**.
4. Click **OK**:

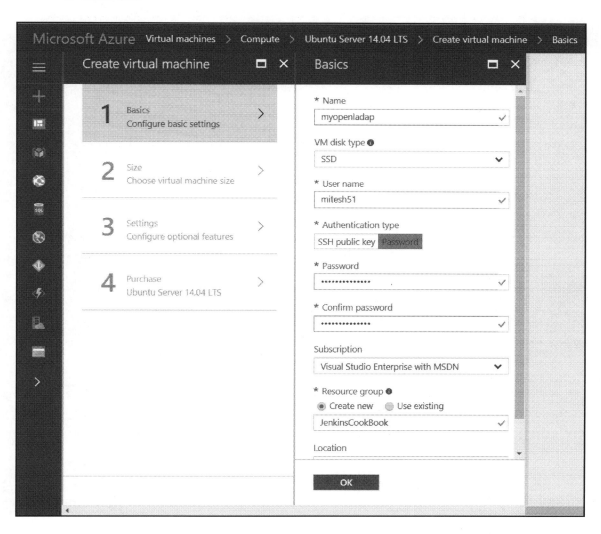

5. Select **Choose virtual machine size**:

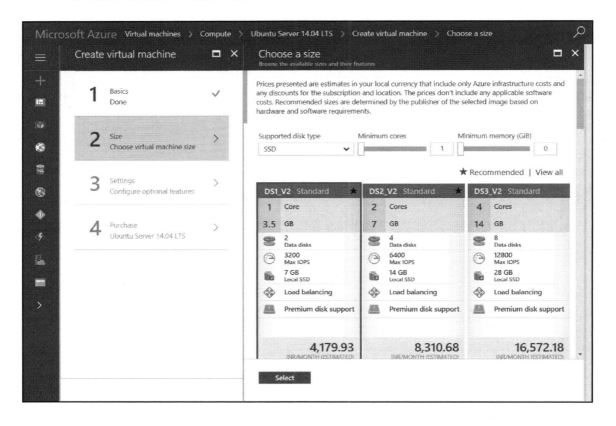

6. Keep the default settings:

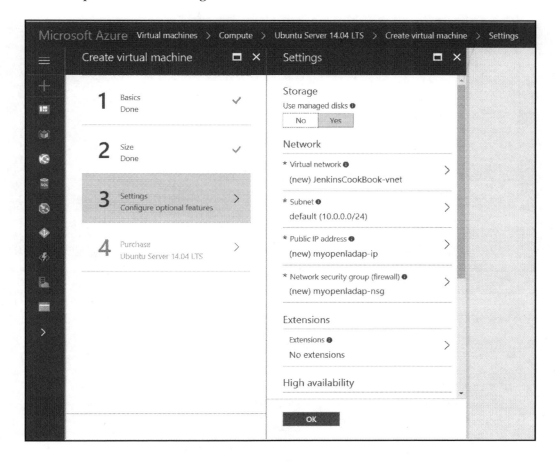

7. Click on **Purchase** in the next pane. Note the IP Address allocated:

Virtual Machine in Microsoft Azure

8. Open PuTTY to remotely access the Ubuntu virtual machine you have created:

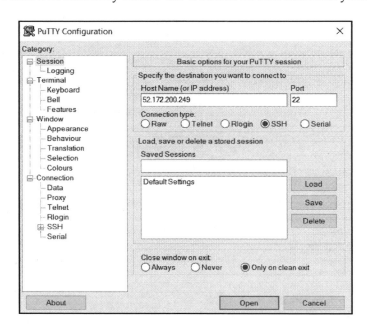

9. Log in to the console with the credential provided during the VM creation.

```
login as: mitesh51
mitesh51@52.172.200.249's password:
Welcome to Ubuntu 14.04.5 LTS (GNU/Linux 4.4.0-91-generic
x86_64)
* Documentation: https://help.ubuntu.com/
System information as of Sat Aug 12 12:31:29 UTC 2017
System load: 0.24 Memory usage: 2% Processes: 82
Usage of /: 41.0% of 1.94GB Swap usage: 0% Users logged in: 0
Graph this data and manage this system at:
https://landscape.canonical.com/
Get cloud support with Ubuntu Advantage Cloud Guest:
http://www.ubuntu.com/business/services/cloud
0 packages can be updated.
0 updates are security updates.
```

10. Your **Hardware Enablement Stack (HWE)** is supported until April 2019.
11. The programs included with the Ubuntu system are free software; the exact distribution terms for each program are described in the individual files in /usr/share/doc/*/copyright.

12. Ubuntu comes with *ABSOLUTELY NO WARRANTY,* to the extent permitted by applicable law.

13. The OpenLDAP server is in Ubuntu's default repositories under the package `slapd`. Execute `apt-get install slapdldap-utils` in the PuTTY console, where you are connected to the virtual machine:

    root@myopenladap:/home/mitesh51# apt-get installslapdldap-utils

14. The installation process needs some configuration. Enter the admin password:

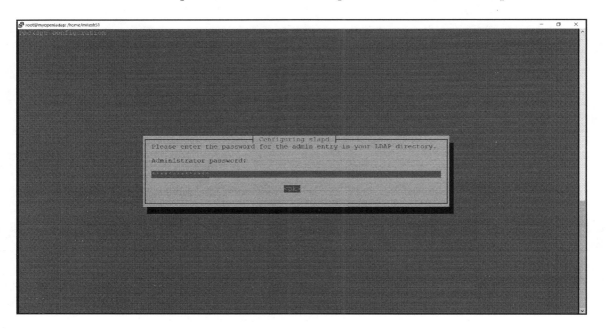

15. Confirm the admin password for the admin entry in your LDAP directory:

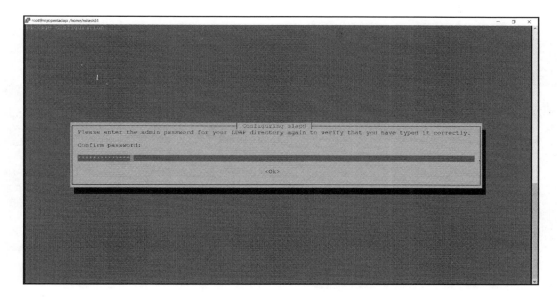

16. Select **No** in **Omit OpenLDAP server configuration**:

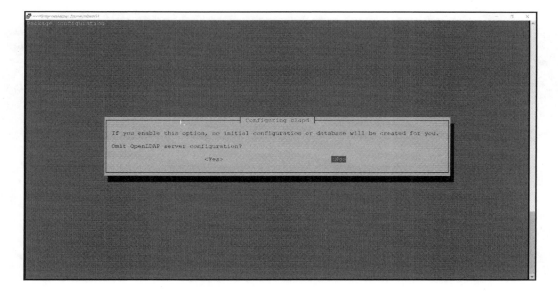

17. Give the **DNS domain name** that provides the base structure of your directory path.
18. Click **OK**:

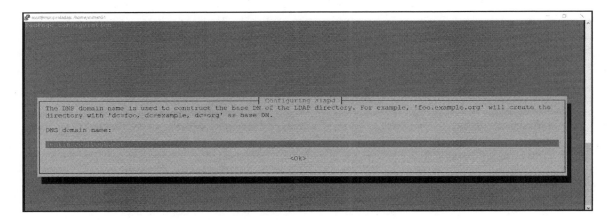

19. Provide the **Organization name** and click **OK**:

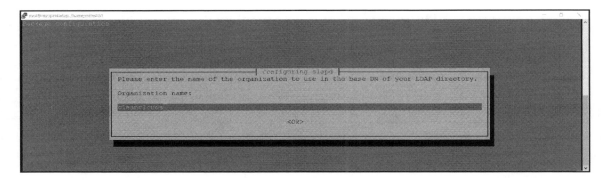

20. Select **HDB** as the database:

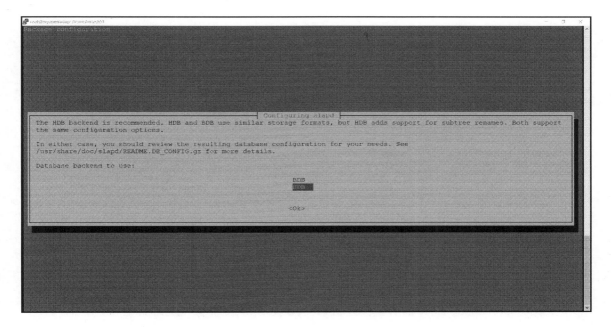

21. Select **No** in remove the database when the `slapd` package is purged:

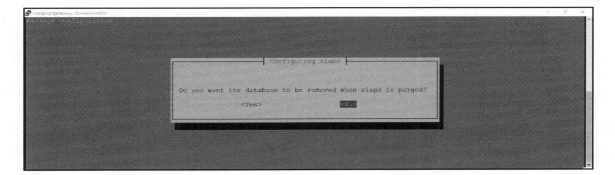

22. Select **Yes** in the **Move Old Database** dialog box:

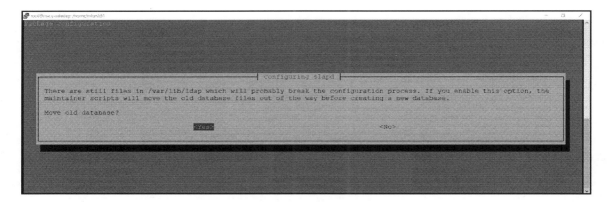

23. Select **No** for not allowing LDAPv2 protocol:

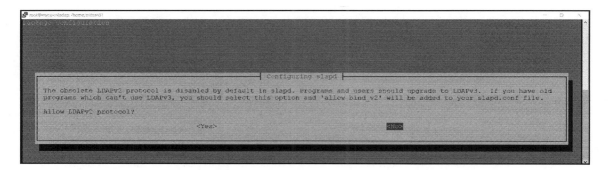

24. After all the configurations, the installation process will be completed.

```
Creating initial configuration... done.
Creating LDAP directory... done.
* Starting OpenLDAPslapd[ OK ]
Setting up ldap-utils (2.4.31-1+nmu2ubuntu8.4) ...
Processing triggers for libc-bin (2.19-0ubuntu6.13) ...
Processing triggers for ufw (0.34~rc-0ubuntu2) ...
Processing triggers for ureadahead (0.100.0-16) ...
root@myopenladap:/home/mitesh51#
root@myopenladap:/home/mitesh51# sudodpkg-reconfigure slapd
* Stopping OpenLDAPslapd[ OK ]
Moving old database directory to /var/backups:
- directory unknown... done.
Creating initial configuration... done.
Creating LDAP directory... done.
* Starting OpenLDAPslapd[ OK ]
Processing triggers for libc-bin (2.19-0ubuntu6.13) ...
root@myopenladap:/home/mitesh51#
```

You will install PHPldapadmin to administrate OpenLDAP. Install it with the command sudo apt-get install phpldapadmin in the PuTTY console:

```
root@myopenladap:/home/mitesh51# sudo apt-get install phpldapadmin
Reading package lists... Done
Building dependency tree
Reading state information... Done
The following extra packages will be installed:
apache2apache2-bin apache2-data libapache2-mod-php5libapr1libaprutil1
libaprutil1-dbd-sqlite3libaprutil1-ldapphp5-cli php5-common php5-json
php5-ldapphp5-readlinessl-cert
Suggested packages:
apache2-doc apache2-suexec-pristine apache2-suexec-custom apache2-utils
php-pear php5-user-cache openssl-blacklist
The following new packages will be installed:
apache2apache2-bin apache2-data libapache2-mod-php5libapr1libaprutil1
libaprutil1-dbd-sqlite3libaprutil1-ldapphp5-cli php5-common php5-json
php5-ldapphp5-readlinephpldapadminssl-cert
0 upgraded, 15 newly installed, 0 to remove and 0 not upgraded.
Need to get 6,881 kB of archives.
After this operation, 30.9 MB of additional disk space will be used.
Do you want to continue? [Y/n] Y
Get:1 http://azure.archive.ubuntu.com/ubuntu/ trusty/main libapr1amd64
1.5.0-1 [85.1 kB]
Get:2 http://azure.archive.ubuntu.com/ubuntu/ trusty/main libaprutil1amd64
1.5.3-1 [76.4 kB]
Get:3 http://azure.archive.ubuntu.com/ubuntu/ trusty/main php5-jsonamd64
1.3.2-2build1 [34.4 kB]
```

```
Get:4 http://azure.archive.ubuntu.com/ubuntu/ trusty-updates/main php5-
common amd645.5.9+dfsg-1ubuntu4.22 [449 kB]
Get:5 http://azure.archive.ubuntu.com/ubuntu/ trusty-updates/main php5-
ldapamd645.5.9+dfsg-1ubuntu4.22 [19.1 kB]
Get:6 http://azure.archive.ubuntu.com/ubuntu/ trusty-updates/main php5-cli
amd645.5.9+dfsg-1ubuntu4.22 [2,154 kB]
Get:7 http://azure.archive.ubuntu.com/ubuntu/ trusty-updates/main php5-
readlineamd645.5.9+dfsg-1ubuntu4.22 [12.1 kB]
Get:8 http://azure.archive.ubuntu.com/ubuntu/ trusty/main libaprutil1-dbd-
sqlite3amd64 1.5.3-1 [10.5 kB]
Get:9 http://azure.archive.ubuntu.com/ubuntu/ trusty/main libaprutil1-
ldapamd64 1.5.3-1 [8,634 B]
Get:10 http://azure.archive.ubuntu.com/ubuntu/ trusty-updates/main apache2-
bin amd64 2.4.7-1ubuntu4.17 [845 kB]
Get:11 http://azure.archive.ubuntu.com/ubuntu/ trusty-updates/main apache2-
data all 2.4.7-1ubuntu4.17 [160 kB]
Get:12 http://azure.archive.ubuntu.com/ubuntu/ trusty-updates/main
apache2amd64 2.4.7-1ubuntu4.17 [87.4 kB]
Get:13 http://azure.archive.ubuntu.com/ubuntu/ trusty-updates/main
libapache2-mod-php5amd645.5.9+dfsg-1ubuntu4.22 [2,194 kB]
Get:14 http://azure.archive.ubuntu.com/ubuntu/ trusty/main ssl-cert all
1.0.33 [16.6 kB]
Get:15 http://azure.archive.ubuntu.com/ubuntu/ trusty-updates/universe
phpldapadmin all 1.2.2-5ubuntu1.1 [730 kB]
Fetched 6,881 kB in 5s (1,305 kB/s)
Preconfiguring packages ...
Selecting previously unselected package libapr1:amd64.
(Reading database ... 29206 files and directories currently installed.)
Preparing to unpack .../libapr1_1.5.0-1_amd64.deb ...
Unpacking libapr1:amd64 (1.5.0-1) ...
...
Processing triggers for man-db (2.6.7.1-1ubuntu1) ...
Processing triggers for ureadahead (0.100.0-16) ...
Processing triggers for ufw (0.34~rc-0ubuntu2) ...
Setting up libapr1:amd64 (1.5.0-1) ...
Setting up libaprutil1:amd64 (1.5.3-1) ...
...
Setting up apache2 (2.4.7-1ubuntu4.17) ...
Enabling module mpm_event.
.
.
Enabling site 000-default.
* Starting web server apache2AH00558: apache2: Could not reliably determine
the server's fully qualified domain name, using 10.0.0.4. Set the
'ServerName' directive globally to suppress this message
*
Setting up ssl-cert (1.0.33) ...
sent invalidate(group) request, exiting
```

```
Setting up php5-common (5.5.9+dfsg-1ubuntu4.22) ...


Creating config file /etc/php5/mods-available/pdo.ini with new version
php5_invoke: Enable module pdo for apache2 SAPI
php5_invoke: Enable module pdo for cli SAPI
.
.
Enabling module mpm_prefork.
apache2_switch_mpm Switch to prefork
* Restarting web server apache2AH00558: apache2: Could not reliably
determine the server's fully qualified domain name, using 10.0.0.4. Set the
'ServerName' directive globally to suppress this message
[ OK ]
apache2_invoke: Enable module php5
* Restarting web server apache2AH00558: apache2: Could not reliably
determine the server's fully qualified domain name, using 10.0.0.4. Set the
'ServerName' directive globally to suppress this message
[ OK ]
Processing triggers for libc-bin (2.19-0ubuntu6.13) ...
root@myopenladap:/home/mitesh51#
```

Open /etc/phpldapadmin/config.php in edit mode and update the following:

- $servers->setValue('server','host','52.172.200.249') with the IP address of the virtual machine you have created

- $servers->setValue('server','base',array('dc=jenkinscookbook,dc =net'));

- $servers->setValue('login','bind_id','cn=admin,dc=jenkinscookbo ok,dc=net');

- $config->custom->appearance['hide_template_warning'] = true;

Go to the **Resource group** in which you have created the virtual machine. Find the **Network Security Group**.

Click on **Add Inbound security rule** and add the **HTTP** rule:

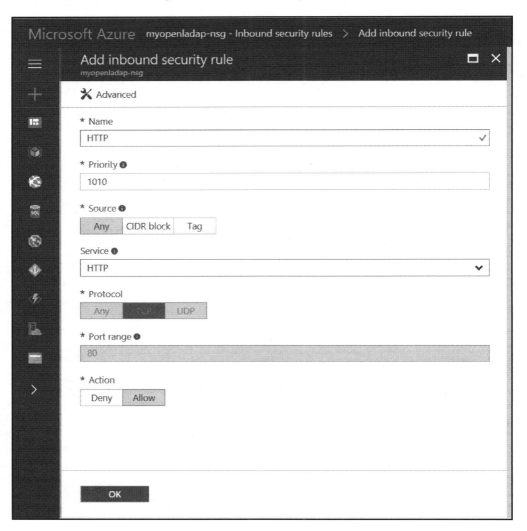

Add the `Ping` command as well so that we can test whether the VM's IP address is accessible or not:

Inbound Security Rules in Network Security Group

Now you are ready to use OpenLDAP using the `phpldapadmin` web interface. Log in with the IP address or DNS/`phpldapadmin`.

Click on **Login**:

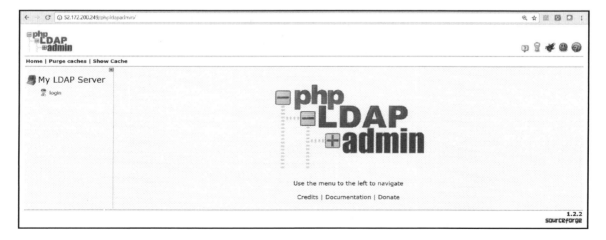

Log in with the admin username and password provided during the OpenLDAP installation and configuration:

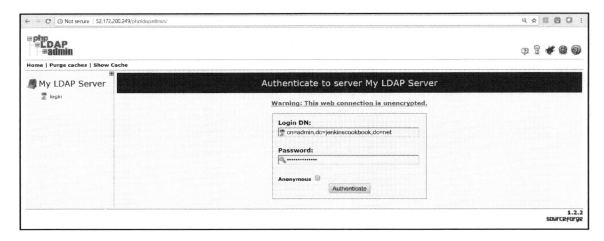

Here you have the `phpldapadmin` web interface:

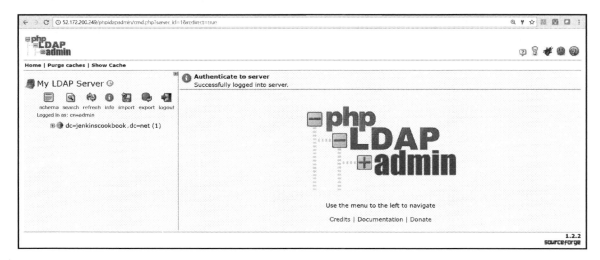

Click on the domain components to see the login you are using:

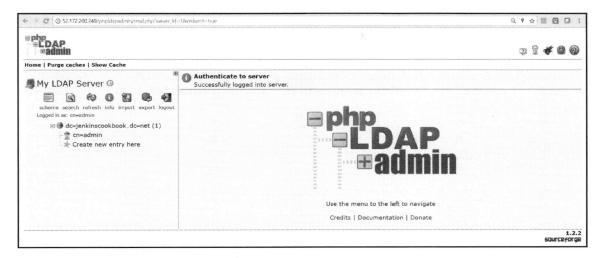

Now you need to add **Organizational Units**, **Groups**, and **Users**. Click on **Create new entry here**. Select the **Generic: Organizational Unit** template:

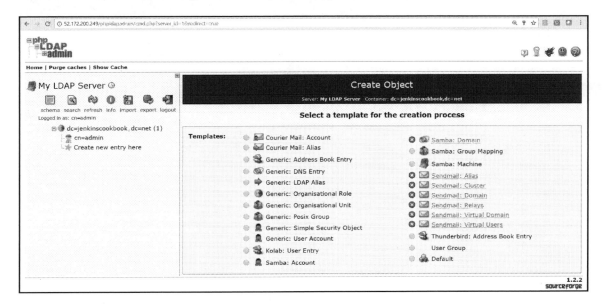

Type `groups` and click on **Create Object**:

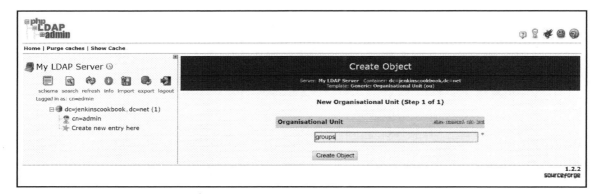

Click on **Commit**:

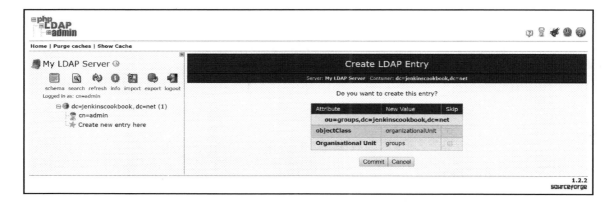

Select the newly created organization unit and verify the content:

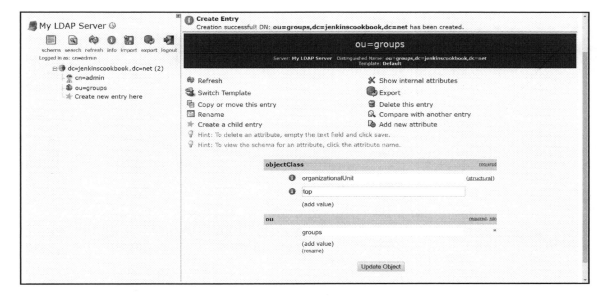

Similarly, create users in the **Organisational unit**:

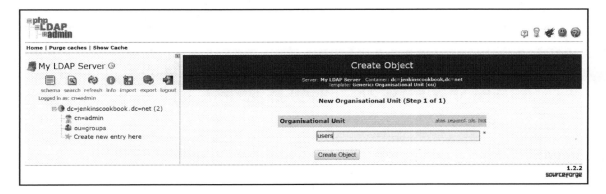

Commit and verify the object in the `phpldapadmin` web interface:

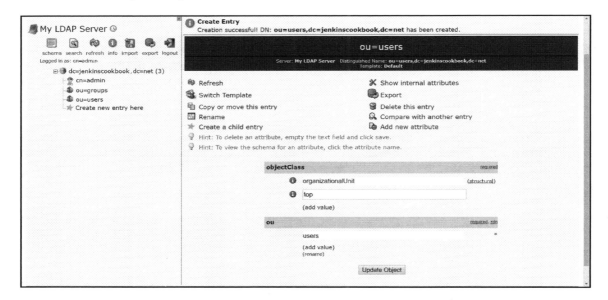

Now, you need to create specific groups within the groups. Select **groups** and click on
Create a child entry:

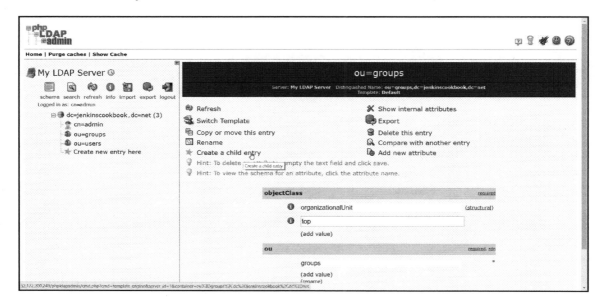

Select **Generic: Posix Group**:

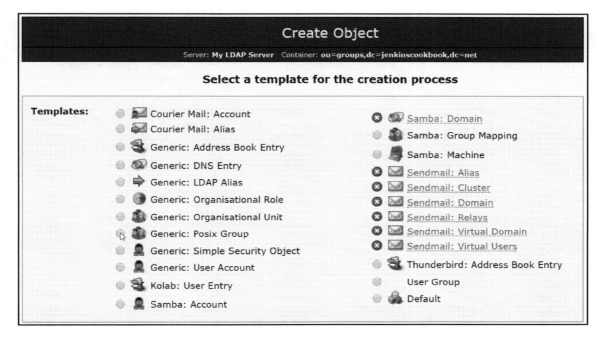

Give the **Group** name and click on **Create Object**:

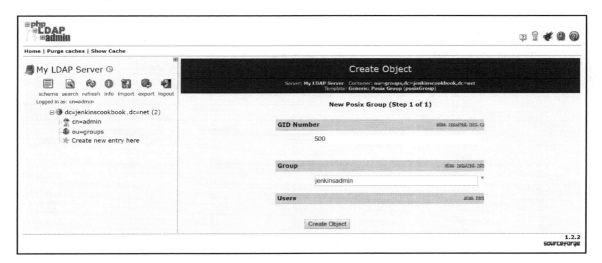

Commit the changes:

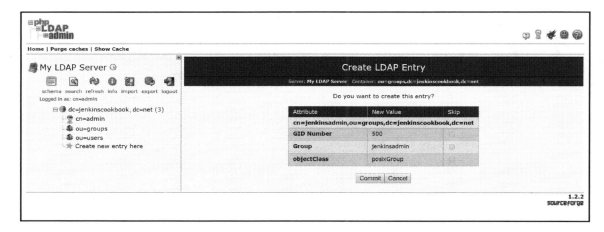

Similarly, create the `jenkinsusers` group:

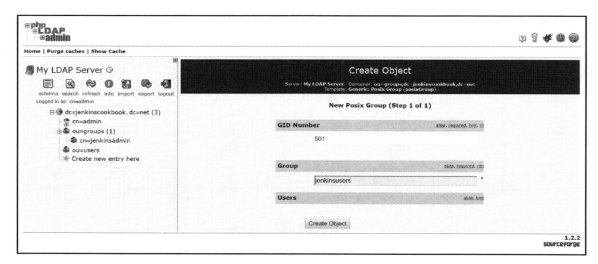

Verify both groups in the `phpldapadmin` web interface:

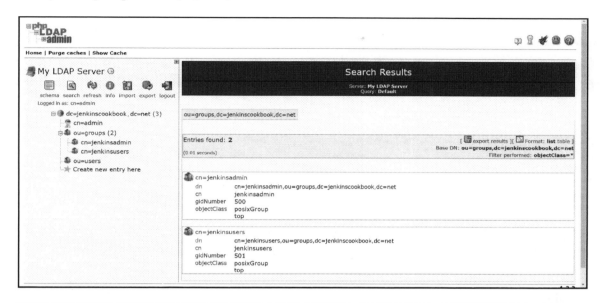

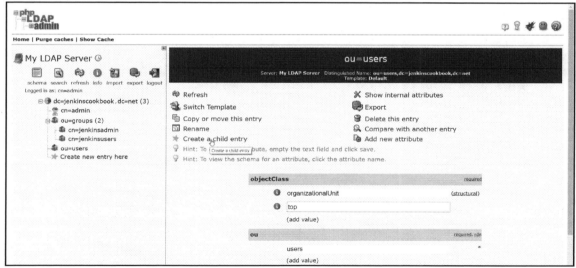

Now it is time to create users. Click on **Create new entry here**.

Select **Generic: User Account**:

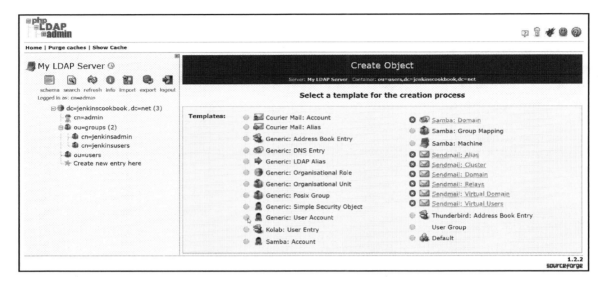

Provide all the required details for a user:

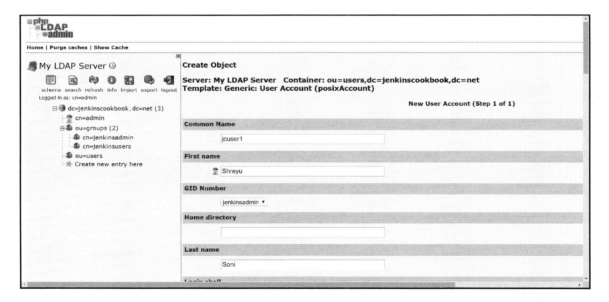

If you get an error while setting the password field when creating a generic user account in `phpldapadmin`, open `/usr/share/phpldapadmin/lib/TemplateRender.php` in edit mode and change `password_hash` to `password_hash_custom` on line 2469:

Give the password and user ID details and click on **Create Object**:

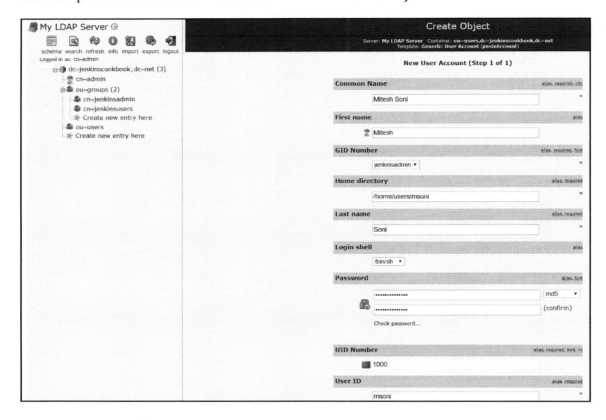

Click on **Commit**:

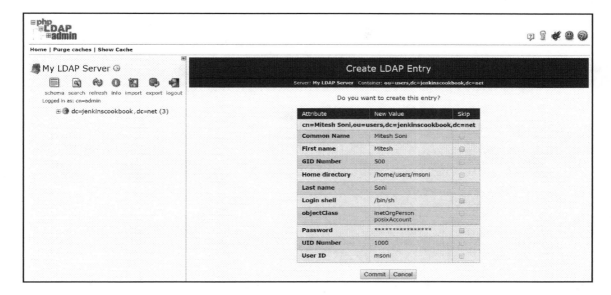

Similarly, create another user with the user ID ssoni:

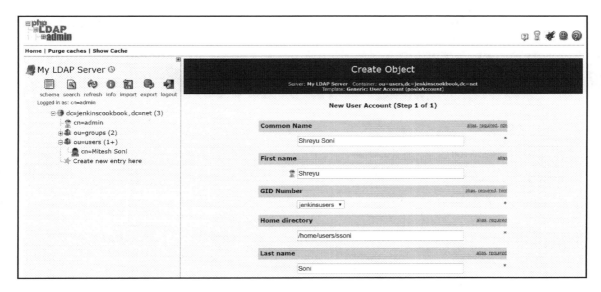

Click on **Commit**:

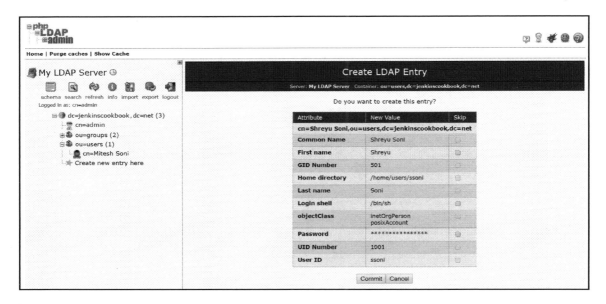

Now you have the groups and users ready. The next step is to assign users to the groups.

Click on **Add new attribute**. Select **memberUid**:

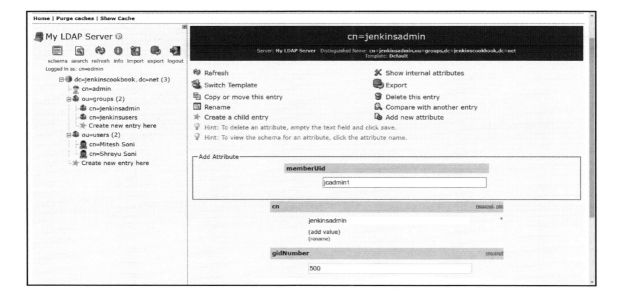

Click on **Update Object**:

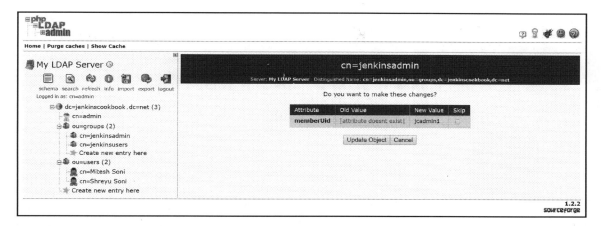

Click on **Modify group** members and add users to the group:

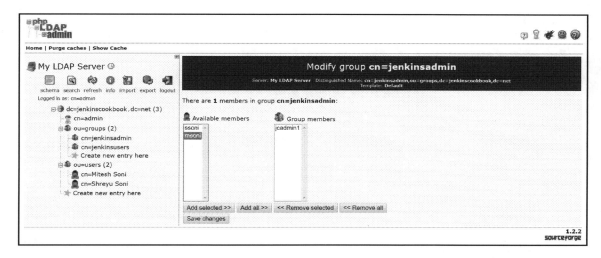

Click on **Save changes**:

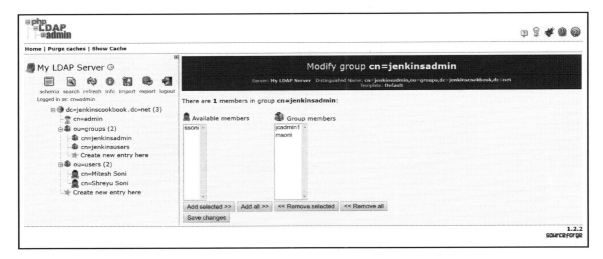

Click on **Update Object**:

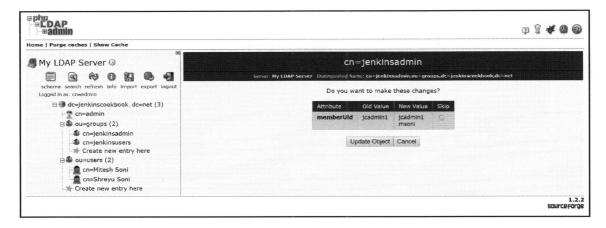

Now, you are ready to integrate OpenLDAP with Jenkins, as we have users available.

How to do it...

1. Go to the **Jenkins** dashboard I **Manage Jenkins** I **Configure Global Security**.
2. Click on **Advanced** and fill in the data as you have configured it in the OpenLDAP installation:

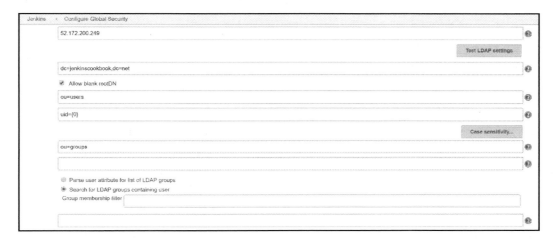

3. Click on **Test LDAP settings**. Give the **User** and **Password**. Click on **Test**:

4. Verify that the authentication is successful:

5. In the **Authorization** section, go to **Project-based Matrix Authorization Strategy** and add the user we created in OpenLDAP:

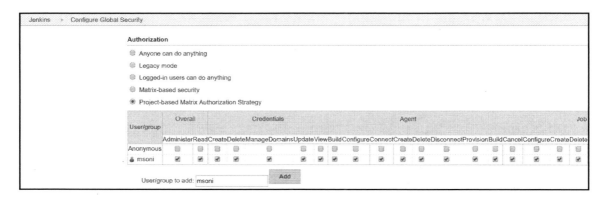

6. Save the changes and Jenkins will be logged out. Log in with your LDAP user credentials and you will be able to log in:

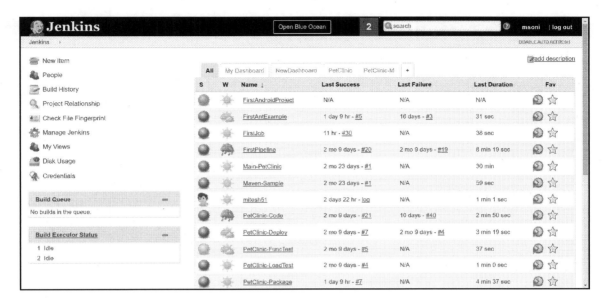

7. Give the `ssoni` user **Read** rights only to verify the access:

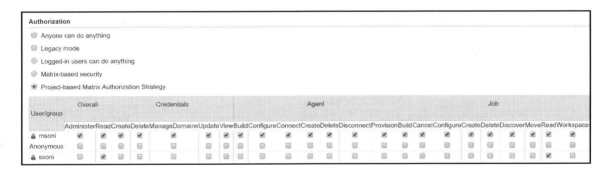

8. Login with the `ssoni` user who has limited access and see that the **Manage Jenkins** section is not available:

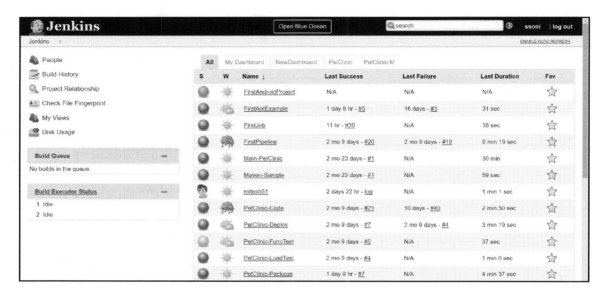

9. Click on the projects available on the Jenkins dashboard and check that only **Read** rights are available:

There's more...

The test that the LDAP server supports anonymous binding, you can search the server without authenticating. Most LDAP servers allow this approach. However, some servers are configured to enforce specific information security policies. For example, your policy might enforce being able to anonymously verify that a user's record exists, but you may not be able to retrieve specific attributes, such as their email or postal address.

Anonymous binding simplifies configuration; otherwise, you will need to add account details for a user in LDAP that has the rights to perform the searches. This account has great LDAP powers, should never be shared, and can present a chink in your security armor.

The user search filter, *uid={0}*, searches for users whose UIDs equal their usernames. Many organizations prefer to use cn instead of UID; the choice of attribute is a matter of taste. You can even imagine an email attribute being used to uniquely identify a person, as long as that attribute cannot be changed by the user.

Jenkins and Active Directory integration

In this section, we will configure Active Directory, which is already available to integrate with Jenkins so all available users in a specific domain of Active Directory can utilize Jenkins with their own Active Directory credentials based on the given access.

Getting ready

Go to the Jenkins dashboard | **Manage Jenkins** | **Manage Plugins** | **Available**.

Install the **Active Directory plugin**:

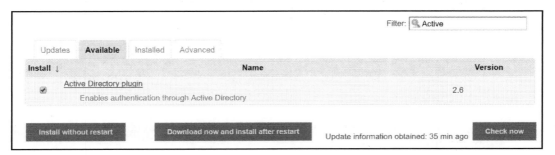

Now you can configure the **Active Directory** settings in **Configure Global Security**.

How to do it...

1. Go to the Jenkins dashboard | **Manage Jenkins** | **Configure Global Security** | **Enable security** | Select **Active Directory**:

2. Select **Specify custom Active Directory domain name**, click on **Add Domain**, provide the **Domain Name**, and save it:

3. If the configuration and access is correct, then we can use all the users in the domain directly in Jenkins.

Jenkins and OWASP Zed Attack Proxy integration

OWASP Zed Attack Proxy(ZAP) is an open source web application security scanner. You can integrate ZAP security tool with the Jenkins CI environment.

Getting ready

Go to `https://github.com/zaproxy/zaproxy/wiki/Downloads` and download the Windows (64) Installer.

Install it on Windows.

Open OWASP ZAP in Windows, click on **File | Persist Session** and save it in the Jenkins workspace in the directory of the build job:

Now you are good to configure ZAP plugins in Jenkins.

How to do it...

1. Go to the Jenkins dashboard | **Configure system** | **Global properties** | **Environment variables** and create the ZAPPROXY_HOME variable:

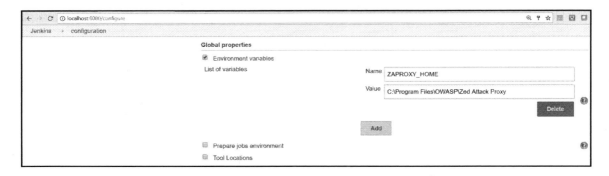

2. Go to the Jenkins dashboard | **Zap project** | **Build** | **Add build step** | **Execute ZAP**.
3. Keep the host and port settings as default or change them according to your installation of OWAASP ZAP:

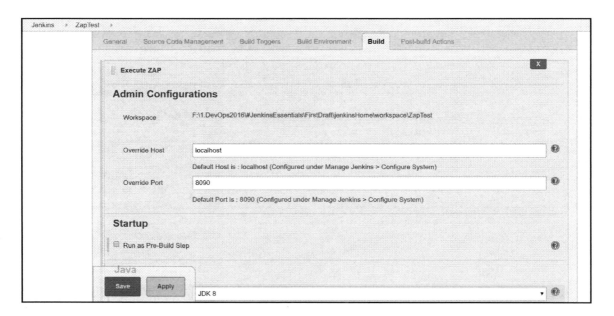

4. Provide `ZAPROXY_HOME`:

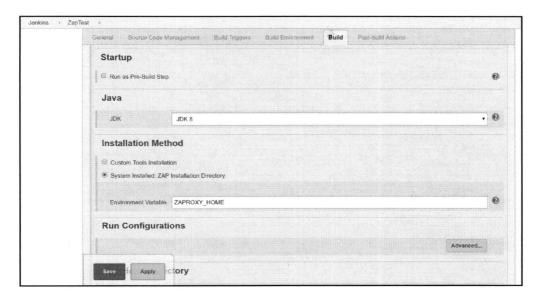

5. Give the **Path** to the ZAP home directory that is not the installation directory.
6. Give the session name that you saved in the workspace:

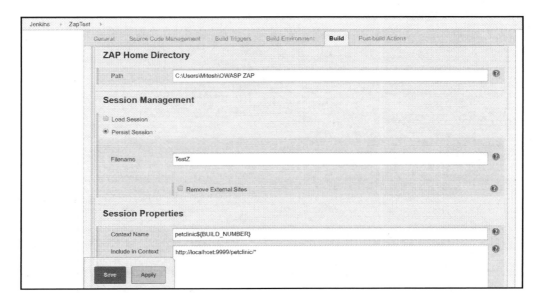

7. Configure the **Attack Mode**:

8. Configure the **Generate Report** section:

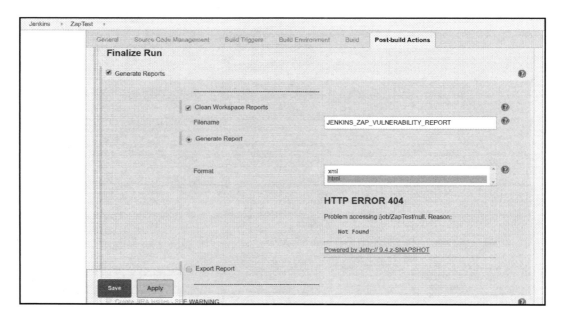

9. **Publish HTML Reports**. Click on **Save**:

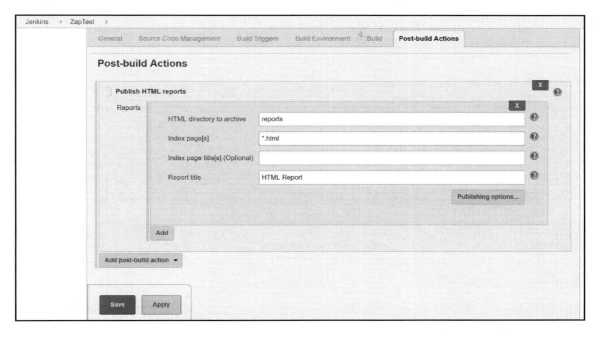

10. Make sure the application is running in the local or remote environment.

See also

- Run the Jenkins build and it will create an HTML report. Navigate to the HTML report and verify the scanning report:

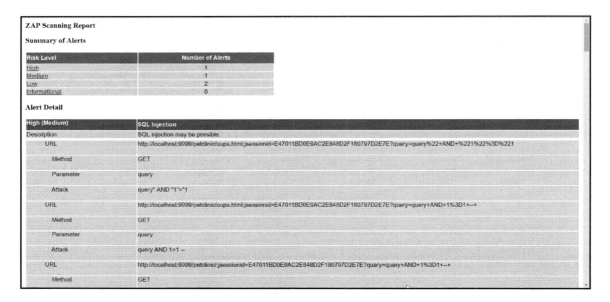

- You have integrated Jenkins and OWASP ZAP for security testing using Jenkins and you can integrate it in the pipeline too.

Testing for OWASP's top 10 security issues

This recipe details the automatic testing of Jenkins for well-known security issues with w3af, a penetration testing tool from the **Open Web Application Security Project (OWASP)**. For more information, visit `http://w3af.sourceforge.net`. OWASP's purpose is to make application security visible. The OWASP's top 10 lists of insecurities for 2010 include the following:

- **A2-Cross-site Scripting (XSS)**: An XSS attack can occur when an application returns an unescaped input to a client's browser. The Jenkins administrator can do this by default through the job description.

- **A6-Security Misconfiguration**: A Jenkins plugin gives you the power to write custom authentication scripts. It is easy to get scripts wrong through misconfiguration.
- **A7-Insecure Cryptographic Storage**: There are over 600 plugins for Jenkins, each storing its configuration in separate XML files. It is quite possible that there could be a rare mistake with the storage of passwords in plain text. You will need to double-check.
- **A9-Insufficient Transport Layer Protection**: Jenkins runs over HTTP by default. It can be a hassle and involves extra costs to obtain a trusted certificate. You might be tempted not to implement TLS, leaving your packets open.

You will find that OWASP's top 10 lists of insecurities for 2013 have some changes compared with the 2010 version. The most significant change is the inclusion of **A9-Using Known Vulnerable Components**. If your software depends on older libraries, then there is a window of opportunity for the manipulation of known weaknesses.

Jenkins has a large set of plugins written by a motivated, diffuse, and hardworking community. It is possible, due to the large churn of code, that security defects are inadvertently added. Examples include leaving passwords in plain text in configuration files or using unsafe rendering that does not remove suspicious JavaScript. You can find the first type of defect by reviewing the configuration files manually. The second type is accessible to a wider audience and is thus more readily crackable. You can attack the new plugins by hand. There are helpful cheat sheets available on the internet (`http://hackers.org/xss.html`). The effort required is tedious; automated tests can cover more ground and can be scheduled as part of a Jenkins job.

In the recipe named *Exploring the OWASP dependency-check plugin*, you will configure Jenkins to give you warning of known attack vectors, based on automatically reviewing your code dependencies.

OWASP storefront:

OWASP publish a list of the top 10 most common security attack vectors for web applications each year. They publish this document and a wide range of books through `http://lulu.com`. At Lulu, you have free access to PDF versions of OWASP's documents, or you can buy cheap, on-demand printed versions. You can find the official storefront at:
`http://stores.lulu.com/owasp`.

Getting ready

Penetration tests have the potential to damage a running application. Make sure that you have a backed-up copy of your Jenkins workspace. You might have to reinstall. Also, turn off any enabled security within Jenkins: this allows w3af to freely roam the security surface.

Download the newest version of w3af from SourceForge (`http://w3af.org/download/`) and also download and read OWASP's top 10 list of well-known attacks from `https://www.owasp.org/index.php/Category:OWASP_Top_Ten_Project`.

w3af has both Windows and *NIX installation packages; use the OS installation of your choice. However, the Windows Installer is no longer supported and the installation process without the Installer is complex. Therefore, it's better to use a *NIX version of the tool.

The `Debian` package for w3af is older and more unstable than the `SourceForge` package for Linux. Therefore, do not use the `apt-get` and `yum` methods of installation, but rather, use the downloaded package from `SourceForge`.

How to do it...

1. To install w3af, follow the instructions given on the developer site (`http://w3af.org/download/`). If there are any unsolvable dependency issues for Ubuntu, fall back to the `apt-get` installation approach and install an older version of the tool as follows:

   ```
   sudo apt-get install w3af
   ```

2. Run `w3af`.
3. Under the **Profiles** tab, select **OWASP_TOP10**.
4. Under the **Target** address window, fill in `http://localhost:8080/`, changing the hostname to suit your environment.
5. Click on the **Start** button. The penetration tests will now take place and the **Start** button will change to **Stop**. At the end of the scan, the **Stop** button will change to **Clear**.
6. View the **attack history** by selecting the **Log** tab.
7. Review the results by clicking on the **Results** tab.

8. After the first scan, select **full_audit** under **Profiles**.
9. Click on the **Clear** button.
10. Type `http://localhost:8080/` in the **Target** address window.
11. Click on the **Start** button.
12. Wait until the scan has finished and review the **Results** tab.

How it works...

w3af is written by security professionals. It is a pluggable framework with extensions written for different types of attacks. The profiles define which plugins and their associated configurations you are going to use in the penetration test.

You first attack using the **OWASP_TOP10** profile and then attack again with a fuller set of plugins.

The results will vary according to your setup. Depending on the plugin, security issues are occasionally flagged that do not exist. You will need to verify any issues mentioned by hand.

At the time of writing, no significant defects were found using this approach. However, the tool pointed out slow links and generated server-side exceptions. This is the sort of information you would like to note in bug reports.

There's more...

Consistently securing your applications requires experienced attention to detail. Here are a few more things for you to review.

Target practice with WebGoat

The top 10 list of security defects can at times seem difficult to understand. If you have some spare time and would like to practice against a deliberately insecure application, you should try WebGoat (`https://www.owasp.org/index.php/Category:OWASP_WebGoat_Project`).

WebGoat is well-documented with a hints system and links to video tutorials; it leaves little room for misunderstanding the attacks.

More tools of the trade

w3af is a powerful tool, but works better in conjunction with the following tools:

- **Nmap** (`http://nmap.org/`): A simple to use, highly popular, award-winning network scanner.
- **Nikto** (`http://cirt.net/nikto2`): A Perl script that quickly summarizes system details and looks for the most obvious defects.
- **Skipfish** (`https://code.google.com/p/skipfish/downloads/list`): A C program that bashes away at many requests over a prolonged period. You can choose from different dictionaries of attacks. This is an excellent poor man's stress test; if your system stays up, you know that it has reached a minimal level of stability.
- **Wapiti** (`http://wapiti.sourceforge.net/`): A Python-based script that discovers attackable URLs and then cycles through a list of evil parameters.

Jenkins is flexible, so you can call a wide range of tools through scripts running in jobs, including the security tools mentioned:

 There are a number of great resources for securing native OSes, including the Debian security how-to (`https://www.debian.org/doc/manuals/securing-debian-howto/`); for Windows, articles found underneath the MSDN security center (`http://msdn.microsoft.com/en-us/security/`); and for Mac, Apple's official security guides (`https://www.apple.com/support/security/guides/`). Online services need vigorous attention to their security surface.

See also

- The *Finding 500 errors and XSS attacks in Jenkins through fuzzing* recipe
- The *Exploring the OWASP dependency-check plugin* recipe

Finding 500 errors and XSS attacks in Jenkins through fuzzing

This recipe describes using a fuzzer to find server-side errors and XSS attacks in your Jenkins servers.

A fuzzer goes through a series of URLs, appends different parameters blindly, and checks the server's response. The inputted parameters are variations on scripting commands, such as `<script>alert("random string");</script>`. An attack vector is found if the server's response includes the unescaped version of the script.

Cross-site scripting attacks are currently one of the more popular forms of attack (`http://en.wikipedia.org/wiki/Cross-site_scripting`). The attack involves injecting script fragments into the client's browser so that the script runs as if it comes from a trusted website. For example, once you have logged in to an application, it is probable that your session ID is stored in a cookie. The injected script might read the value in the cookie and then send the information to another server ready for an attempt at reuse.

A fuzzer discovers the links on the site it is attacking and the form variables that exist within the site's web pages. For the web pages discovered, it repeatedly sends input based on historic attacks and lots of minor variations. If responses are returned with the same random strings sent, the fuzzer knows it has found an evil URL.

To fully integrate with the build process of a web-based application, you will need to build the application, deploy and run the application, run the fuzzer from a script, and finally, use log parsing to fail the build if evil URLs are mentioned in the output. This process will be similar for other command-line tools you wish to integrate. For more information about log parsing, refer to the *Deliberately failing builds through log parsing* recipe in Chapter 1, Getting Started with Jenkins.

Getting ready

Back up your sacrificial Jenkins server and turn off its security. Expect the application to be unstable by the end of the attack.

You will need the Python programming language installed on your computer. To download and install Wapiti, you will need to follow the instructions found at `http://wapiti.sourceforge.net`.

If you're attacking your local machine from your local machine, then you can afford to turn off its networking. The attack will stay in the loopback network driver and no packets should escape to the internet.

In this recipe, the methodology and command-line options are correct. However, at the time of writing, the results mentioned may not exist. Jenkins goes through a rapid life cycle where developers remove bugs rapidly.

How to do it...

1. Within the `wapiti` bin directory, run the following command:

   ```
   python wapiti  http://localhost:8080 -m "-all,xss,exec" -x
   http://localhost:8080/pluginManager/* -v2
   ```

2. When the command has finished running, you will see the location of the final report on the console output:

   ```
   Report
   ------
   A report has been generated in the file
   ~/.wapiti/generated_report
   ~/.wapiti/generated_report/index.html with a browser to see
   this report.
   ```

3. Open the report in a web browser and review it.
4. Click on the **Internal Server Error** link.
5. For one of the items named **Anomaly** found in **/iconSize**, copy the URL from the **URL command line** tab:
6. Open the URL in a web browser. You will now see a newly generated Jenkins bug report page, as shown in the following screenshot:
7. Run the following command:

   ```
   python wapiti http://localhost:8080 -m "-all,xss,permanentxss"
   -x http://localhost:8080/pluginManager/*
   ```

8. View the output to verify that the `permanentxss` module was run:

```
[*] Loading modules :
mod_crlf, mod_exec, mod_file, mod_sql, mod_xss,
mod_backup, mod_htaccess, mod_blindsql,    mod_permanentxss,
mod_nikto
[+] Launching module xss
[+] Launching module permanentxss
```

How it works...

Wapiti loads in different modules. By default, all modules are used. You will have to be selective; for Version 2.2.1 on Ubuntu Linux, this causes Wapiti to crash or timeout.

To load in specific modules, use the -m option.

The -m `"-all,xss,exec"` statement tells Wapiti to ignore all modules except the xss and exec modules.

The exec module is very good at finding 500 errors in Jenkins. This is mostly due to unexpected input, which Jenkins does not handle well. This is purely a cosmetic set of issues. However, if you start to see errors associated with resources such as files or database services, then you should give the issues higher priority and send in bug reports.

The -x option specifies which URLs to ignore. In this case, we don't want to cause work for the plugin manager. If we do, it will then generate a lot of requests to an innocent external service.

Wapiti crawls websites. If you are not careful, the tool might follow a link to locations that you do not want testing. To avoid embarrassment, carefully use the exclude URL's option, -x.

The -v2 option sets the verbosity of logging up to its highest so that you can see all the attacks.

In the second run of Wapiti, you also used the `permanentxss` module, which at times finds bonafide XSS attacks, depending on the race between developers building features and cleaning bugs:

 Fuzzers are good at covering a large portion of an application's URL space, triggering errors that would be costly in terms of time to search out. Consider automating through a Jenkins job as part of a project's QA process.

There's more...

The reports you generated in this recipe mention many more server errors than XSS attacks. This is because many of the errors generated are due to unexpected input causing failures that are only caught by the final layer of error handling; in this case, the bug report page. If you consider the error worth reporting, then follow the instructions found on the bug report page.

Here are some guidelines for the meaning behind the output of the stack traces:

- `java.lang.SecurityException`: If a Jenkins user is doing something that the programmer considers insecure, such as hitting a URL, this should only be reachable once you have logged in.
- `java.lang.IllegalArgumentException`: Jenkins checked for a valid range for your parameter and the parameter value was outside that range. This is a deliberately thrown exception.
- `java.lang.NumberFormatException`: Jenkins did not check for a valid string and then tried to parse a non-conformant string to a number.
- `java.lang.NullPointerException`: This normally happens when you hit a URL without all the parameters set that Jenkins expects. In programmer's language, the code is expecting an object that does not exist, and then tries to call a method of the nonexistent object without checking that the object exists. The programmer needs to add more error-checking. Write a bug report.

See also

- The *Testing for OWASP's top 10 security issues* recipe

Avoiding sign-up bots with JCaptcha

CAPTCHA stands for **Completely Automated Public Turing test to tell Computers and Humans Apart**. The most commonly viewed CAPTCHAs are sequential letters and numbers displayed as graphics that you have to correctly feed into a text input.

If you let anyone sign up for an account on your Jenkins server, then the last thing you want are bots (automated scripts) creating accounts. Bots have an economy of scale, being able to scan the internet rapidly and never getting bored. CAPTCHAs are a necessary defense against these dumb attacks.

The negative purposes of bots are as follows:

- Performing a **Denial Of Service (DOS)** attack on your server, for example, by automatically creating numerous heavyweight jobs
- **Distributed Denial Of Service attack (DDOS)** on other servers by harvesting many Jenkins servers to fire off large numbers of requests
- Injecting unwanted advertisements or content that then points to malicious sites
- Adding scripts that are stored permanently and run when a user accidentally browses the Jenkins site

> There are commercial motivations for criminals to circumvent CAPTCHAs that have led to well-documented law cases. You can find one such law case at `http://www.wired.com/2010/10/hacking-captcha/`.

Getting ready

Make sure you have backed up your sacrificial Jenkins server. You are going to modify its security settings. It is easy to make a service-changing mistake.

> The `JCaptcha` plugin is based on Java implementation that you can find at `https://jcaptcha.atlassian.net/wiki/display/general/Home`.

How to do it...

1. Log in as an administrator.
2. Click on the **Configure Global Security** link.
3. Select **Jenkins' own user database** under **Security Realm**.
4. Select **Allow users to sign up**:
5. Press **Save**.
6. Browse to the signup location, `http://localhost:8080/signup`.
7. Click on the **Manage Plugins** link in the **Manage Jenkins** page.
8. Select the **Available** tab.
9. Install the `JCaptcha` plugin.
10. Click on the **Configure Global Security** link under the **Manage Jenkins** page.
11. Select **Jenkins' own user database** under **Security Realm**.
12. Select **Enable captcha on sign up**.
13. Press **Save** and then click on the **Log Out** link.
14. Browse to the signup location, `http://localhost:8080/signup`. The page is now defended by a CAPTCHA.

How it works...

Installing the plugin adds the CAPTCHA image to the signup process. The image needs pattern recognition to decipher it. Humans are very good at this; automated processes are a lot worse, but improving.

4

Improving Code Quality

In this chapter, we will cover the following recipes:

- Integrating Jenkins with SonarQube
- The updating center in SonarQube
- Quality gates, quality profiles, and rules
- Verifying HTML, CSS, and JavaScript validity using SonarQube
- Verifying Java code using SonarQube
- Configuring SonarQube as a Windows service

Introduction

This chapter explores the use of Jenkins plugins to display code metrics and failed builds. Automation lowers costs and improves consistency. The process does not get tired. If you decide the success and failure criteria before a project starts, then this will remove a degree of subjective debate from release meetings.

In 2002, NIST estimated that software defects were costing America around 60 billion dollars per year (`http://www.abeacha.com/NIST_press_release_bugs_cost.html`). Expect the cost to have increased considerably since. To save money and improve quality, you need to remove defects as early in the software lifecycle as possible.

You will also find recipes in this chapter on static code review through SonarQube. Static means that you can look at the code without running it. Good documentation and source code structure aid the maintainability and readability of your code.

There are a number of good introductions to software metrics. These include a Wikibook on the details of the metrics (`http://en.wikibooks.org/wiki/Introduction_to_Software_Engineering/Quality/Metrics`) and a well-written book called *Code Quality: The Open Source Perspective*, by Diomidis Spinellis.

In the *Integrating Jenkins with SonarQube* recipe of this chapter, you will link Jenkins projects to Sonar reports. Sonar is a specialized tool that collects software metrics and breaks them down into understandable reports. Sonar details the quality of a project. It uses a wide range of metrics including the results of tools such as FindBugs and PMD, mentioned in this chapter. The project itself is evolving rapidly. Consider using Jenkins for early warnings and to spot obvious defects, such as a bad commit. You can then use Sonar for a deeper review.

Download SonarQube from `https://www.sonarqube.org/downloads/` and extract it in the system:

Name	Date modified	Type	Size
lib	01-08-2017 08:31	File folder	
InstallNTService.bat	11-04-2017 13:55	Windows Batch File	2 KB
StartNTService.bat	11-04-2017 13:55	Windows Batch File	2 KB
StartSonar.bat	11-04-2017 13:55	Windows Batch File	2 KB
StopNTService.bat	11-04-2017 13:55	Windows Batch File	2 KB
UninstallNTService.bat	11-04-2017 13:55	Windows Batch File	2 KB
wrapper.exe	11-04-2017 13:39	Application	216 KB

SonarQube supports 20+ programming languages: Java Android, JavaScript, HTML, CSS, Objective-C, C#, C/C++, PHP, Python, PL/SQL, Flex, Groovy, COBOL, Swift (paid plugin), and so on. It allows reports on bugs, vulnerabilities, code smells, duplicate code, code coverage, comments, and so on.

1. Java 8 is a prerequisite for running SonarQube.
2. In the Windows OS, go to the `bin` directory and, based on the operating system and platform of the operating system, go to the specific directory.

3. Execute `StartSonar.bat` in the command window, as we are using the Windows OS:

You will find the **SonarQube is up** message in the console if it starts successfully.

- Once SonarQube is up and running, open the browser at `http://localhost:9000` to visit the SonarQube dashboard
- You may want to check the requirements at `https://docs.sonarqube.org/display/SONAR/Requirements` and set up and upgrade at `https://docs.sonarqube.org/display/SONAR/Setup+and+Upgrade`

Integrating Jenkins with SonarQube

SonarQube, previously known as Sonar, is a rapidly evolving application for reporting quality metrics and finding code hotspots. This recipe details how to generate code metrics through a Jenkins plugin, and then push them directly to a Sonar database.

Getting ready...

1. Go to the Jenkins dashboard and click on **Manage Jenkins**. Go to **Manage Plugins** and in the **Available** tab find the SonarQube plugin.

2. Click on **Install without restart**:

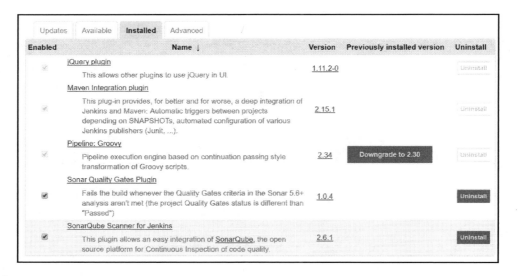

3. Go to the Jenkins dashboard and click on **Manage Jenkins**.
4. Click on **Configure system** and find the **SonarQube** section.
5. Now, let's go to SonarQube to get the token to integrate Jenkins and SonarQube.
6. Once SonarQube is up and running, open the browser at
   `http://localhost:9000` to visit the SonarQube dashboard:

7. Click on **Login** and give the default username and password as `admin` and `default` to log in as an administrator.

8. Click on **Login**:

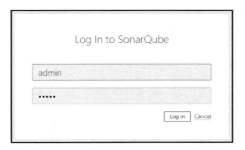

9. As of now, there is no project available in the SonarQube dashboard.

10. Click on the **Administration** tab and in the **Security** menu click on **Users**:

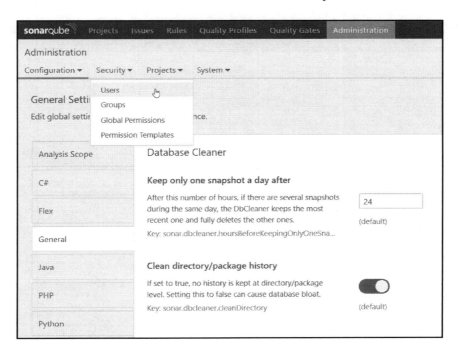

11. Initially, there are no tokens issued; there is a **0** token for **Administrator**:

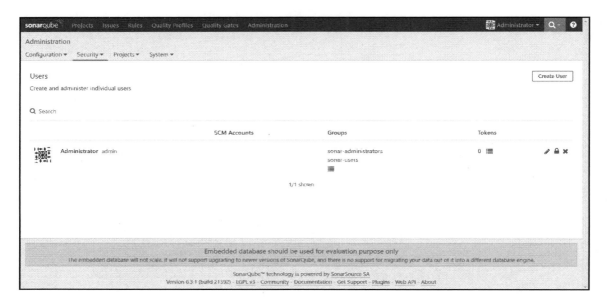

12. Click on **Tokens**:

13. Give a name in the **Generate Tokens** section and click on **Generate**:

14. Copy the newly created token. Click on **Done**:

15. Verify the number of **Tokens** for the **Administrator** user:

16. Now we have all the required parameters to integrate Jenkins and SonarQube:

How to do it...

1. Go to the Jenkins dashboard and click on **Manage Jenkins**.
2. Click on **Configure system** and find the **SonarQube** section.
3. Click on **Add SonarQube**.
4. Provide the **Name**, **Server URL**, and **Server version**.
5. Paste the token value in Jenkins and save it:

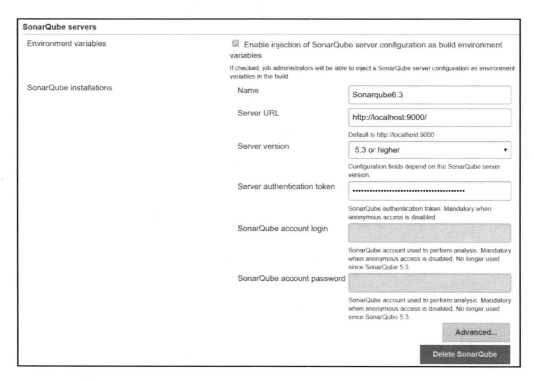

6. Go to **Global Tool Configuration** and configure **Add SonarQube Scanner**:

7. Now, you are ready for the static code analysis of the project.

There's more

The default SonarQube instance is preconfigured with an in-memory database. The Jenkins plugin already knows the default configuration and requires little extra configuration.

Just for troubleshooting, if you come across a Jenkins job failure due to SCM blame, you need to fix that by configuring it in SonarQube.

Go to **SonarQube** and **Disable the SCM sensor**:

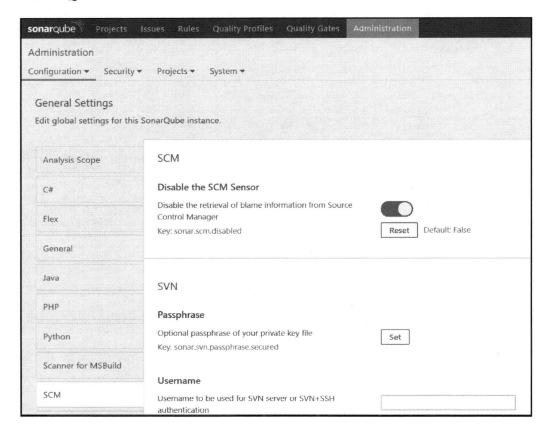

Sonar is a dedicated application for measuring software-quality metrics. Like Jenkins, it has a dedicated and active community. You can expect an aggressive roadmap of improvements. Features such as its ability to point out hotspots of suspicious code, a visually appealing report dashboard, ease of configuration, and detailed control of inspection rules to view, all currently differentiate it from Jenkins.

The updating center in SonarQube

Administrators can utilize the **Update Center** to keep SonarQube up to date by installing plugins and updating plugins.

Getting ready

1. Go to **Administration** | **System** | **Update Center**:

2. The **Update Center** contains four tabs: **Installed, Updates Only, Available,** and **System Upgrades**:

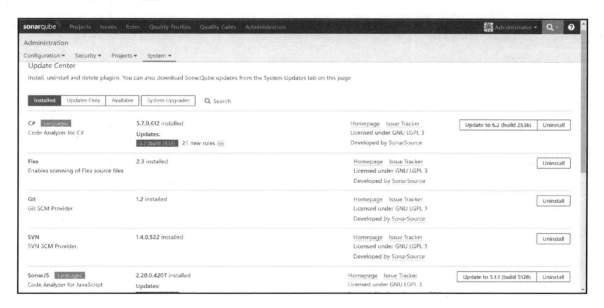

3. As mentioned earlier, we can install and update different plugins so we can perform static code analysis.

How to do it...

1. Go to **Administration** | **System** | **Update Center**.
2. Click on **Update** or **Uninstall** to perform those operations in the SonarQube portal:

3. Updates will be pending if you don't **Restart** SonarQube:

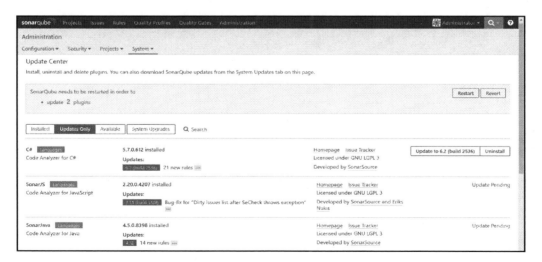

4. Go to **Administration** | **System** | **Update Center** | **Available** to install new plugins:

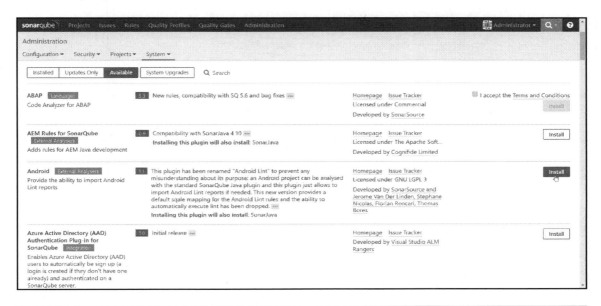

5. Click on **Restart**:

6. **Restart** SonarQube:

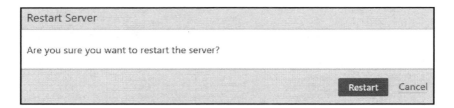

7. Wait until the server restarts:

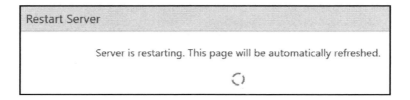

8. This is how we can use the **Update Center** to install, uninstall, and update the plugins available in SonarQube.

There's more...

1. Go to the **Administration** | **System** | **Update Center** | **Installed** tab to verify all the newly installed plugins:

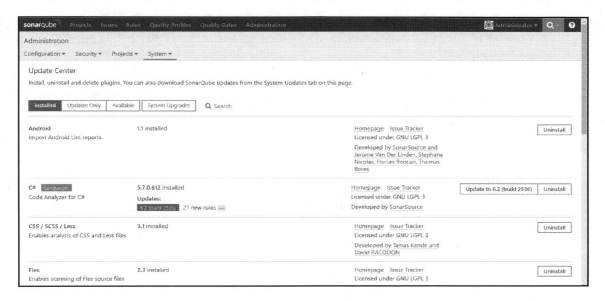

2. You can uninstall plugins from the **Installed** tab also.

Quality gates, quality profiles, and rules

In this section, we will look at the default quality gate that defines the base level for passing or failing code analysis, and quality profiles is rule specific to a particular programming language.

How to do it...

1. As of now there is no project available in the SonarQube dashboard:

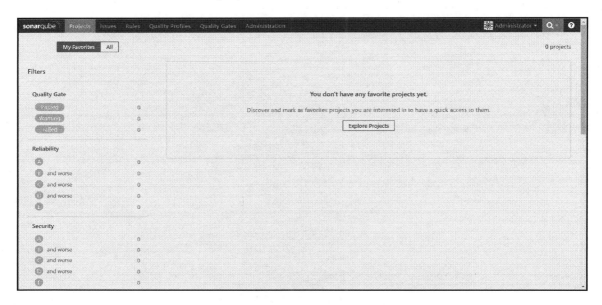

2. **Quality Gate** is used to enforce policy in the organization for static code analysis.
3. The SonarQube way is the default **Quality Gate** and you assign it to different projects based on the policies required.
4. You can also add conditions based on your requirement and policies you want to enforce:

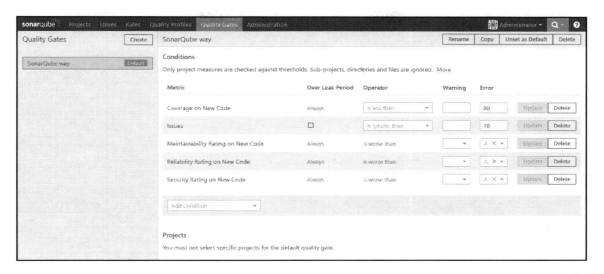

5. Click on the **Quality Profiles** tab to get details on the default quality profiles available in SonarQube.

6. **Quality Profiles** is at the heart of SonarQube; it is just a set of rules specific to a language. If not mentioned explicitly, all the projects are analyzed with default profiles. However, it is ideal to have a profile for each project so that specific rules can be set or deactivated. Each language has a default profile named Sonar way:

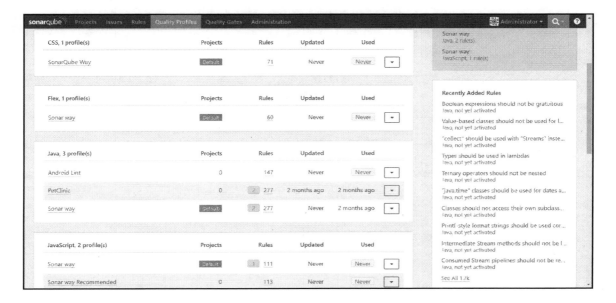

7. Click on the **Rules** tab to get more details about the existing rules available in profiles:

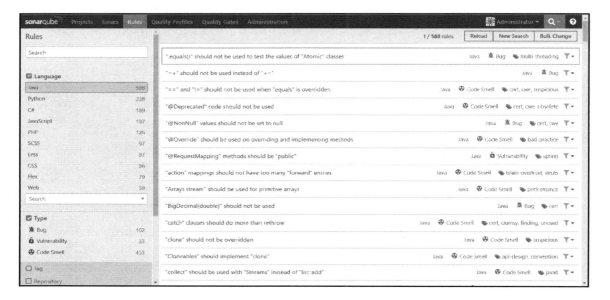

8. Click on rule to get more insight into it:

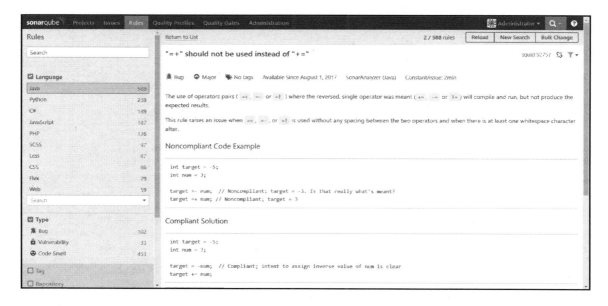

9. Go to **Quality Profiles** and select the Sonar way default profile. Observe the total **Active and Inactive Rules**.

Verifying HTML, CSS and JavaScript validity using SonarQube

You are going to perform static code analysis on the sample application that comprises HTML, CSS, and JavaScript files.

Getting ready

1. Go to the Jenkins dashboard and click on **New Item**.
2. Give the **Name** and select **Freestyle project**:

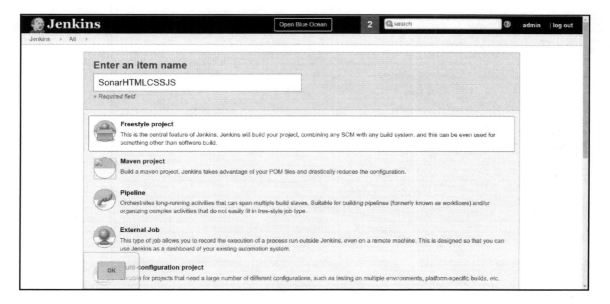

3. Provide the **Repository URL** in the **Source Code Management** section:

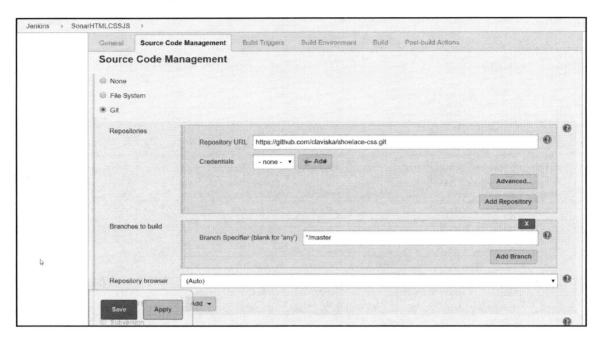

4. Any project that has HTML, CSS, and JavaScript files can be utilized.

How to do it...

1. Go to the **Build** section and select **Execute SonarQube Scanner**:

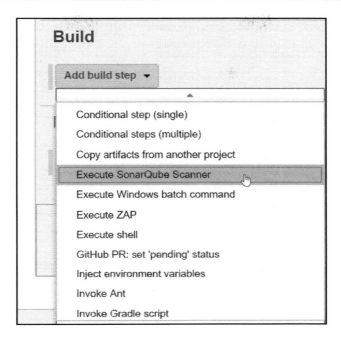

2. You can provide the location of `sonar-project.properties` or provide details directly for static code analysis.

```
# Required metadata
sonar.projectKey=SonarHTMLCSSJS
sonar.projectName=Simple HTML CSS JS project analyzed with the
SonarQube
sonar.projectVersion=1.0
# Comma-separated paths to directories with sources (required)
sonar.sources=.
# Encoding of the source files
sonar.sourceEncoding=UTF-8
```

3. `sonar.sources` is the main property for static code analysis. With this property, you inform SonarQube which directory needs to be analyzed:

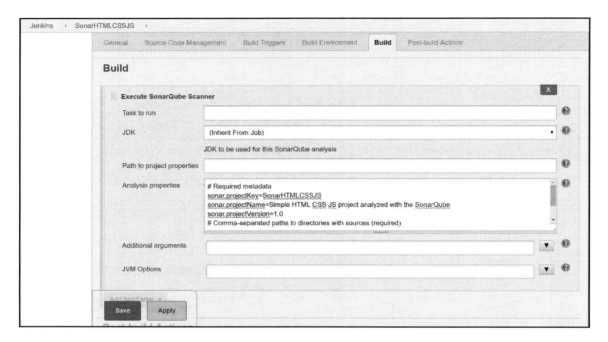

4. Click on **Save**.
5. Go to Jenkins Project and click on **Build now**.
6. Go to **Console output** to check the logs.
7. Just observe the logs given in the following code.
8. You will notice that based on the available files, SonarQube automatically selects different quality profiles and analyzes the code:
9. Started by user admin.
10. `[EnvInject]` - Loading node environment variables.
11. Building in workspace:
    `F:\1.DevOps2016\#JenkinsEssentials\FirstDraft\jenkinsHome\works`
    `pace\SonarHTMLCSSJS`

12. Cloning the remote Git repository:

```
Cloning repository https://github.com/claviska/shoelace-css.git
>git.exe init
F:\1.DevOps2016\#JenkinsEssentials\FirstDraft\jenkinsHome\works
pace\SonarHTMLCSSJS # timeout=10
```

13. Fetching upstream changes from `https://github.com/claviska/shoelace-css.git`:

```
> git.exe --version # timeout=10
>git.exe fetch --tags --progress
https://github.com/claviska/shoelace-css.git
+refs/heads/*:refs/remotes/origin/*
>git.exe config remote.origin.url
https://github.com/claviska/shoelace-css.git # timeout=10
>git.exe config --add remote.origin.fetch
+refs/heads/*:refs/remotes/origin/* # timeout=10
>git.exe config remote.origin.url
https://github.com/claviska/shoelace-css.git # timeout=10
```

14. Fetching upstream changes from `https://github.com/claviska/shoelace-css.git`:

```
>git.exe fetch --tags --progress
https://github.com/claviska/shoelace-css.git
+refs/heads/*:refs/remotes/origin/*
>git.exe rev-parse "refs/remotes/origin/master{commit}" #
timeout=10
>git.exe rev-parse "refs/remotes/origin/origin/master{commit}"
# timeout=10
```

15. Checking out revision `39b44e9519e5050675e01527c421c5e0f3a046b7` (`refs/remotes/origin/master`):

```
>git.exe config core.sparsecheckout # timeout=10
>git.exe checkout -f 39b44e9519e5050675e01527c421c5e0f3a046b7
```

16. First time build. Skipping changelog:

```
[SonarHTMLCSSJS] $
F:\1.DevOps2016\#JenkinsEssentials\FirstDraft\jenkinsHome\tools
\hudson.plugins.sonar.SonarRunnerInstallation\SonarQube_Scanner
_3.0.3\bin\sonar-scanner.bat -e -
Dsonar.host.url=http://localhost:9000/ ******** "-
Dsonar.projectName=Simple HTML CSS JS project analyzed with the
SonarQube" -Dsonar.projectVersion=1.0 -
```

```
Dsonar.sourceEncoding=UTF-8 -Dsonar.projectKey=SonarHTMLCSSJS -
Dsonar.sources=. -
Dsonar.projectBaseDir=F:\1.DevOps2016\#JenkinsEssentials\FirstD
raft\jenkinsHome\workspace\SonarHTMLCSSJS

INFO: Option -e/--errors is no longer supported and will be
ignored
INFO: Scanner configuration file:
F:\1.DevOps2016\#JenkinsEssentials\FirstDraft\jenkinsHome\tools
\hudson.plugins.sonar.SonarRunnerInstallation\SonarQube_Scanner
_3.0.3\bin\..\conf\sonar-scanner.properties
INFO: Project root configuration file: NONE
INFO: SonarQube Scanner 3.0.3.778
INFO: Java 1.8.0_111 Oracle Corporation (64-bit)
INFO: Windows 10 10.0 amd64
INFO: User cache:
C:\WINDOWS\system32\config\systemprofile\.sonar\cache
INFO: Load global settings
INFO: Load global settings (done) | time=557ms
INFO: User cache:
C:\WINDOWS\system32\config\systemprofile\.sonar\cache
INFO: Load plugins index
INFO: Load plugins index (done) | time=113ms
INFO: Download sonar-csharp-plugin-5.7.0.612.jar
INFO: Download sonar-python-plugin-1.7.0.1195.jar
INFO: Download sonar-css-plugin-3.1.jar
INFO: Download sonar-java-plugin-4.12.0.11033.jar
INFO: Download sonar-scm-git-plugin-1.2.jar
INFO: Download sonar-android-plugin-1.1.jar
INFO: Download sonar-php-plugin-2.9.2.1744.jar
INFO: Download sonar-scm-svn-plugin-1.4.0.522.jar
INFO: SonarQube server 6.3.1
INFO: Default locale: "en_IN", source code encoding: "UTF-8"
INFO: Process project properties
INFO: Load project repositories
INFO: Load project repositories (done) | time=140ms
INFO: Load quality profiles
INFO: Load quality profiles (done) | time=437ms
INFO: Load active rules
INFO: Load active rules (done) | time=6984ms
INFO: Load metrics repository
INFO: Load metrics repository (done) | time=752ms
INFO: Publish mode
INFO: Project key: SonarHTMLCSSJS
INFO: ------------ Scan Simple HTML CSS JS project analyzed
with the SonarQube
INFO: Load server rules
INFO: Load server rules (done) | time=1241ms
```

```
INFO: Initializer GenericCoverageSensor
INFO: Initializer GenericCoverageSensor (done) | time=0ms
INFO: Base dir:
F:\1.DevOps2016\#JenkinsEssentials\FirstDraft\jenkinsHome\works
pace\SonarHTMLCSSJS
INFO: Working dir:
F:\1.DevOps2016\#JenkinsEssentials\FirstDraft\jenkinsHome\works
pace\SonarHTMLCSSJS\.scannerwork
INFO: Source paths: .
INFO: Source encoding: UTF-8, default locale: en_IN
INFO: Index files
INFO: 30 files indexed
INFO: Quality profile for css: SonarQube Way
INFO: Quality profile for js: Sonar way
INFO: Quality profile for web: Sonar way
INFO: Sensor NoSonar Sensor [php]
INFO: Sensor NoSonar Sensor [php] (done) | time=0ms
INFO: Sensor Coverage Report Import [csharp]
INFO: Sensor Coverage Report Import [csharp] (done) | time=0ms
INFO: Sensor Coverage Report Import [csharp]
INFO: Sensor Coverage Report Import [csharp] (done) | time=0ms
INFO: Sensor Unit Test Results Import [csharp]
INFO: Sensor Unit Test Results Import [csharp] (done) |
time=1ms
INFO: Sensor CSS Analyzer Sensor [css]
INFO: 15 source files to be analyzed
INFO: Sensor CSS Analyzer Sensor [css] (done) | time=8774ms
INFO: 15/15 source files have been analyzed
INFO: Sensor Embedded CSS Analyzer Sensor [css]
INFO: 1 source files to be analyzed
INFO: Sensor Embedded CSS Analyzer Sensor [css] (done) |
time=631ms
INFO: Sensor SonarJavaXmlFileSensor [java]
INFO: Sensor SonarJavaXmlFileSensor [java] (done) | time=0ms
INFO: Sensor Web [web]
INFO: 1/1 source files have been analyzed
INFO: Sensor Web [web] (done) | time=3667ms
INFO: Sensor Analyzer for "php.ini" files [php]
INFO: Sensor Analyzer for "php.ini" files [php] (done) |
time=0ms
INFO: Sensor JavaScript Squid Sensor [javascript]
INFO: 2 source files to be analyzed
INFO: Unit Test Coverage Sensor is started
INFO: 2/2 source files have been analyzed
INFO: Integration Test Coverage Sensor is started
INFO: Overall Coverage Sensor is started
INFO: Sensor JavaScript Squid Sensor [javascript] (done) |
time=1949ms
```

```
INFO: Sensor Zero Coverage Sensor
INFO: Sensor Zero Coverage Sensor (done) | time=334ms
INFO: Sensor Code Colorizer Sensor
INFO: Sensor Code Colorizer Sensor (done) | time=4ms
INFO: Sensor CPD Block Indexer
INFO:
org.sonar.scanner.cpd.deprecated.DefaultCpdBlockIndexer@511a307
e is used for css
INFO:
org.sonar.scanner.cpd.deprecated.DefaultCpdBlockIndexer@511a307
e is used for js
INFO:
org.sonar.scanner.cpd.deprecated.DefaultCpdBlockIndexer@511a307
e is used for web
INFO: Sensor CPD Block Indexer (done) | time=3ms
INFO: SCM Publisher is disabled
INFO: Calculating CPD for 18 files
INFO: CPD calculation finished
INFO: Analysis report generated in 1401ms, dir size=475 KB
INFO: Analysis reports compressed in 244ms, zip size=111 KB
INFO: Analysis report uploaded in 13680ms
INFO: ANALYSIS SUCCESSFUL, you can browse
http://localhost:9000/dashboard/index/SonarHTMLCSSJS
INFO: Note that you will be able to access the updated
dashboard once the server has processed the submitted analysis
report
INFO: More about the report processing at
http://localhost:9000/api/ce/task?id=AV2b4vtMnc_wgjAawYBq
INFO: Task total time: 56.134 s
INFO: ------------------------------------------------------
---------------
INFO: EXECUTION SUCCESS
INFO: ------------------------------------------------------
---------------
INFO: Total time: 1:09.022s
INFO: Final Memory: 50M/219M
INFO: ------------------------------------------------------
---------------
Started calculate disk usage of build
Finished Calculation of disk usage of build in 0 seconds
Started calculate disk usage of workspace
Finished Calculation of disk usage of workspace in 0 seconds
Finished: SUCCESS
```

17. Go to http://localhost:9000/ where SonarQube is available and check whether static code analysis for our project is available or not.

18. Click on the Project link in SonarQube:

19. The default **Quality Profiles** and **Quality Gate** are used in static code analysis.
20. There are **Bugs &Vulnerabilities**, and **Code Smells** related details available. Click on each of them to get more details based on the files.
21. **Quality Gate** has **Failed** here and conditions are not met:

22. Go to the **Code** tab to get the file and directory **Bugs & Vulnerabilities** and **Code Smells**:

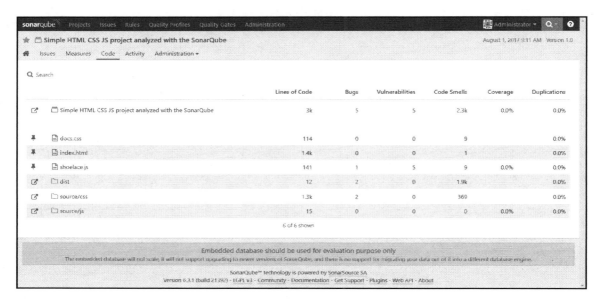

23. Click on **Activity** to get the history of project analysis:

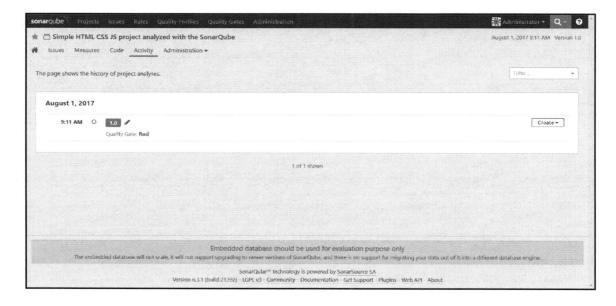

24. Go to **Measures** | **Maintainability** to get details on rating and technical debt:

25. Go to **Measures** | **Size** to get the chart for code smell size:

26. Go to different subsections of the same hierarchy and observe the details in depth to gain more understanding.

There's more

1. Go to **Issues Unresolved** I **Errors** and click on it to get more details:

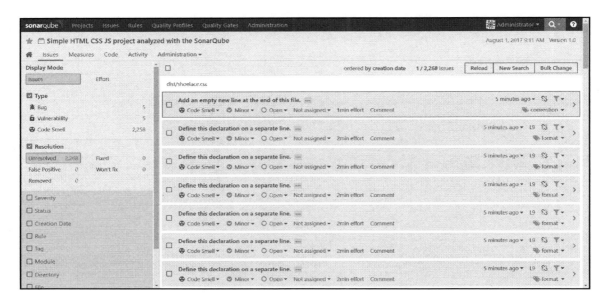

2. There are situations where some issues are false positives. In such cases, configure themes fixed from the SonarQube dashboard.

Verifying Java code using SonarQube

Now let's create a new **Quality Profile** and assign the project so every time static code analysis is performed, the default profile is not used but a custom profile is utilized.

Getting ready

1. Go to **Quality Profiles** and in the Java section, copy the default profile:

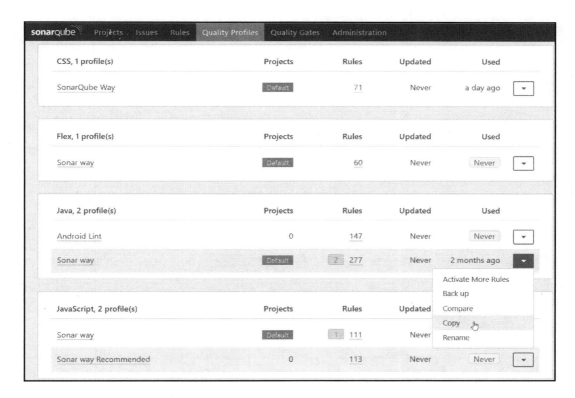

2. Give a specific name to it and click on **Copy**:

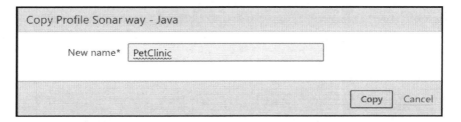

3. We can specify projects for a specific **Quality Profile** by clicking on **Change Projects** as well:

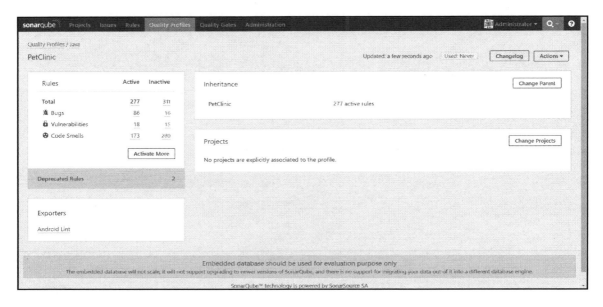

4. Assign a Quality Profile to your project so that the same profile is used every time a static code analysis is performed. Hence, we can use different profiles for different projects based on our requirements.

How to do it...

1. Go to the Jenkins dashboard and click on **New Item**.
2. Give the **Name** and select **Freestyle project**.
3. Provide the **Repository URL** in the **Source Code Management** section.
4. Go to the **Build** section and select **Execute SonarQube Scanner**.
5. You can provide the location of `sonar-project.properties` or provide details directly for static code analysis:

```
# Required metadata sonar.projectKey=java-sonar-runner-simple
sonar.projectName=Java project analyzed with the SonarQube
Runner sonar.projectVersion=1.0 # Comma-separated paths to
directories with sources (required) sonar.sources=src #
Encoding of the source files sonar.sourceEncoding=UTF-8
```

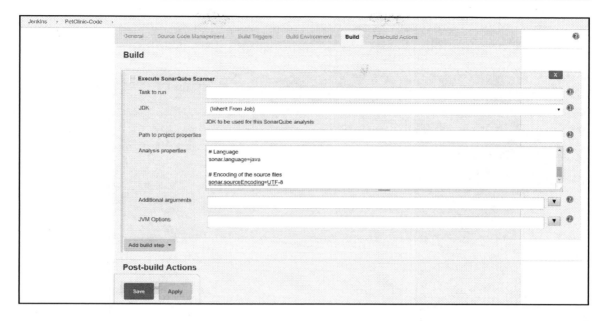

6. Click on **Save** and then **Build now**.
7. Go to the SonarQube dashboard and check **Quality Gate** and **Quality Profiles**:

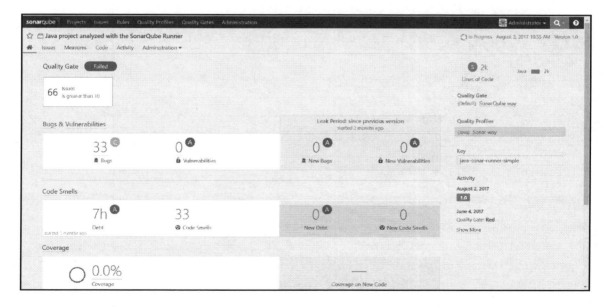

8. Now go to **PetClinic Quality Profile** and click on **Change Projects**.

9. Select **Java project analyzed with the SonarQube Runner** and click on **Close**:

10. Check the **Projects** in **PetClinic Quality Profiles**:

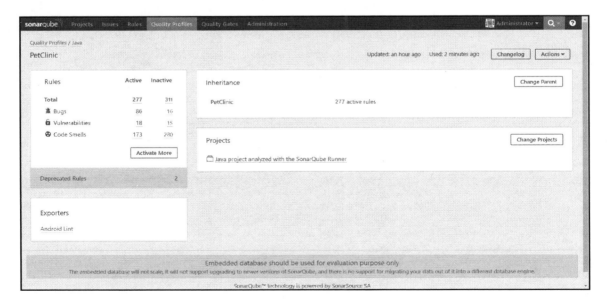

11. Go to Jenkins and click on **Build now**:

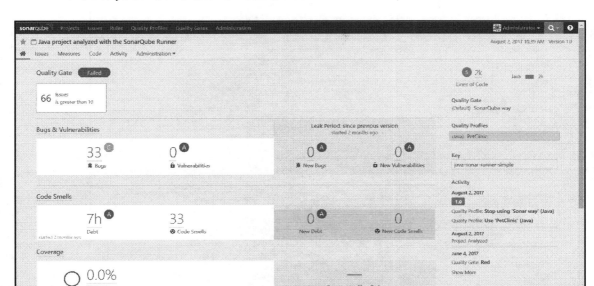

12. Create a new quality gate and assign the quality gate to the Java project.
13. We don't need to mention the language explicitly as SonarQube is intelligent enough to find the programming language and analyze it based on the default profiles.

Configuring SonarQube as a Windows service

It is a pain to start SonarQube every time we start the system. It is better to have a situation where SonarQube has started automatically when the system is started.

Getting ready

Open **Command Prompt** by selecting **Run as administrator**:

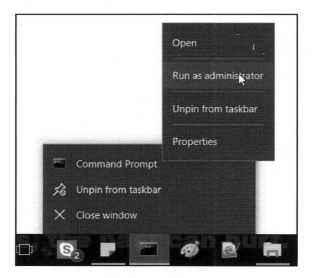

It is important to start **Command Prompt** as **Administrator**.

How to do it...

1. Go to SonarQube | bin | Specific OS Directory | Execute InstallNTService:

```
Administrator: Command Prompt                                                    —    □    ✕
F:\#A.Books\#JenkinsCookBook\sonarqube-6.3.1\bin\windows-x86-64>dir
 Volume in drive F is New Volume
 Volume Serial Number is 6A72-42C1

 Directory of F:\#A.Books\#JenkinsCookBook\sonarqube-6.3.1\bin\windows-x86-64

01-08-2017  08:31    <DIR>          .
01-08-2017  08:31    <DIR>          ..
11-04-2017  13:55             1,272 InstallNTService.bat
01-08-2017  08:31    <DIR>          lib
11-04-2017  13:55             1,262 StartNTService.bat
11-04-2017  13:55             1,424 StartSonar.bat
11-04-2017  13:55             1,260 StopNTService.bat
11-04-2017  13:55             1,276 UninstallNTService.bat
11-04-2017  13:39           220,672 wrapper.exe
               6 File(s)        227,166 bytes
               3 Dir(s)  242,244,472,832 bytes free

F:\#A.Books\#JenkinsCookBook\sonarqube-6.3.1\bin\windows-x86-64>StartNTService.bat
wrapper  | The SonarQube service is not installed - The specified service does not exist
 as an installed service. (0x424)
Press any key to continue . . .

F:\#A.Books\#JenkinsCookBook\sonarqube-6.3.1\bin\windows-x86-64>InstallNTService.bat
wrapper  | SonarQube installed.

F:\#A.Books\#JenkinsCookBook\sonarqube-6.3.1\bin\windows-x86-64>StartNTService.bat
wrapper  | Starting the SonarQube service...
wrapper  | Waiting to start...
wrapper  | SonarQube started.

F:\#A.Books\#JenkinsCookBook\sonarqube-6.3.1\bin\windows-x86-64>
```

2. Execute `StartNTService.bat`.

There's more

Go to **Services** in Windows, and verify whether the SonarQube service is available now or not:

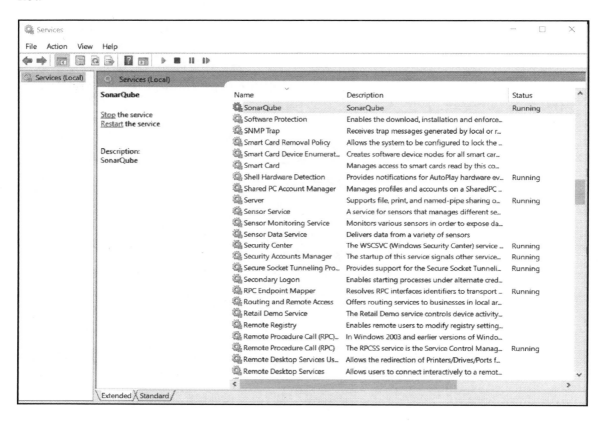

You can start, stop, or restart services once it is available.

5

Building Applications in Jenkins

In this chapter, we will cover the following recipes:

- Configuring an Ant project for execution
- Configuring a Maven project for execution
- Configuring an Android project for execution
- Manipulating environmental variables
- Running Ant through Groovy in Maven
- Failed Jenkins jobs based on JSP syntax errors
- Remotely triggering jobs through the Jenkins API

Introduction

This chapter reviews the relationship between Jenkins, Ant, Gradle, and Maven builds, and there is also a small amount of scripting with Groovy and Ant.

Jenkins is the master of flexibility. It works well across multiple platforms and technologies. Jenkins has an intuitive interface with clear configuration settings. This is great for getting the job done. However, it is also important that you clearly define the boundaries between Jenkins plugins and Maven build files. A lack of separation will make you unnecessarily dependent on Jenkins. If you know that you will always run your builds through Jenkins, then you can afford to place some of the core work in Jenkins plugins, gaining interesting extra functionality.

Jenkins is technology agnostic and can glue together project technologies across the organization, development teams, and software position in their life cycle. Jenkins lets you run scripting languages of choice, and makes it easy to pull in source code using Git, Subversion, CVS, and a number of other version control systems. If Jenkins is not compatible, developers with a little practice can write their own integration.

In this book, you will see both Subversion and Git projects mentioned. This represents a realistic mix. Many consider Git more versatile than Subversion. Feel free to use Git as your repository of choice for the examples in this book. Designed in from the start, Jenkins makes it easy for you to choose between the different revision control systems.

If you look at the relative use of Git and Subversion for a representative collection from Ohoh in early 2014, for Git there were 247,103 repositories (37 percent of the total) and Subversion had 324,895 repositories (48 percent of the total).

Typical enterprises lag behind when using the most modern offerings because of their resistance to changing their working processes. Therefore, expect this category of businesses to have a higher percentage of Subversion repositories compared to smaller organizations.

Configuring an Ant project for execution

Let's configure an Ant project in Jenkins with static code analysis, compilation of files, creation of a package file, and archiving it so you can use it later in another build job or project.

Getting ready

You have already created an Ant project in Jenkins in `Chapter 1`, *Getting Started with Jenkins* in the recipe *Creating a Freestyle Job for an Ant project*.

How to do it...

1. Go to **Jenkins** dashboard | **Ant** project | **General** section.
2. Select **Discard old builds** | Configure **Max # of builds to keep** (to avoid too many builds and save disk space):

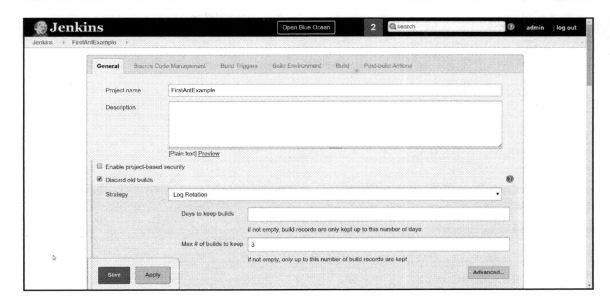

3. Go to **Build** | **Add build step** | **Invoke Ant** | Provide **Targets** based on the `build.xml`:

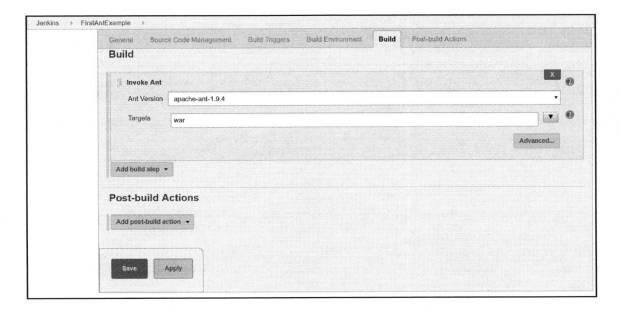

4. Go to **Post-build Actions** | **Add post-build action** | **Archive the artifacts**.

5. Provide the path of the .WAR file that needs to be archived so another project can utilize the package file if required:

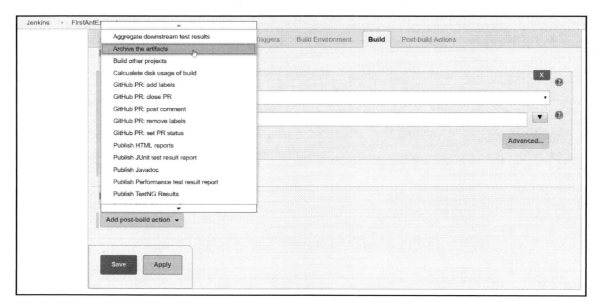

6. Click on **Build now**.

7. Go to **Console Output** (as shown in the following screenshot) and verify the build execution log for all the operations or actions that we have configured:

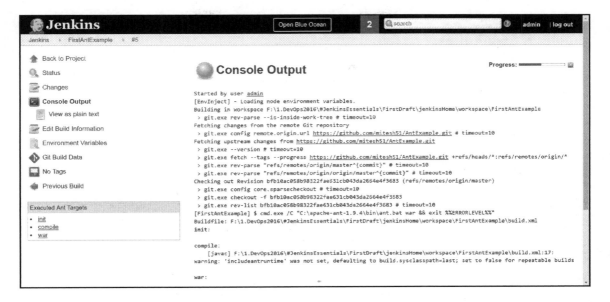

8. Go to **Project** dashboard and verify the number of builds in the **Build History,** in the bottom left-hand corner. Go to Project dashboard and verify **Workspace**. You will find the package file. Both are demonstrated in this screenshot:

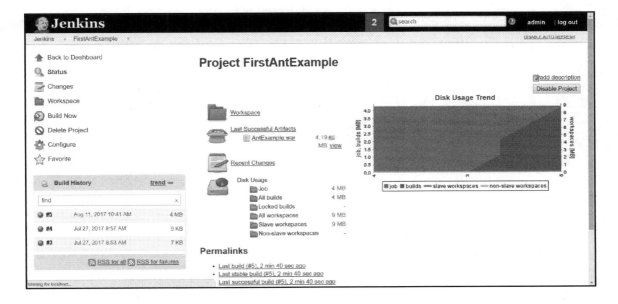

There's more...

- Check the **Console Output**, given here in depth. All the targets mentioned in `build.xml` are available:

```
buildfile:
F:\1.DevOps2016\#JenkinsEssentials\FirstDraft\jenkinsHome\works
pace\FirstAntExample\build.xml
init:
compile:
    [javac]
F:\1.DevOps2016\#JenkinsEssentials\FirstDraft\jenkinsHome\works
pace\FirstAntExample\build.xml:17: warning: 'includeantruntime'
was not set, defaulting to build.sysclasspath=last; set to
false for repeatable builds war:
BUILD SUCCESSFUL
Total time: 1 second
Archiving artifacts
Started calculation of disk usage of build
Finished calculation of disk usage of build in 0 seconds
Started calculation of disk usage of workspace
Finished calculation of disk usage of workspace in 0 seconds
Finished: SUCCESS
```

- Once the build is successful, the artifact or the package file was recovered successfully.

Configuring a Maven project for execution

Let's configure a Maven project in Jenkins with static code analysis, compilation of files, creation of the package file, and archiving it so you can use it later in another build job or project.

Getting ready

You have already created a Maven project in Jenkins in Chapter 1, *Getting Started with Jenkins*, in the recipe, *Creating a Maven Job for a Maven project*.

How to do it...

1. Go to Jenkins dashboard | **Maven Project** | **General Section**.
2. Select **Discard old builds** | Configure **Max # of builds to keep** (to avoid too many builds and save disk space).
3. As the Maven template was selected at the time the build job or project was created, we only need to verify the path of pom.xml and then we can give package as a goal to create a package or WAR file in case of Java.
4. Go to **Post-build Actions** | **Add post-build action** | **Archive the artifacts**.
5. Provide the path of the war file that needs to be archived so another project can utilize the package file if required.
6. Click on **Build now**.
7. Go to **Console Output** and verify the build execution log for all the operations or actions that we have configured.

```
INFO: Task total time: 1:02.260 s
INFO: ------------------------------------------------------------
--------------
INFO: EXECUTION SUCCESS
INFO: ------------------------------------------------------------
--------------
INFO: Total time: 1:37.380s
INFO: Final Memory: 51M/223M
INFO: ------------------------------------------------------------
--------------
Archiving artifacts
Started calculation of disk usage of build
Finished calculation of disk usage of build in 0 seconds
Started calculation of disk usage of workspace
Finished calculation of disk usage of workspace in 0 seconds
Finished: SUCCESS
```

8. Go to the Project dashboard and verify the number of builds in the **Build History**:

9. Go to the Project dashboard and check **Workspace**. You will find the `package` file.

Configuring an Android project for execution

You have already created a Freestyle project in Jenkins in `Chapter 1`, *getting Started with Jenkins*, in the recipe *Creating a Freestyle Job for an Ant project*. You need to create Freestyle project for an Android project.

Getting ready

You can use Android Lint for static code analysis. Before configuring Continuous Integration, install the required plugins.

Go to Jenkins dashboard | **Manage Jenkins** | **ManagePlugins** | **Available**

Install the Android Lint plugin:

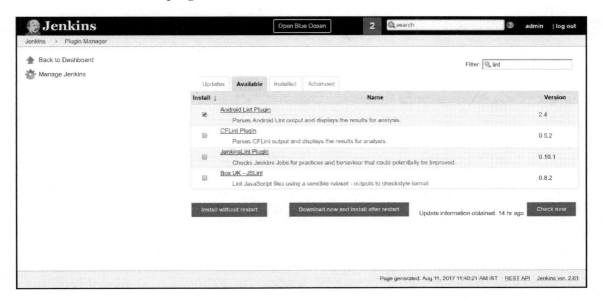

Wait until the plugin has been installed successfully:

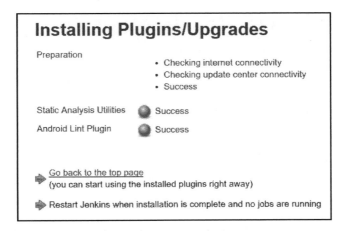

Go to Jenkins dashboard I **Manage Jenkins** I **Global Tool Configuration** I **Gradle** I **Add Gradle**, as shown in this screenshot:

Go to Jenkins dashboard I **Manage Jenkins** I **Configure system** I **Global properties** I **Environment variables**.

Provide the Android SDK path for ANDROID_HOME:

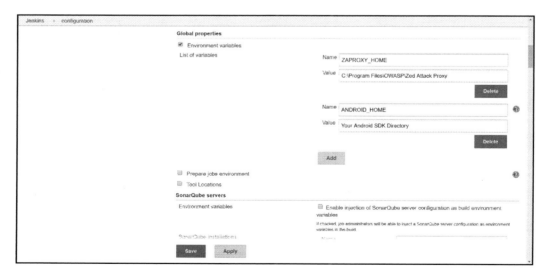

Now, you can configure the Android build and code analysis using Lint and publish the Android Lint results in Jenkins.

How to do it...

1. Go to Jenkins dashboard | **New Item** | **Freestyle project**:

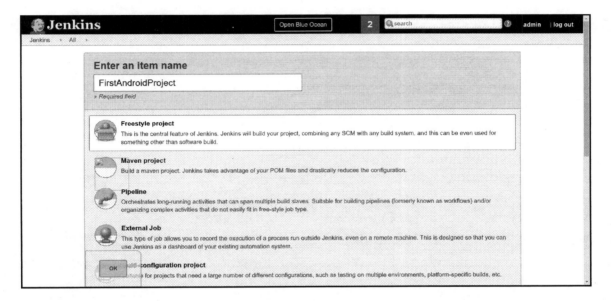

2. Go to **Build Environment** | **Add build step** | **Invoke Gradle script**:

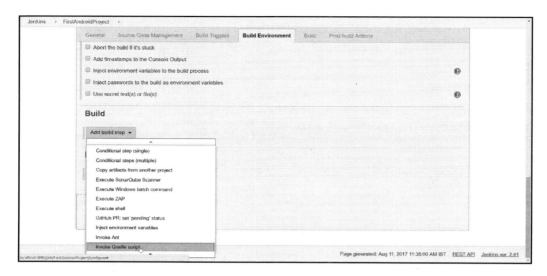

3. Select **Gradle version**.

4. Write `build` in the **Tasks** bar and then click **Save**. Click on **Build now** to execute the Android build and create an APK file:

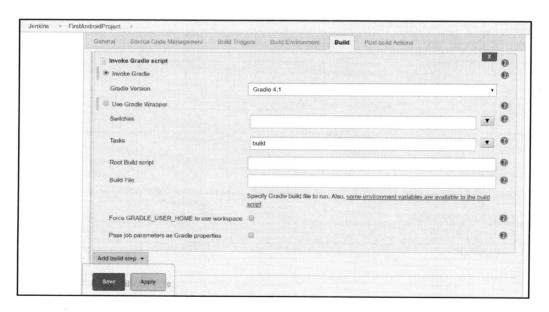

5. To analyze the code with Android Lint, use **lint** in the **Tasks** bar:

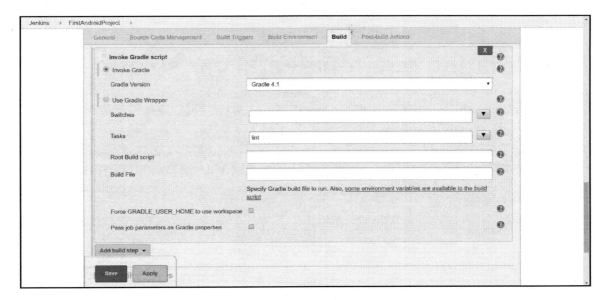

6. **Publish Android Lint results** from **Post-build Actions,** as demonstrated in the following screenshot:

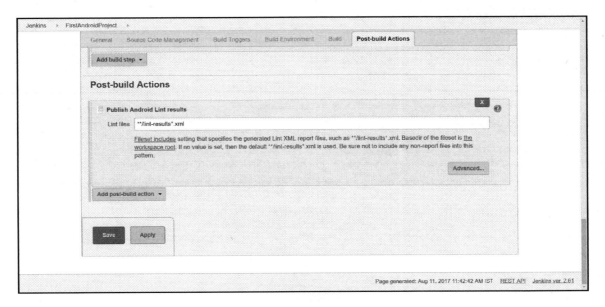

7. In this way, we can configure Ant, Maven, and Android projects for Continuous Integration or execution to create a package file that we can distribute or deploy.

Manipulating environmental variables

This recipe shows you how to pass variables from Jenkins to your build job, and how different variables are overwritten. It also describes one way of failing the build if crucial information has not been correctly passed.

In a typical development/acceptance/production environment, you will want to keep the same pom.xml files, but pass different configurations. One example is the extension names of property files such as .dev, .acc, and .prd. You would want to fail the build if critical configuration values are missing due to human error.

Jenkins has a number of plugins for passing information to builds, including the EnvFile plugin (https://wiki.jenkins-ci.org/display/JENKINS/Envfile+Plugin) and the EnvInject plugin (https://wiki.jenkins-ci.org/display/JENKINS/EnvInject+Plugin). The EnvInject plugin was chosen for this recipe as it is reported to work with nodes and offers a wide range of property injection options.

Getting ready

Install the EnvInject plugin (https://wiki.jenkins-ci.org/display/JENKINS/EnvInject+Plugin). Create a recipe directory named ch3.building_software/environment.

How to do it...

1. Create a pom.xml file that is readable by Jenkins with the following lines of code:

```
<project xmlns="http://maven.apache.org/POM/4.0.0"
xmlns:xsi="http://www.w3.org/2001/XMLSchema-instance"
xsi:schemaLocation="http://maven.apache.org/POM/4.0.0
http://maven.apache.org/maven-v4_0_0.xsd">
<modelVersion>4.0.0</modelVersion>
<groupId>org.berg</groupId>
<artifactId>ch3.jenkins.builds.properties</artifactId>
<version>1.0-SNAPSHOT</version>
<name>${name.from.jenkins}</name>
```

```
<properties><project.build.sourceEncoding>UTF8</project.build.s
ourceEncoding>
</properties>
<build>
<plugins><plugin>
<groupId>org.codehaus.gmaven</groupId>
<artifactId>gmaven-plugin</artifactId>
<version>1.3</version>
<executions><execution>
<id>run-myGroovy</id>
<goals><goal>execute</goal></goals>
<phase>verify</phase>
<configuration>
<source>
def environment = System.getenv()
println "----Environment"
environment.each{println it }
println "----Property"
println(System.getProperty("longname"))
println "----Project and session"
println "Project: ${project.class}"
println "Session: ${session.class}"
println "longname: ${project.properties.longname}"
println "Project name: ${project.name}"
println "JENKINS_HOME: ${project.properties.JENKINS_HOME}"
</source>
</configuration>
</execution></executions>
</plugin></plugins>
</build>
</project>
```

2. Create a file named `my.properties` and place it in the same directory as the `pom.xml` file. Then, add the following lines of code in the `my.properties` file:

```
project.type=prod
secrets.file=/etc/secrets
enable.email=true
JOB_URL=I AM REALLY NOT WHAT I SEEM
```

3. Create a blank Freestyle job with the job name `ch3.environment`.

4. In the **Source Code Management** section, check **File System** and add a fully qualified path for your directory, such as `/var/lib/jenkins/cookbook/ch3.building_software/environment`, in the **Path** field.

5. In the **Build** section, select **Add a build step** for **Invoke top-level Maven targets**. In the newly expanded section, add the following details:

```
Maven Version: 3.2.1
Goals: verify
```

6. Click on the **Advanced** button and type `longname=SuperGood` in **Properties**.

7. Inject the values in my.properties by selecting the **Prepare an environment for the job** checkbox (near the top of the job configuration page).

8. For the **Properties** filepath, add `/full_path/my.properties`, for example,`/home/var/lib/cookbook/ch3.building_software/environment/my.properties`.

9. Run the job. The build will fail:

```
----Project and session
Project: class org.apache.Maven.model.Model
Session: class org.apache.Maven.execution.MavenSession
longname: SuperGood
[INFO] -------------------------------------------------------
[ERROR] BUILD ERROR[INFO] --------------------------------------
------------------
[INFO] Groovy.lang.MissingPropertyException: No such property:
namefor class: script1315151939046
```

10. In the **Build** section, for **Invoke top-level Maven targets**, click on the **Advanced** button. In the newly expanded section, add an extra property, `name.from.jenkins=The build with a name`.

11. Run the job. It should now succeed.

How it works...

The `EnvInject` plugin is useful for injecting properties into a build.

During the recipe, Maven is run twice. The first time, it is run without the `name.from.jenkins` variable defined, and the Jenkins job fails. The second time, it is run with the variable defined, and the Jenkins job now succeeds.

Maven expects that the `name.from.jenkins` variable is defined, or the name of the project will also not be defined. Normally, this would not be enough to stop your job succeeding. However, when running the Groovy code, the `println "Project name: ${project.name}"` line, specifically the `project.name` call, will fail the build. This is great for protecting against missing property values.

The Groovy code can see instances of the `org.apache.Maven.model.Model` project and the `org.apache.Maven.execution.MavenSession` class. The project instance is a model of the XML configuration that you can programmatically access. You can get the longname property by referencing it through `project.properties.longname`. Your Maven goal will fail if the property does not exist. You can also get to the property through the `System.getProperty("longname")` call. However, you cannot get to the property by using the `System.getenv()` environment call.

It is well worth learning the various options:

- **Keep Jenkins environment variables and keep Jenkins build variables**: Both these options affect the Jenkins-related variables that your job sees. It is good to keep your environment as clean as possible as it will aid you in debugging later.
- **Properties content**: You can override specific values in the properties files.
- **Environment script file path**: This option points to a script that will set up your environment. This is useful if you want to detect specific details of the running environment and configure your build accordingly.
- **Populate build cause**: You enable Jenkins to set the `BUILD_CAUSE` environment variable. The variable contains information about the event that triggered the job.

There's more...

Maven has a plugin for reading properties (`http://mojo.codehaus.org/properties-maven-plugin/`). To choose between property files, you will need to set a variable in the plugin configuration and call it as part of the Jenkins job, as follows:

```
<build>
<plugins>
<plugin>
<groupId>org.codehaus.mojo</groupId>
<artifactId>properties-maven-plugin</artifactId>
<version>1.0-alpha-2</version>
<executions>
<execution>
```

```
<phase>initialize</phase>
<goals>
<goal>read-project-properties</goal>
</goals>
<configuration>
<files>
<file>${fullpath.to.properties}</file>
</files>
</configuration>
</execution>
</executions>
</plugin>
</plugins>
</build>
```

If you use a relative path to the `properties` file, then the file can reside in your source code. If you use a full path, then the `properties` file can be stored on the Jenkins server. The second option is preferable if sensitive passwords, such as those for database connections, are included.

Jenkins has the ability to ask for variables when you run a job manually. This is called a parameterized build (`https://wiki.jenkins-ci.org/display/JENKINS/Parameterized+Build`). At build time, you can choose your property files by selecting from a choice of property file locations.

See also

- The *Running Ant through Groovy in Maven* recipe

Running Ant through Groovy in Maven

Jenkins interacts with an audience with a wide technological background. There are many developers who became proficient in Ant scripting before moving on to using Maven, developers who might be happier with writing an Ant task than editing a `pom.xml` file. There are mission-critical Ant scripts that still run in a significant proportion of organizations.

In Maven, you can run Ant tasks directly with the `AntRun` plugin (`http://maven.apache.org/plugins/maven-antrun-plugin/`), or through Groovy (`http://docs.codehaus.org/display/GROOVY/Using+Ant+from+Groovy`). AntRun represents a natural migration path. This is the path of least initial work.

The Groovy approach makes sense for Jenkins administrators who use Groovy as part of their tasks. Groovy, being a first-class programming language, has a wide range of control structures that are hard to replicate in Ant. You can partially do this by using the `Ant-contrib` library (http://ant-contrib.sourceforge.net). However, Groovy, as a feature-rich programming language, is much more expressive.

This recipe details how you can run two Maven POMs involving Groovy and Ant. The first POM shows you how to run the simplest of Ant tasks within Groovy, and the second performs an Ant-Contrib task to securely copy files from a large number of computers.

Getting ready

Create a directory named `ch3.building_software/antbuilder`.

How to do it...

1. Create a template file and name it `pom_ant_simple.xml`.
2. Change the values of `groupId`, `artifactId`, `version`, and name to suit your preferences.
3. Add the following XML fragment just before the `</project>` tag:

```xml
<build>
<plugins><plugin>
<groupId>org.codehaus.gmaven</groupId>
<artifactId>gmaven-plugin</artifactId>
<version>1.3</version>
<executions>
<execution>
<id>run-myGroovy-test</id>
<goals><goal>execute</goal></goals>
<phase>test</phase>
<configuration>
<source>
def ant = new AntBuilder()
ant.echo("\n\nTested ----> With Groovy")
</source>
</configuration>
</execution>
<execution>
<id>run-myGroovy-verify</id>
<goals><goal>execute</goal></goals>
<phase>verify</phase>
```

```
<configuration>
<source>
def ant = new AntBuilder()
ant.echo("\n\nVerified at ${new Date()}")
</source>
</configuration>
</execution>
</executions>
</plugin></plugins>
</build>
```

4. Run mvn test -f pom_ant_simple.xml. Review the output (note that there are no warnings about empty JAR files):

5. Run mvn verify -f pom_ant_simple.xml. Review the output; it should look similar to the following screenshot:

```
T E S T S

Results :

Tests run: 0, Failures: 0, Errors: 0, Skipped: 0

[INFO]
[INFO] --- gmaven-plugin:1.3:execute (run-myGroovy-test) @ ch3.jenkins.builds ---
    [echo]
    [echo]
    [echo] Tested ----> With Groovy
[INFO]
[INFO] --- maven-jar-plugin:2.2:jar (default-jar) @ ch3.jenkins.builds ---
[WARNING] JAR will be empty - no content was marked for inclusion!
[INFO] Building jar: /home/user/antbuilder/target/ch3.jenkins.builds-1.0-SNAPSHOT.jar
[INFO]
[INFO] --- gmaven-plugin:1.3:execute (run-myGroovy-verify) @ ch3.jenkins.builds ---
    [echo]
    [echo]
    [echo] Verified at Fri Nov 21 17:04:59 CET 2014
[INFO] ------------------------------------------------------------------------
[INFO] BUILD SUCCESS
[INFO] ------------------------------------------------------------------------
[INFO] Total time: 3.601s
[INFO] Finished at: Fri Nov 21 17:04:59 CET 2014
[INFO] Final Memory: 14M/177M
[INFO] ------------------------------------------------------------------------
```

4. Create a second template file named pom_ant_contrib.xml.

5. Change the values of `groupId`, `artifactId`, `version`, and name to suit your preferences.

6. Add the following XML fragment just before the `</project>` tag:

```
<build>
<plugins><plugin>
<groupId>org.codehaus.gmaven</groupId>
<artifactId>gmaven-plugin</artifactId>
<version>1.3</version>
<executions><execution>
<id>run-myGroovy</id>
<goals><goal>execute</goal></goals>
<phase>verify</phase>
<configuration>
<source>
def ant = new AntBuilder()
host="Myhost_series"
print "user: "
user = new String(System.console().readPassword())
print "password: "
pw = new String(System.console().readPassword())

for ( i in 1..920) {
counterStr=String.format('%02d',i)
ant.scp(trust:'true',file:"${user}:${pw}${host}${counterStr}:/$
{full_path_to_location}",
localTofile:"${myfile}-${counterStr}", verbose:"true")
}
</source>
</configuration>
</execution></executions>
<dependencies>
<dependency>
<groupId>ant</groupId>
<artifactId>ant</artifactId>
<version>1.6.5</version>
</dependency>
<dependency>
<groupId>ant</groupId>
<artifactId>ant-launcher</artifactId>
<version>1.6.5</version>
</dependency>
<dependency>
<groupId>ant</groupId>
<artifactId>ant-jsch</artifactId>
<version>1.6.5</version>
</dependency>
```

```
<dependency>
<groupId>com.jcraft</groupId>
<artifactId>jsch</artifactId>
<version>0.1.42</version>
</dependency>
</dependencies>
</plugin></plugins>
</build>
```

This is only representative code, unless you have set it up to point to real files on real servers:

```
mvn verify -f pom_ant_simple.xml will fail
```

How it works...

Groovy runs basic Ant tasks without the need for extra dependencies. An `AntBuilder` instance (http://groovy.codehaus.org/Using+Ant+Libraries+with+AntBuilder) is created and then the Ant echo task is called. Under the bonnet, Groovy calls the Java classes that Ant uses to perform the `echo` command. Within the `echo` command, a date is printed by directly creating an anonymous object:

```
ant.echo("\n\nVerified at ${new Date()}").
```

You configured the `pom.xml` file to fire off the Groovy scripts in two phases: the test phase, and then later in the verify phase. The test phase occurs before the generation of a JAR file, and thus avoids creating a warning about an empty JAR file. As the name suggests, this phase is useful for testing before packaging.

The second example script highlights the strength of combining Groovy with Ant. The SCP task (http://ant.apache.org/manual/Tasks/scp.html) is run many times across many servers. The script first asks for the username and password, avoiding storage on your filesystem or your revision control system. The Groovy script expects you to inject the `host`, `full_path_to_location`, and `myfile` variables.

Observe the similarity between the Ant SCP task and the way it is expressed in the `pom_ant_contrib.xml` file.

There's more...

Another example of running Ant through Groovy is the creation of custom property files on the fly. This allows you to pass on information from one Jenkins job to another.

You can create property files through AntBuilder using the echo task. The following lines of code create a value.properties file with two lines, x=1 and y=2:

```
def ant = new AntBuilder()
ant.echo(message: "x=1\n", append: "false", file: "values.properties")
ant.echo(message: "y=2\n", append: "true", file: "values.properties")
```

The first echo command sets append to false, so that every time a build occurs, a new properties file is created. The second echo appends its message.

 You can remove the second append attribute as the default value is set to true.

See also

- The *Running Groovy scripts through Maven* recipe

Failed Jenkins jobs based on JSP syntax errors

JavaServer Pages (JSP)

(http://www.oracle.com/technetwork/java/overview-138580.html) is a standard that makes the creation of simple web applications straightforward. You write HTML, such as pages with extra tags interspersed with Java coding, into a text file. If you do this in a running web application, then the code recompiles on the next page call. This process supports agile programming practices, but the risk is that developers make messy, hard-to-read JSP code that is difficult to maintain. It would be nice if Jenkins could display metrics about the code to defend quality.

JSP pages are compiled on the fly the first time a user request for the page is received. The user will perceive this as a slow loading of the page, and this may deter them from future visits. To avoid this situation, you can compile the JSP page during the build process and place the compiled code in the WEB-INF/classes directory, or packaged in the WEB-INF/lib directory of your web app. This approach has the advantage of a faster first-page load.

A secondary advantage of having compiled source code is that you can run a number of statistical code review tools over the code base and obtain testability metrics. This generates testing data ready for Jenkins plugins to display.

This recipe describes how to compile JSP pages based on the maven-jetty-jspc-plugin (http://www.eclipse.org/jetty/documentation/current/jetty-jspc-maven-plugin.html). The compiled code will work with the Jetty server, which is often used for integration tests.

 The JSP mentioned in this recipe is deliberately insecure, and hence ready for testing later in this book.

A complementary plugin specifically for Tomcat deployment is the Tomcat Maven plugin (http://tomcat.apache.org/maven-plugin.html).

Getting ready

Create a directory named ch3.building_software/jsp_example.

How to do it...

1. Create a WAR project from a Maven archetype by typing the following command:

   ```
   mvnarchetype:generate –DarchetypeArtifactId=maven-archetype-
   webapp
   ```

2. Enter the following values:

- groupId: ch3.packt.builds
- artifactId: jsp_example
- version: 1.0-SNAPSHOT
- package: ch3.packt.builds<build>
  <finalName>jsp_example</finalName>

3. Click on **Enter** to confirm the values.

4. Edit the jsp_example/pom.xml file by adding the following build section:

```
<build>
<finalName>jsp_example</finalName>
<plugins>
<plugin>
<groupId>org.mortbay.jetty</groupId>
<artifactId>maven-jetty-jspc-plugin</artifactId>
<version>6.1.14</version>
<executions>
<execution>
<id>jspc</id>
<goals>
<goal>jspc</goal>
</goals>
<configuration>
</configuration>
</execution>
</executions>
</plugin>
<plugin>
<groupId>org.apache.maven.plugins</groupId>
<artifactId>maven-war-plugin</artifactId>
<version>2.4</version>
<configuration>
<webXml>${basedir}/target/web.xml</webXml>
</configuration>
</plugin>
</plugins>
</build>
```

5. Replace the code snippet in the `src/main/webapp/index.jsp` file with the following lines of code:

```
<html>
<head>
<meta http-equiv="Content-Type" content="text/html;
charset=UTF-8">
<title>Hello World Example</title>
</head>
<body>
<%
        String evilInput= null;
evilInput =
  request.getParameter("someUnfilteredInput");
if (evilInput==null){evilInput="Hello Kind Person";}
    %>
<form action="index.jsp">
      The big head says: <%=evilInput%><p>
      Please add input:<input type='text'
         name='someUnfilteredInput'>
<input type="submit">
</form>
</body>
</html>
```

6. Create a WAR file by using the `mvn package` command.

7. Modify `./src/main/webapp/index.jsp` by adding `if (evilInput==null)` underneath the line starting with if, so that it is no longer a valid JSP file.

8. Run the `mvn package` command. The build will now fail with the following error message:

```
[ERROR] Failed to execute goal org.mortbay.jetty:maven-jetty-
jspc-plugin:6.1.14:jspc (jspc) on project jsp_example: Failure
processing jsps -> [Help 1]
```

How it works...

You created a template project using an archetype.

The Maven plugin, upon seeing the `index.jsp` page, compiles it into a class with the name `jsp.index_jsp`, placing the compiled class under `WEB-INF/classes`. The plugin then defines the class as a servlet in `WEB-INF/web.xml` with a mapping to `/index.jsp`. Let's take a look at the following example:

```
<servlet>
<servlet-name>jsp.index_jsp</servlet-name>
<servlet-class>jsp.index_jsp</servlet-class>
</servlet>

<servlet-mapping>
<servlet-name>jsp.index_jsp</servlet-name>
<url-pattern>/index.jsp</url-pattern>
</servlet-mapping>
```

The list of archetypes is increasing over time. You can find the full list at `http://maven-repository.com/archetypes`. If you are running Ubuntu, you will find a local XML catalog listing all the archetypes named `archetype-catalog.xml` in the~/.m2 directory.

There's more...

Here are a few things you should consider.

Different server types

By default, the Jetty Maven plugin (Version 6.1.14) loads JSP 2.1 libraries with JDK 1.5. This will not work for all server types. For example, if you deploy the WAR file generated by this recipe to a Tomcat 7 server, it will fail to deploy properly. If you look at logs/catalina.out, you will see the following error:

```
javax.servlet.ServletException: Error instantiating servlet class
jsp.index_jsp
Root Cause
java.lang.NoClassDefFoundError:
Lorg/apache/jasper/runtime/ResourceInjector;
```

This is because different servers have different assumptions about how JSP code is compiled, and which libraries they depend on to run. For Tomcat, you will need to tweak the compiler used and the Maven plugin dependencies. For more details, visit `http://wiki.eclipse.org/Jetty/Feature/Jetty_Maven_Plugin`.

Eclipse templates for JSP pages

Eclipse is a popular open source IDE for Java developers (`http://www.eclipse.org/`). If you are using Eclipse with its default template for JSP pages, then your pages may fail to compile. This is because, at the time of writing, the default compiler does not like the meta-information mentioned before the `<html>` tag, as follows:

```
<%@ page language="java" contentType="text/html;charset=UTF-8"
pageEncoding="UTF-8"%>
<!DOCTYPE html PUBLIC "-//W3C//DTD HTML 4.01 Transitional//EN"
"http://www.w3.org/TR/html4/loose.dtd">
```

As the meta-information follows the JSP specification, it is likely that later the JSP compiler will accept the information. Until that day, simply remove the lines before compiling, or change the JSP compiler that you use.

Remotely triggering jobs through the Jenkins API

Jenkins has a remote API that allows you to enable, disable, run, and delete jobs; it also lets you change the configuration. The API is increasing with each Jenkins version. To get the most up-to-date details, you will need to review `http://yourhost/job/Name_of_Job/api/`. Where `yourhost` is the location of your Jenkins server, `Name_of_Job` is the name of a job that exists on your server.

This recipe details how you can trigger builds remotely by using security tokens. This will allow you to run other jobs from within Maven.

Getting ready

This recipe expects Jenkins security to be turned on so that you can log in as a user. It also assumes you have a modern version of `wget` (`http://www.gnu.org/software/wget/`) installed.

How to do it...

1. Create a Freestyle project with the project name ch3.RunMe.

2. Check **This Build** is parameterized, select **String Parameter**, and add the following details:
    1. **Name**: myvariable
    2. **DefaultValue**: Default
    3. **Description**: This is my example variable

3. Under the **Build Triggers** section, check **Trigger builds remotely** (for example, from scripts).

4. In the **Authentication Token** textbox, add changeme.

5. Click on the **Save** button.

6. Click on the **Build with Parameters link**.

7. You will be asked for the variable named myvariable. Click on **Build**.

8. Visit your personal configuration page, such as http://localhost:8080/, where you replace your_user with your Jenkins username.

9. In the **API Token** section, click on the **Show API Token...** button.

10. Copy the token to apiToken.

11. From a terminal console, run wget to log in and run the job remotely:

    ```
    wget --auth-no-challenge --http-user=username --http-
    password=apiToken
    http://localhost:8080/job/ch3.RunMe/build?token=changeme
    ```

12. Check the Jenkins job to verify that it has not run and returns a 405 HTTP status code:

    ```
    Resolving localhost (localhost)... 127.0.0.1
    Connecting to localhost (localhost)|127.0.0.1|:8080...
    connected.
    HTTP request sent, awaiting response... 405 Method Not Allowed
    2014-08-14 15:08:43 ERROR 405: Method Not Allowed.
    ```

13. From a terminal console, run `wget` to log in and run the job, returning a `201` HTTP status code:

```
wget --auth-no-challenge --http-user=username --http-
password=apiToken
http://localhost:8080/job/ch3.RunMe/buildWithParameters?token=c
hangeme\&myvariable='Hello World'
Connecting to localhost (localhost)|127.0.0.1|:8080...
connected.
HTTP request sent, awaiting response... 201 Created
```

HTTP can be packet-sniffed by a third party. Use HTTPS when transporting passwords.

How it works...

To run a job, you need to authenticate as a user and then obtain permission to run the specific job. This is achieved through `apiTokens`, which you should consider to be the same as passwords.

There are two remote method calls. The first is `build`, which is used to run the build without passing parameters. The method is currently not accepted. The second working method is `buildWithParameters`, which expects you to pass at least one parameter to Jenkins. The parameters are separated by `\&`.

The `wget` tool does the heavy lifting; otherwise, you would have to write some tricky Groovy code. We have chosen simplicity and OS dependence for the sake of a short recipe. Running an executable risks making your build OS-specific. The executable will depend on how the underlying environment has been set up. However, sometimes you will need to make compromises to avoid complexity.

For more details, visit
https://wiki.jenkins-ci.org/display/JENKINS/Authenticating+scripted+clients.

You can find the equivalent Java code at the following URL:
https://wiki.jenkins-ci.org/display/JENKINS/Remote+access+API.

There's more...

Here are a few things you should consider.

Running jobs from within Maven

With little fuss, you can run `wget` through the `Maven-AntRun` plugin. The following is the equivalent `pom.xml` fragment:

```
<build>
<plugin>
<groupId>org.apache.maven.plugins</groupId>
<artifactId>maven-antrun-plugin</artifactId>
<version>1.7</version>
<executions><execution>
<phase>compile</phase>
<configuration>
<tasks>
<exec executable="wget">
<arg line="--auth-no-challenge --http-user=username --http-
password=apiToken http://localhost:8080/job/ch3.RunMe/build?token=changeme"
/>
</exec>
</tasks>
</configuration>
<goals><goal>run</goal></goals>
</execution></executions>
</plugin>
</build>
```

You can use the Exec Maven plugin for the same purpose as the `Maven-AntRun` plugin. For more details, visit `http://mojo.codehaus.org/exec-maven-plugin/`.

Remotely generating jobs

There is also a project that allows you to create Jenkins jobs through Maven remotely (`https://github.com/evgeny-goldin/maven-plugins/tree/master/jenkins-maven-plugin`). The advantage of this approach is its ability to enforce consistency and reuse between jobs. You can use one parameter to choose a Jenkins server and populate it. This is useful for generating a large set of consistently structured jobs.

See also

- The *Running Ant through Groovy in Maven* recipe

6
Continuous Delivery

In this chapter, we will cover the following recipes:

- Archiving artifacts
- Copying an artifact from another build job
- Integrating Jenkins with Artifactory
- Deploying a WAR file from Jenkins to Tomcat
- Deploying a WAR file from Jenkins to AWS Beanstalk
- Deploying a WAR file from Jenkins to Azure App Services
- Promoting builds

Introduction

Continuous Delivery (CD) is a DevOps practice that is used to deploy an application quickly while maintaining a high quality with an automated approach in a non-production environment. It is about the way application package is deployed in the Web Server or in the Application Server in environment such as dev, test or staging. Deployment of an application can be done using shell script, batch file, or plugins available in Jenkins. Approach of automated deployment in case of Continuous Delivery and Continuous Deployment will be always same most of the time. In the case of Continuous Delivery, the application package is always production ready.

Archiving artifacts

Artifact archiving is useful when you want to use an installable or distribution package in another project or build job. Normally, you create a different project to achieve a pipeline for end-to-end automation.

Getting ready

You need to have a project in Jenkins that creates a package file or distribution file, or any artifact that you want to utilize later from another project.

How to do it...

1. Go to **Jenkins** dashboard I Jenkins project or build job I **Post-build Actions** I **Add post-build action** I **Archive the artifacts**:

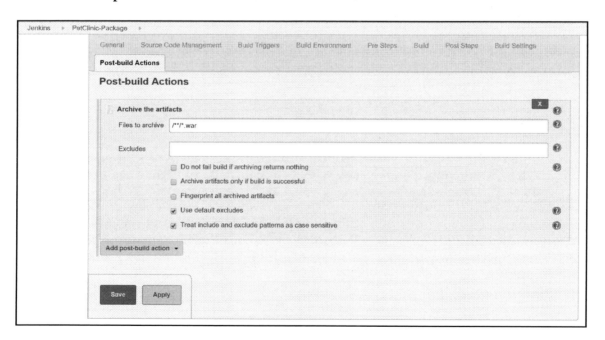

2. You can use wildcards, such as `module/dist/**/*.zip`. The artifact archiver uses `Ant org.apache.tools.ant.DirectoryScanner`, which excludes the following patterns by default:
`**/%*%,**/.git/**,**/SCCS,**/.bzr,**/.hg/**,**/.bzrignore,**/.git,**/SCCS/**,**/.hg,**/.#,**/vssver.scc,**/.bzr/**,**/._*,**/#*#,**/*~,**/CVS,**/.hgtags,**/.svn/**,**/.hgignore,**/.svn,**/.gitignore,**/.gitmodules,**/.hgsubstate,**/.gitattributes,**/CVS/**,**/.hgsub,**/.DS_Store,**/.cvsignore`

See also

- The *Copying an artifact from other build job* recipe is useful for copying an archived artifact from another project into Jenkins

Copying an artifact from another build job

n this recipe, we will copy artifact/file/package from one build to other. It helps in the deployment or copy operations. Even with Master/Agent architecture, we can copy artifacts effortlessly using the `Copy Artifact` Plugin.

Getting ready

You need to allow read access to anonymous users, as the `Copyartifact` plugin treats builds running as an anonymous. To allow read access to anonymous, do the following:

Go to **Manage Jenkins** | **Global Security Configuration**:

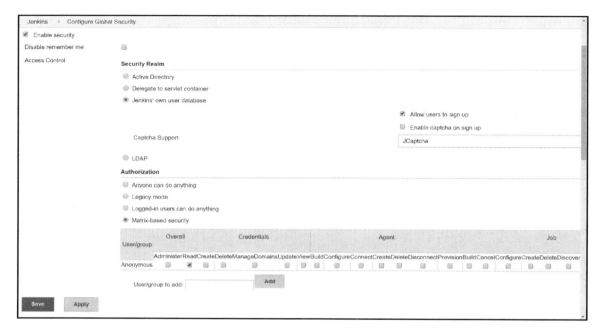

Click on **Save**.

How to do it...

1. Go to Jenkins dashboard | **Project** | **Configure** | **Build** | **Add build step** | **Copy artifacts from another project**.
2. Give the **Project name** from which you want to copy the artifact.
3. For the **Which build** field, select appropriate options from the available list:

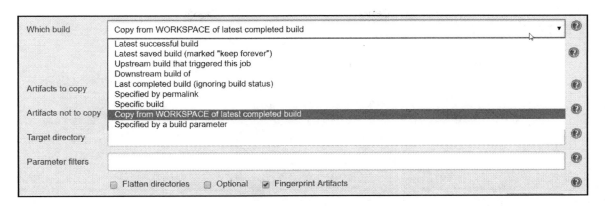

4. Provide the name of the **Artifacts to copy**:

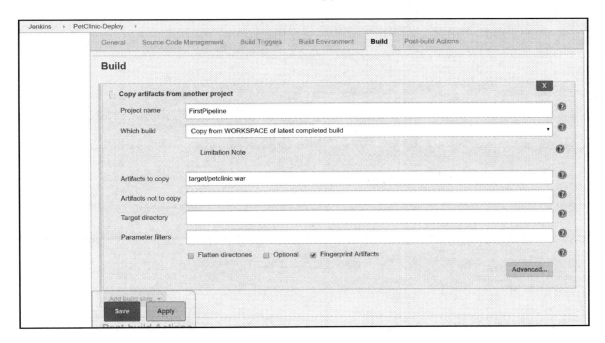

5. Click on **Save**.

There's more...

- You can also specify projects that can copy artifacts.
- For example, in the `PetClinic-Package` project you can create a WAR file that you can deploy to the application server.
- In the **General** section of `PetClinic-Package`, check **Permission to Copy Artifact** and provide the name of the project that can copy the artifact:

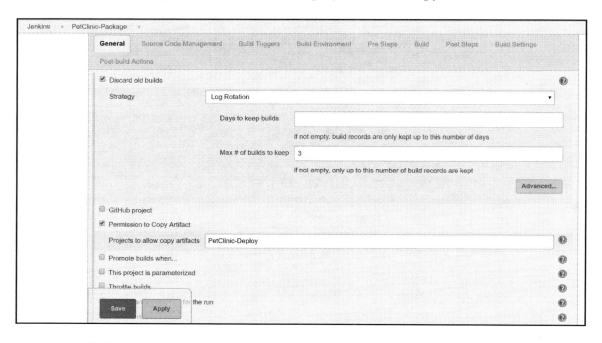

- Click on **Save**.

Integrating Jenkins with Artifactory

Artifactory is a repository manager that allows you to store and retrieve artifacts, such as dependencies or package files. It is like a local repository in the organization.

Getting ready

In this recipe,
`https://bintray.com/jfrog/artifactory/jfrog-artifactory-oss-zip/4.15.0` is used
for Artifactory.

To start Artifactory, go to **artifactory-oss-4.15.0** | **bin** and execute `artifactory.bat`. Use a
`.sh` script to start Artifactory if the operating system is Linux-based.

Go to your browser and visit `IP_ADDRESS:8081` to visit Artifactory in the browser:

Create a **Local** repository to store package files created by the Jenkins project:

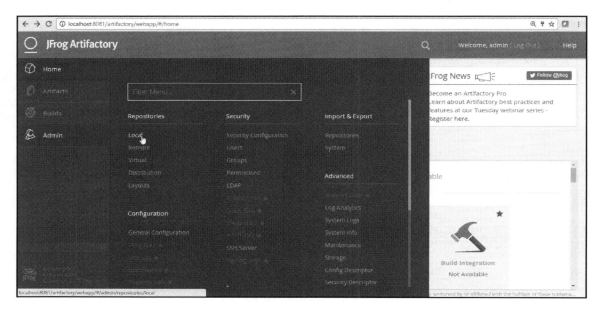

Click on **New**:

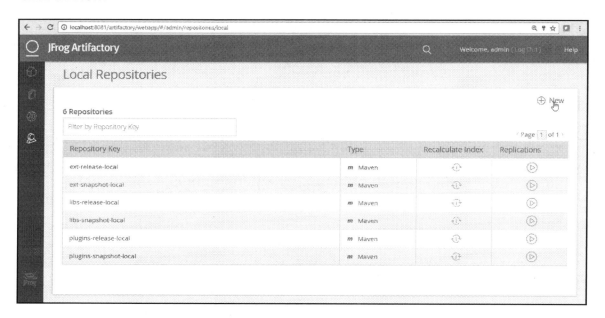

Select **Maven as a Project Type**:

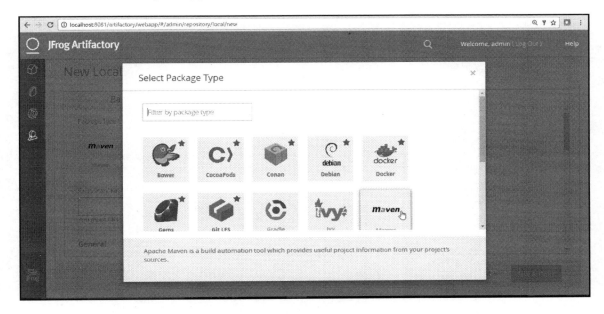

Give a **Repository Key *** and click on **Save and Finish**:

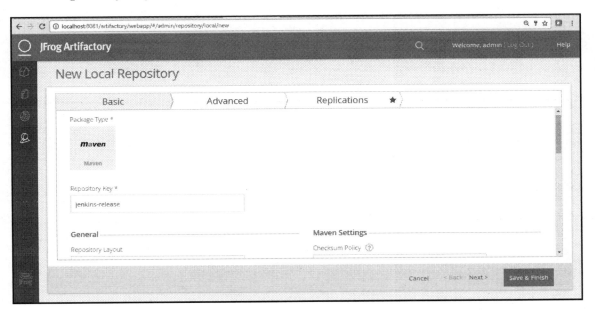

Similarly, create a `Jenkins-snapshot` repository:

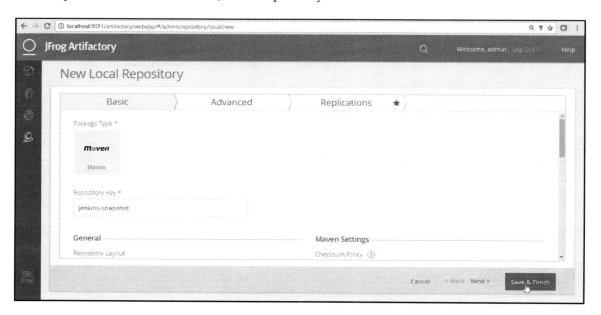

Verify all repositories in the list:

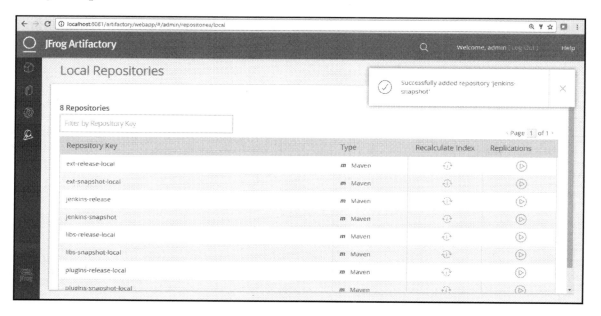

Create a user that you can utilize from Jenkins to access Artifactory:

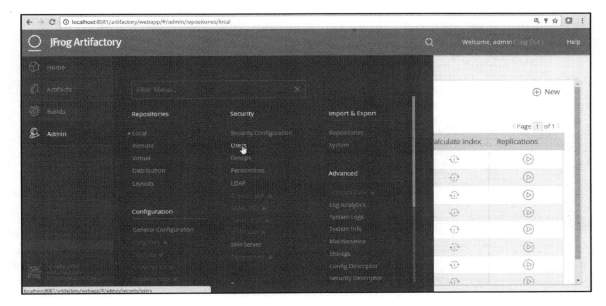

Click on **New**:

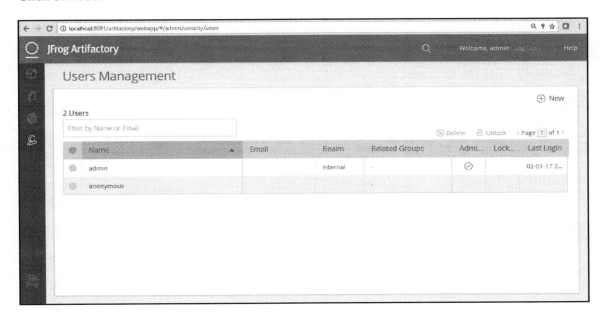

Provide user details and **Save**:

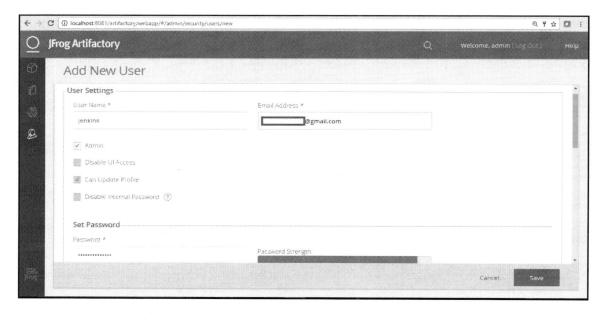

Verify the list of users:

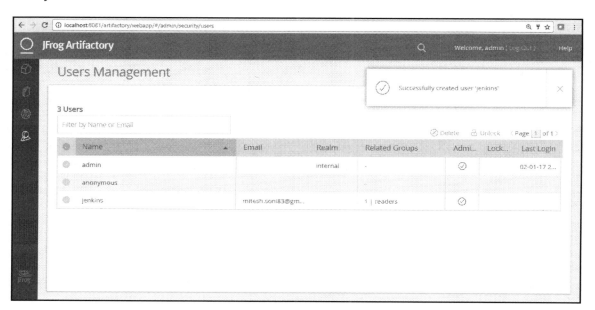

Provide the newly created user with permissions to the repositories:

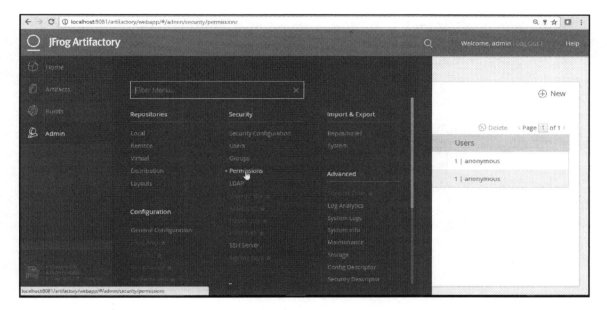

Select **Repositories** and click on **Save & Finish**:

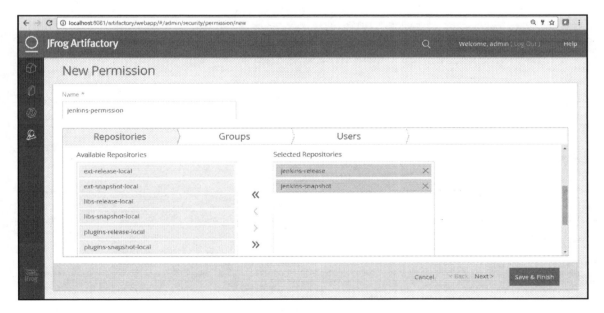

Check the **Permissions Management** section in Artifactory for recent changes:

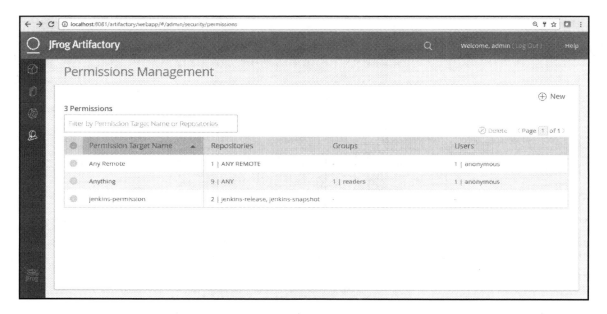

Edit the permissions and assign the user:

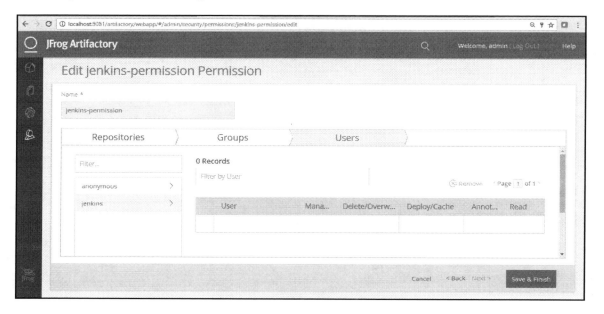

Click on **Save & Finish**:

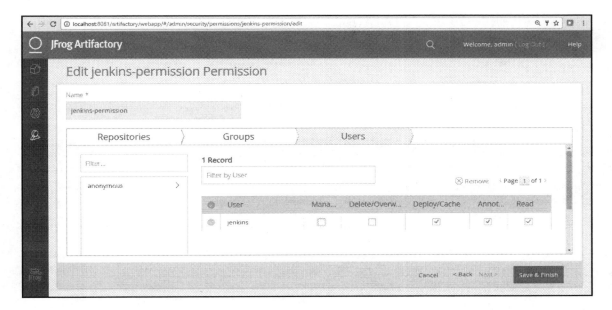

Check the **Permissions Management** section in Artifactory for recent changes:

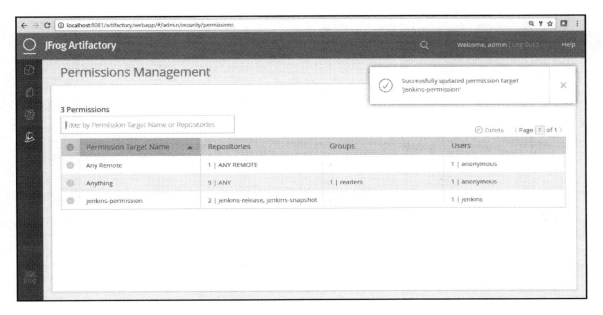

Now, you are ready to integrate Artifactory with Jenkins.

Install the **Artifactory Plugin** in Jenkins:

Once plugin installation is successful, you can configure Artifactory-related settings in Jenkins:

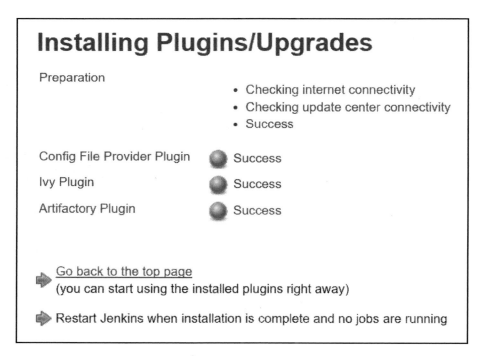

Configure **Artifactory** in Jenkins:

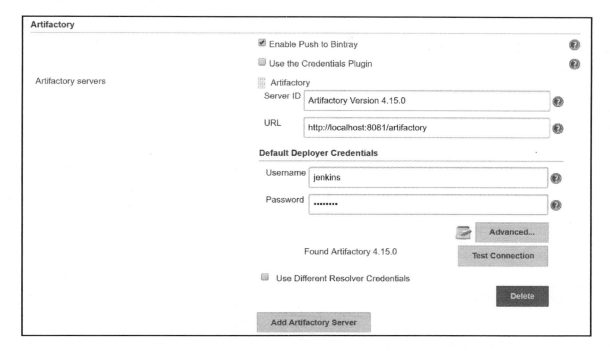

When you use Maven as a build tool, it creates the .m2 directory. This keeps all the dependencies in the repository directory when it downloads dependencies from Maven repositories available on the internet.

For the sake of verification, change the directory name in the .m2 directory to repository1:

The moment Jenkins build execution starts, it will fetch dependencies from Artifactory and create a repository directory in .m2.

How to do it...

1. Go to a Jenkins project that creates a package file after compiling all of the source files.

2. Select **Resolve artifacts from Artifactory**:

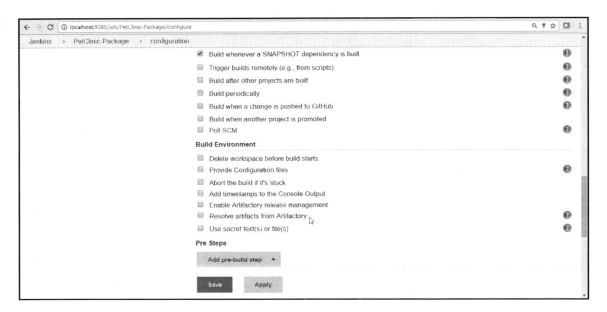

3. Click on **Refresh Repositories** and select the repository in the release and snapshot field from the lists:

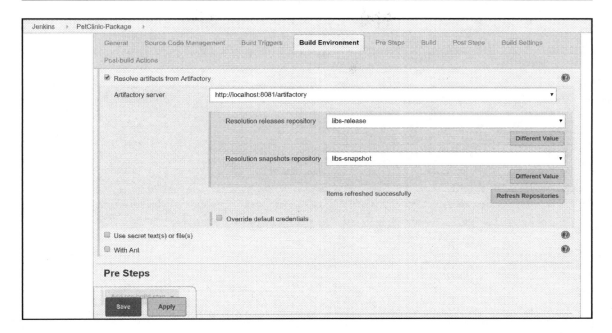

4. Select **Deploy artifacts to Artifactory** from **Add post-build action**:

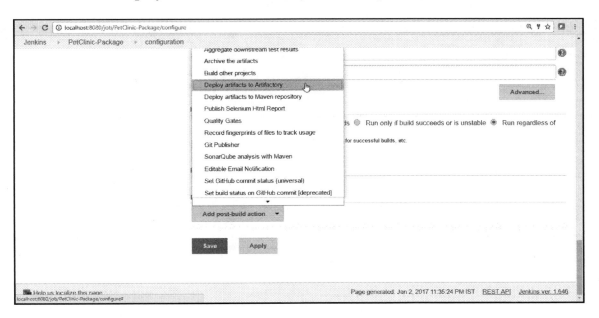

5. Click on **Refresh** and select the repositories you created earlier:

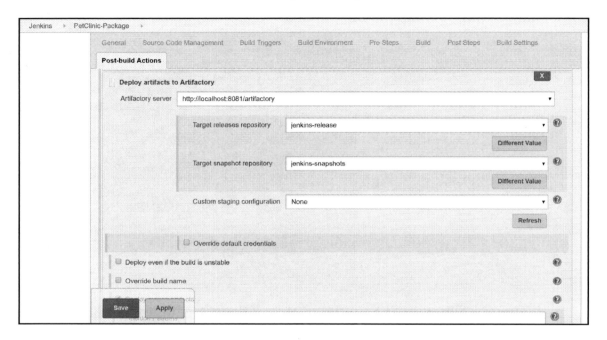

6. Click on **Save**.

7. Click on **Build now** and verify logs in the **Console Output**. Jar files are resolved from the local repository or Artifactory:

```
Jenkins   ▸  PetClinic-Package  ▸  #13
[INFO] Scanning for projects...
[INFO] Initializing Artifactory Build-Info Recording
[HUDSON] Collecting dependencies info
[INFO]
[INFO] ------------------------------------------------------------------------
[INFO] Building petclinic 4.2.5-SNAPSHOT
[INFO] ------------------------------------------------------------------------
[INFO] Downloading: http://localhost:8081/artifactory/libs-release/com/itextpdf/itextpdf/5.4.5/itextpdf-
5.4.5.pom
log4j:WARN No appenders could be found for logger
(org.apache.maven.wagon.providers.http.httpclient.client.protocol.RequestAddCookies).
log4j:WARN Please initialize the log4j system properly.
log4j:WARN See http://logging.apache.org/log4j/1.2/faq.html#noconfig for more info.
[INFO] Downloaded: http://localhost:8081/artifactory/libs-release/com/itextpdf/itextpdf/5.4.5/itextpdf-
5.4.5.pom (9 KB at 3.7 KB/sec)
[INFO] Downloading: http://localhost:8081/artifactory/libs-release/com/itextpdf/itext-parent/1.0.0/itext-
parent-1.0.0.pom
[INFO] Downloaded: http://localhost:8081/artifactory/libs-release/com/itextpdf/itext-parent/1.0.0/itext-
parent-1.0.0.pom (4 KB at 9.3 KB/sec)
[INFO] Downloading: http://localhost:8081/artifactory/libs-release/com/itextpdf/itextpdf/5.4.5/itextpdf-
5.4.5.jar
[INFO] Downloaded: http://localhost:8081/artifactory/libs-release/com/itextpdf/itextpdf/5.4.5/itextpdf-
5.4.5.jar (2054 KB at 137.0 KB/sec)
[INFO]
[INFO] --- maven-resources-plugin:2.6:resources (default-resources) @ spring-petclinic ---
[INFO] Downloading: http://localhost:8081/artifactory/libs-release/org/apache/maven/maven-plugin-
api/2.0.6/maven-plugin-api-2.0.6.pom
[INFO] Downloaded: http://localhost:8081/artifactory/libs-release/org/apache/maven/maven-plugin-
api/2.0.6/maven-plugin-api-2.0.6.pom (2 KB at 0.4 KB/sec)
[INFO] Downloading: http://localhost:8081/artifactory/libs-release/org/apache/maven/maven/2.0.6/maven-
2.0.6.pom
```

8. Once the package is created, it is stored in Artifactory too:

```
Finished Calculation of disk usage of workspace in  2 second
[INFO] Artifactory Build Info Recorder: Saving Build Info to
'F:\1.DevOps2016\#JenkinsEssentials\FirstDraft\jenkinsHome\workspace\PetClinic-Package\target\build-info.json'
[INFO] Deploying artifact: http://localhost:8081/artifactory/jenkins-snapshots/org/springframework/samples/spring-petclinic/4.2.5-SNAPSHOT/spring-petclinic-4.2.5-SNAPSHOT.war
log4j:WARN No appenders could be found for logger (org.apache.http.client.protocol.RequestAddCookies).
log4j:WARN Please initialize the log4j system properly.
log4j:WARN See http://logging.apache.org/log4j/1.2/faq.html#noconfig for more info.
[INFO] Artifactory Build Info Recorder: Deploying build info ...
[INFO] Deploying build descriptor to: http://localhost:8081/artifactory/api/build
[INFO] Build successfully deployed. Browse it in Artifactory under
http://localhost:8081/artifactory/webapp/builds/PetClinic-Package/14
[INFO] ------------------------------------------------------------------------
[INFO] BUILD SUCCESS
[INFO] ------------------------------------------------------------------------
[INFO] Total time: 03:53 min
[INFO] Finished at: 2017-08-14T17:03:32+05:30
[INFO] Final Memory: 35M/245M
[INFO] ------------------------------------------------------------------------
Waiting for Jenkins to finish collecting data
[JENKINS] Archiving F:\1.DevOps2016\#JenkinsEssentials\FirstDraft\jenkinsHome\workspace\PetClinic-Package\pom.xml
to org.springframework.samples/spring-petclinic/4.2.5-SNAPSHOT/spring-petclinic-4.2.5-SNAPSHOT.pom
[JENKINS] Archiving F:\1.DevOps2016\#JenkinsEssentials\FirstDraft\jenkinsHome\workspace\PetClinic-Package\target\petclinic.war to org.springframework.samples/spring-petclinic/4.2.5-SNAPSHOT/spring-petclinic-4.2.5-SNAPSHOT.war
channel stopped
Archiving artifacts
Started calculate disk usage of build
Finished Calculation of disk usage of build in 0 seconds
Started calculate disk usage of workspace
Finished Calculation of disk usage of workspace in  2 second
Finished: SUCCESS
```

9. Go to Artifactory and verify the package:

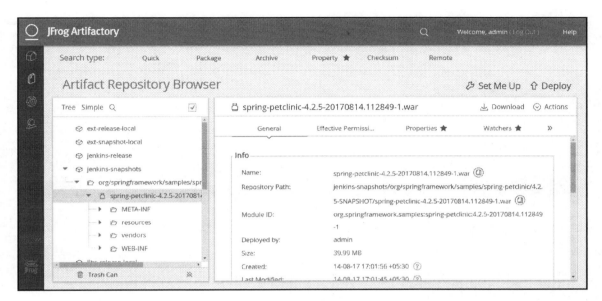

10. Verify the local repository, `libs-release`, in Artifactory and you will find all Jar files available in it.

Deploying a WAR file from Jenkins to Tomcat

For application deployment, we can utilize multiple methods to deploy an application to a web server or application server. We can use a batch script or shell script to copy the Package file created after the Continuous Integration process, or we can use the Jenkins plugin to deploy an application.

Getting ready

Go to **Manage Jenkins** | **Manage Plugins** and install **Deploy to container Plugin**:

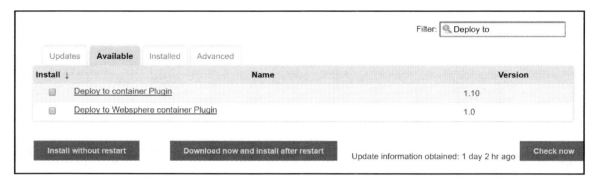

Wait until the plugin has installed successfully.

How to do it...

To allow deployment using the Jenkins plugin, go to the Tomcat installation directory and open `conf\tomcat-users.xml`.

1. Create a new role and a new user, as follows:

```xml
<?xml version='1.0' encoding='utf-8'?>
<!--
<tomcat-users>
<!--
<!--
  NOTE:  The sample user and role entries below are intended for use with the
  examples web application. They are wrapped in a comment and thus are ignored
  when reading this file. If you wish to configure these users for use with the
  examples web application, do not forget to remove the <!.. ..> that surrounds
  them. You will also need to set the passwords to something appropriate.
-->
  <role rolename="manager-script"/>
  <user username="admin" password="admin@123" roles="manager-script"/>
</tomcat-users>
```

2. Restart Tomcat.

3. Create a new Freestyle build in the Jenkins named `PetClinic-Deploy`.

4. What we will do here is copy the artifact created for the `PetClinic-Package` job and deploy it in Tomcat. Install the Copy Artifact plugin to perform this action. Give the **Project name** and path from which we need to copy the WAR file:

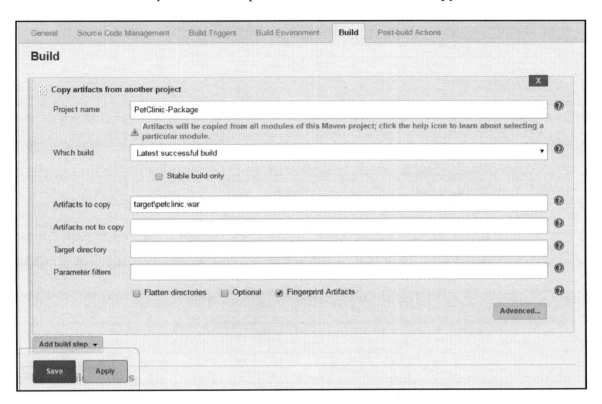

5. Give the path to the WAR file for deployment using the Jenkins plugin. Select **Deploy war/ear to a container** from **Post-build Actions**. Click on **Add Container** and select the latest version of Tomcat. Give the **Tomcat URL**. Give the username and password we have defined in `tomcat-users.xml`:

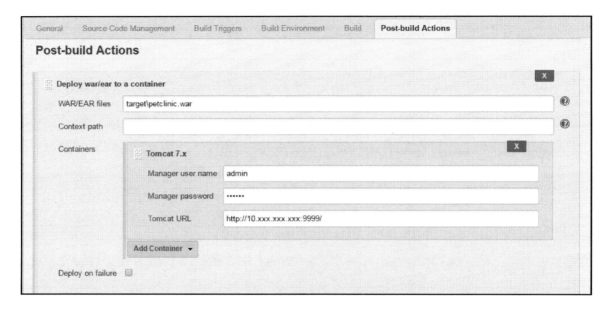

6. Execute the build by clicking **Build now**. Verify the logs for application deployment:

```
Results :

Tests run: 59, Failures: 0, Errors: 0, Skipped: 0

[INFO]
[INFO] --- maven-war-plugin:2.3:war (default-war) @ spring-petclinic ---
[INFO] Packaging webapp
[INFO] Assembling webapp [spring-petclinic] in [d:\jenkins\workspace\PetClinic-Test\target\spring-
petclinic-4.2.5-SNAPSHOT]
[INFO] Processing war project
[INFO] Copying webapp resources [d:\jenkins\workspace\PetClinic-Test\src\main\webapp]
[INFO] Webapp assembled in [1669 msecs]
[INFO] Building war: d:\jenkins\workspace\PetClinic-Test\target\spring-petclinic-4.2.5-SNAPSHOT.war
[INFO] ------------------------------------------------------------------------
[INFO] BUILD SUCCESS
[INFO] ------------------------------------------------------------------------
[INFO] Total time: 28.772 s
[INFO] Finished at: 2016-07-06T22:59:37+05:30
[INFO] Final Memory: 29M/261M
[INFO] ------------------------------------------------------------------------
Deploying d:\jenkins\workspace\PetClinic-Test\target\spring-petclinic-4.2.5-SNAPSHOT.war to container
Tomcat 7.x Remote
  [d:\jenkins\workspace\PetClinic-Test\target\spring-petclinic-4.2.5-SNAPSHOT.war] is not deployed.
Doing a fresh deployment.
  Deploying [d:\jenkins\workspace\PetClinic-Test\target\spring-petclinic-4.2.5-SNAPSHOT.war]
Finished: SUCCESS
```

7. Go to your browser and visit the application with the Tomcat URL and the context of the application:

8. In the next section, we will deploy the PetClinic application to Tomcat, which resides in the AWS EC2 instance.

Deploying a WAR file from Jenkins to AWS Beanstalk

AWS Elastic Beanstalk is a **Platform as a Service (PaaS)**. We will use it to deploy the PetClinic application. These are the steps you need to follow to deploy an application on AWS Elastic Beanstalk:

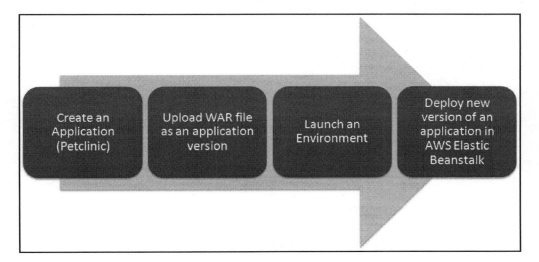

Getting ready

Let's create a sample application in Elastic Beanstalk to understand how Elastic Beanstalk works. Then, we will use the Jenkins plugin to deploy an application into it.

Click on **Services** in the AWS management console and select AWS Elastic Beanstalk. Create a new application named `petclinic`. Select **Tomcat** as a **Platform** and select the **Sample application** radio button:

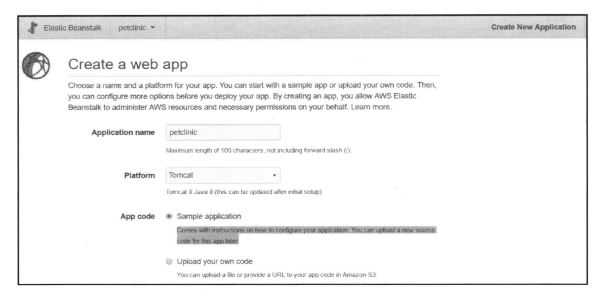

Verify the sequence of events for the creation of a sample application:

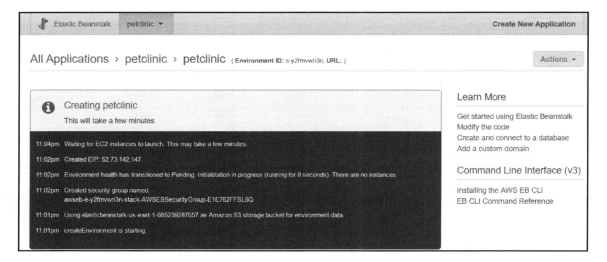

It will take some time and, once the environment has been created, it will be highlighted in green:

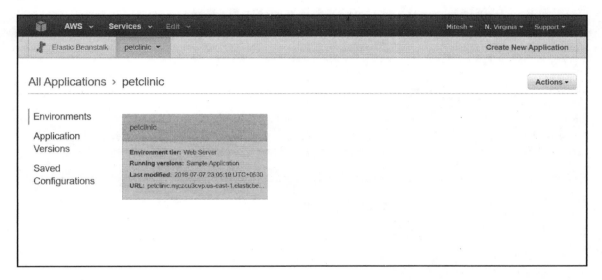

Click on the **petclinic** environment and verify **Health** and **Running Version** in the dashboard:

Verify the environment ID and URL. Click on the **URL** and verify the default page:

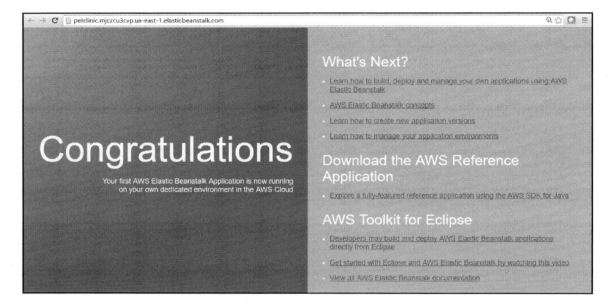

How to do it...

1. Install the AWS Elastic Beanstalk Publisher plugin. For more details, visit
   `https://wiki.jenkins-ci.org/display/JENKINS/AWS+Beanstalk+Publisher+Pl`
   `ugin`:

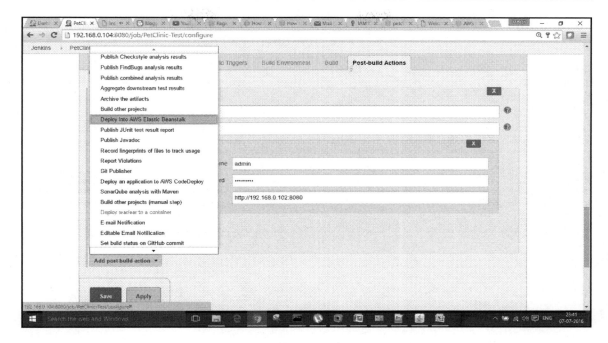

2. A new section will come up in **Post-build Actions** for Elastic Beanstalk.
3. Click on the **Jenkins** dashboard and select **Credentials**; add your **AWS Credentials**.
4. Go to your Jenkins build and select **AWS Credentials**, which is set in the global configuration.
5. Select **AWS Region** from the list and click on **Get Available Applications**. As we have created a sample application, it will show up like this.

6. In **EnvironmentLookup**, provide an environment ID in the **Get Environments By Name** box and click on **Get Available Environments**:

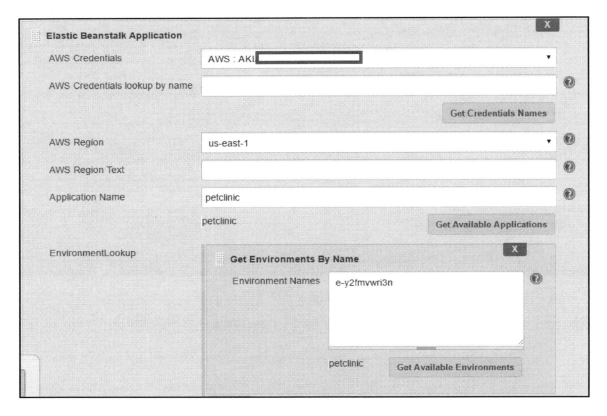

7. Save the configuration and click on **Build now**.
8. Now, let's go to the AWS management console to check whether the WAR file is being copied in Amazon S3 or not:
9. Go to S3 Services and check the available buckets:

10. Since the WAR file is large, it will take a while to upload to Amazon S3. Once it is uploaded, it will be available in the Amazon S3 bucket.

11. Check the build job's execution status in Jenkins. Some sections of the expected output are the following:

    - The test case execution and WAR file creation were successful
    - The build was successful

12. Now, check the AWS management console:

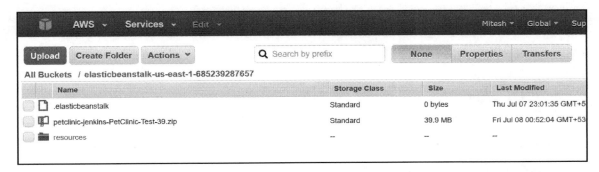

13. Go to **Services**, click on **AWS Elastic Beanstalk**, and verify the environment. The previous version was Sample Application. Now, the version has been updated to what is provided in **Version Label Format** in the Jenkins build job configuration:

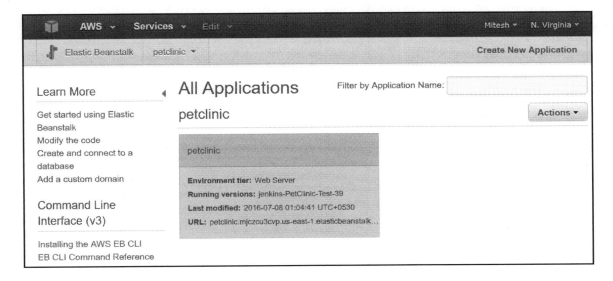

14. Go to the dashboard and verify **Health** and **Running Version** again.

15. Once everything has been verified, click on the URL for the environment, and our PetClinic application will be live:

16. Once the application deployment is successful, terminate the environment. Go to Specific environment and click on Actions to Terminate the environment. We have successfully deployed our application on Elastic Beanstalk.

Deploying a WAR file from Jenkins to Azure App Services

Microsoft Azure App services is a PaaS. In this section, we will look at the Azure web app and how we can deploy our PetClinic application.

Getting ready

We need to have a Microsoft Azure subscription. Go to **App Services** and click **+ Add**:

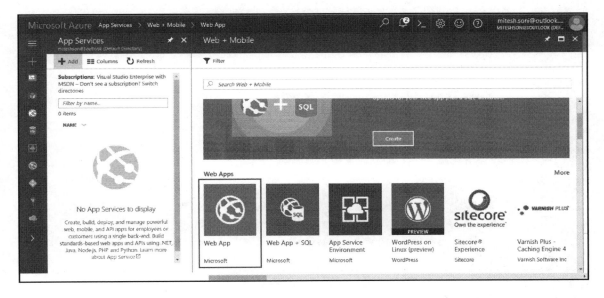

Then, click on **Create**:

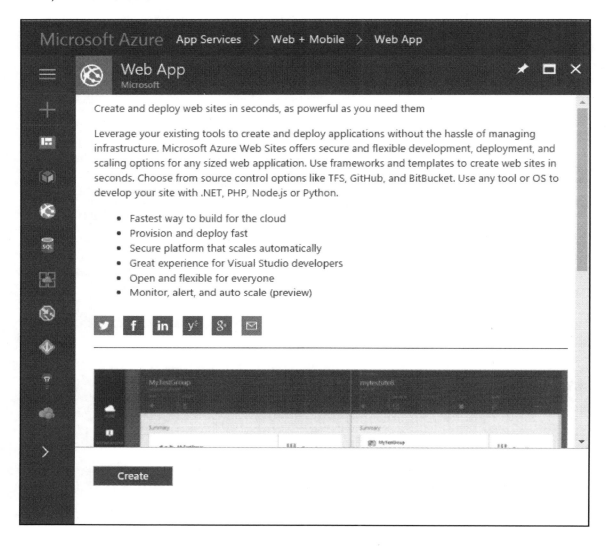

Go to the Microsoft Azure portal at `https://portal.azure.com`. Click on **App Services** and then on **+ Add**. Provide values for **App name**, **Subscription**, **Resource Group**, and **App Service plan/Location**. Then, click on **Create**:

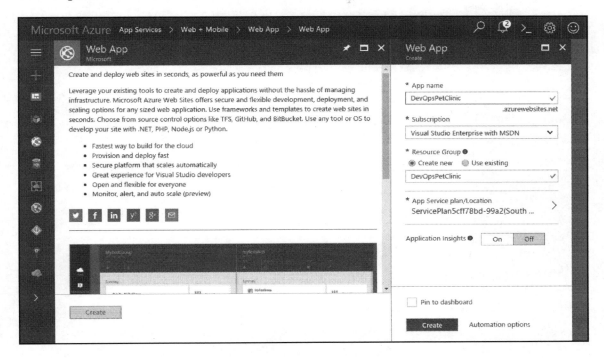

Once the Azure Web App is created, see whether it shows up in the Azure portal. Click on **DevOpsPetClinic** and its details related to the **URL**, **Status**, **Location**, and so on:

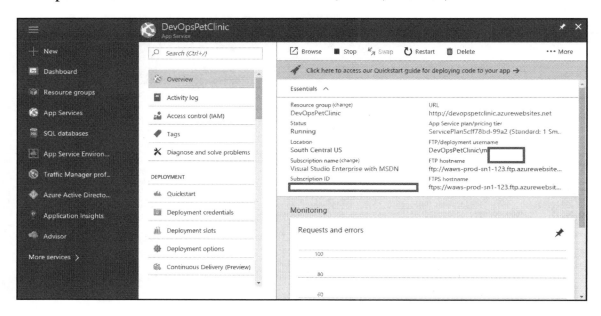

Verify on the **App Services** section too:

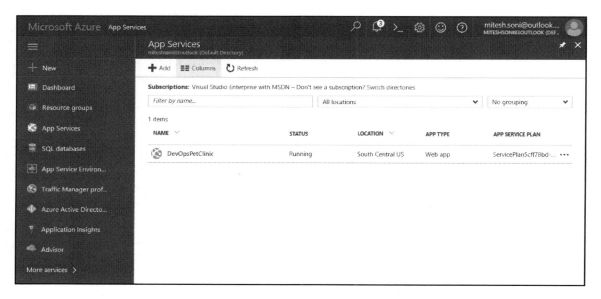

Click on **All Settings**, go to the **SETTINGS** section, and click on **Application settings** to configure the Azure Web App for Java web application hosting. Select the **Java version**, **Java Minor version**, **Web container**, and **Platform**, and click on **Always On**:

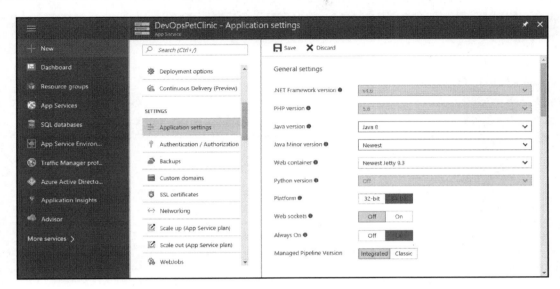

Visit the URL of an Azure Web App from your browser and verify that it is ready for hosting our sample spring application, PetClinic:

Click on **All Settings**, and go to **Deployment credentials** in the **DEPLOYMENT** section. Provide an **FTP/deployment username** and **Password**, and save your changes:

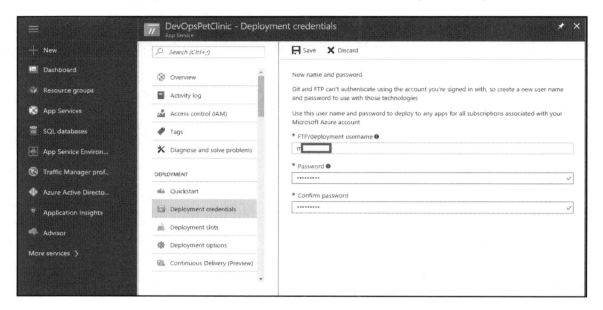

Let's install the `Publish Over FTP` plugin in Jenkins. We will use the Azure Web App's FTP details to publish the `PetClinic WAR` file.

How to do it...

1. Let's go to the Jenkins dashboard. Click on **New Item** and select **Freestyle project**.
2. In Jenkins, go to **Manage Jenkins** and click on **Configure | Configure FTP settings**. Provide a **Hostname**, **Username**, and **Password**, available in the Azure portal.
3. Go to `azurewebsites.net` and go to the Kudu console. Navigate through the different options and find the `site` directory and `webapps` directory. In the App Service URL, add `.scm` after the name of the Web App.

4. Click on Test Configuration and, once you get a Success message, you are ready to deploy the PetClinic application:

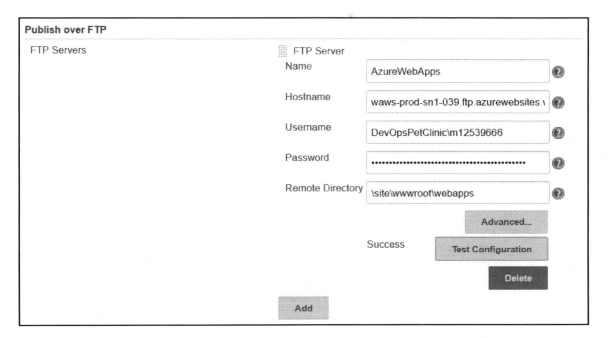

5. In the build job we created, go to the **Build** section and configure **Copy artifacts** from another project. We will copy the WAR file to a specific location on a virtual machine.

6. In **Post-build Actions**, click on **Send build artifacts over FTP**. Select the **FTP Server Name** that is configured in Jenkins. Configure **Source files** and the **Remove prefix** for the deployment of an Azure Web App.

7. Select **Verbose output** in the Console:

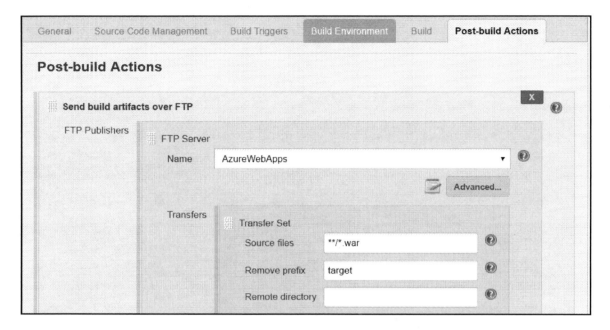

8. Click on **Build now** and see what happens behind the scenes:
9. Go to the Kudu console, click on **DebugConsole**, and go to **Powershell**. Go to **site** | **wwwroot** | **webapps**. Check whether the WAR file has been copied:

8. Now we have an application deployed on an Azure Web App.

Promoting builds

It is essential to differentiate builds from each other, based on verification or passing certain stages.

Getting ready

Go to **Manage Jenkins** | **Manage Plugins** | **Available**.

Install the promoted builds plugin.

How to do it...

1. Go to project configuration and check **Promote builds when...**:

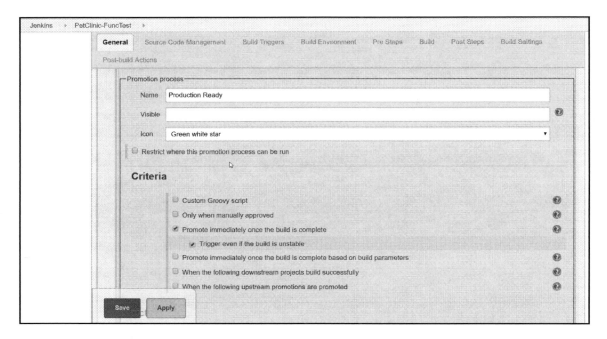

2. This build is promoted immediately once the build is complete, irrespective of its status.
3. You can configure promotion for manual approval too.

7
Continuous Testing

In this chapter, we will cover the following recipes:

- Getting started with continuous testing
- Creating a Selenium test case using Eclipse
- Integrating Jenkins and Selenium for functional testing
- Jenkins and Cucumber test reports
- Creating a load test in Apache JMeter
- Executing a load test from Jenkins
- Reporting JMeter performance metrics
- Testing with FitNesse

Getting started with continuous testing

Continuous testing is one of the most important DevOps practices available for the end-to-end automation of application life cycle management.

It not only considers automation, but it also includes aspects such as culture changes and tools. It is essential to integrate automated tests early in application life cycle management, to test quickly and in a timely manner, and to repeat the test execution process efficiently.

By the end of this chapter, you will have run performance and functional tests against a web application and web services.

This chapter emphasizes the need to make test writing accessible to a large audience. Embracing the largest possible audience improves the chances that testing will defend the intent of the application.

The technologies highlighted include:

- **Selenium**: This is the defacto industry standard for the functional testing of web applications. With Selenium IDE, you can record your actions within Firefox or Chrome, saving them in HTML format to replay later. The tests can be rerun through Maven using Selenium RC (Remote Control). It is common to use Jenkins slaves with different OSes and browser types to run tests. The alternative is to use Selenium Grid (`https://code.google.com/p/selenium/wiki/Grid2`).
- **JMeter**: This is a popular open source tool for stress testing. It can also be used to functionally test through the use of assertions. JMeter has a GUI that allows you to build test plans. The test plans are then stored in XML format. JMeter is executable through a Maven or Ant script. JMeter is very efficient and one instance is normally enough to hit your infrastructure hard. However, for super-high-load scenarios, JMeter can trigger an array of JMeter instances.
- **FitNesse**: This is a wiki with which you can write different types of tests. Having a wiki-like language to express and change tests on the fly gives functional administrators, consultants, and the end user a place to express their needs. You will be shown how to run FitNesse tests through Jenkins. FitNesse is also a framework where you can extend Java interfaces to create new testing types. These testing types are called fixtures; there are a number of fixtures available, including ones for database testing, running tools from the command line, and the functional testing of web applications.

Creating a Selenium test case using Eclipse

Let's go step by step to create a sample functional test case and then execute it using Jenkins.

The `PetClinic` project is a Maven-based Spring application and we will create a test case using Eclipse and Maven. Hence, we will utilize the `m2eclipse` plugin in Eclipse.

Getting ready

You will need Eclipse Java EE IDE for Web Developers, Version: Mars.2 Release (4.5.2), Build ID: 20160218-0600.

Go to the Eclipse Marketplace and install the Maven integration for the Eclipse plugin:

1. Create a **Maven Project** using a wizard in Eclipse IDE:

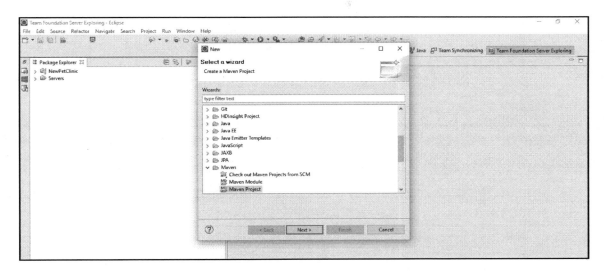

2. Select **Create a simple project (skip archetype selection)** and click on **Next**:

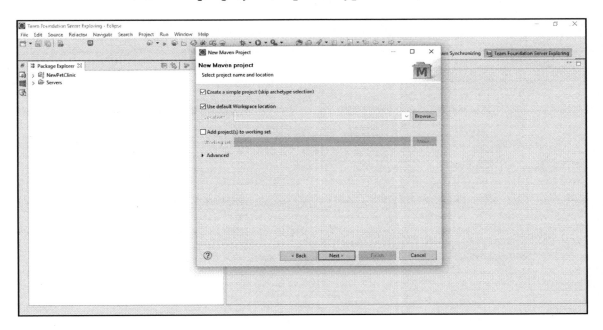

3. Go through the wizard and create a project. It will take some time to create a project in Eclipse. Provide the **Artifact, Version, Packaging, Name,** and **Description.** Click on **Finish.**

4. Wait until the Maven project is created and configured. Make sure that Maven is installed and configured properly. In the case of the Maven behind the proxy, configure the proxy details into `conf.xml`, available in the `Maven` directory.

5. In `Pom.xml`, we need to add Maven, Selenium, TestNG, and JUnit dependencies in the `<project>` node. The following is a modified `Pom.xml`:

```
<project xmlns="http://maven.apache.org/POM/4.0.0"
xmlns:xsi="http://www.w3.org/2001/XMLSchema-instance"
  xsi:schemaLocation="http://maven.apache.org/POM/4.0.0
http://maven.apache.org/xsd/maven-4.0.0.xsd">
  <modelVersion>4.0.0</modelVersion>
  <groupId>com.tiny</groupId>
  <artifactId>test</artifactId>
  <version>0.0.1-SNAPSHOT</version>
  <name>test</name>
  <build>
    <plugins>
      <plugin>
        <groupId>org.apache.maven.plugins</groupId>
        <artifactId>maven-compiler-plugin</artifactId>
        <version>3.6.1</version>
        <configuration>
          <source>1.8</source>
          <target>1.8</target>
        </configuration>
      </plugin>
      <plugin>
        <groupId>org.apache.maven.plugins</groupId>
        <artifactId>maven-surefire-plugin</artifactId>
        <version>2.19.1</version>
        <configuration>
          <suiteXmlFiles>
            <suiteXmlFile>testng.xml</suiteXmlFile>
          </suiteXmlFiles>
        </configuration>
      </plugin>
    </plugins>
  </build>
  <dependencies>
    <dependency>
      <groupId>org.seleniumhq.selenium</groupId>
      <artifactId>selenium-java</artifactId>
      <version>3.6.0</version>
```

```
      </dependency>
      <dependency>
        <groupId>org.testng</groupId>
        <artifactId>testng</artifactId>
        <version>6.10</version>
        <scope>test</scope>
      </dependency>
    </dependencies>
  </project>
```

6. Save Pom.xml after adding these changes and build the project again from the **Project** menu. It will download new dependencies:

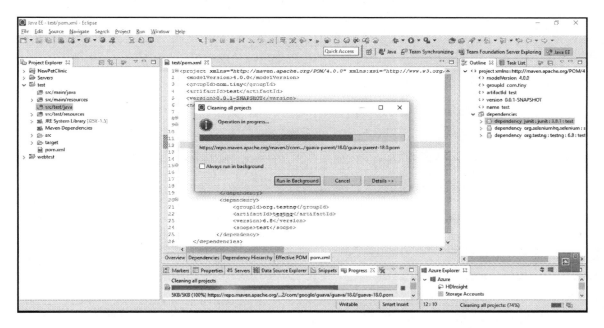

7. Click on the **Details** button of the dialog box to verify the operation in progress.

8. The next task is to write the `TestNG` class. Install the `TestNG` plugin. Go to **Help** and click on **Install New Software**. **Add Repository**:

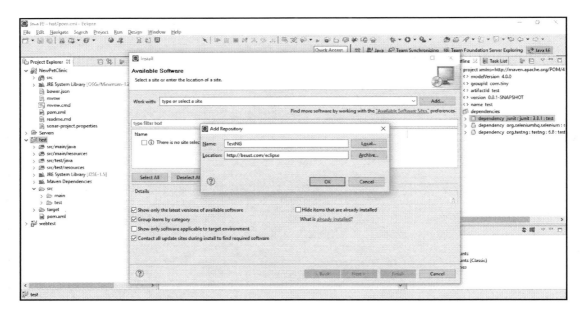

9. Select the items we need to install:

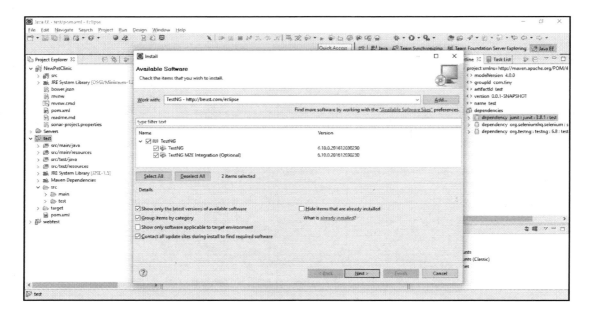

10. Review all the items that need to be installed and click on **Next**.
11. Accept the license and click on **Finish**.
12. Verify the installation progress in Eclipse.

How to do it...

1. Now let's create a **TestNG class**:

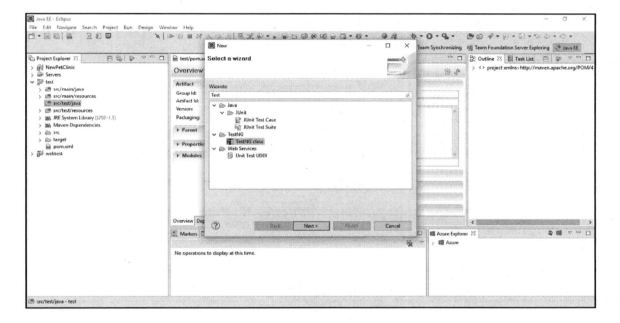

2. Provide a **Class name**:

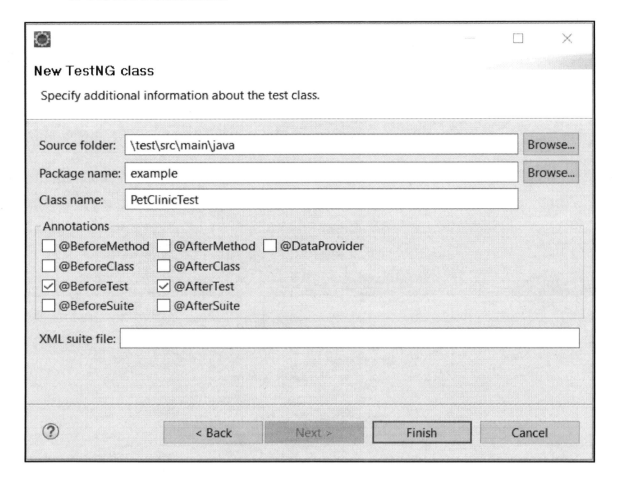

3. Give a **Package name** and click on **Finish**.

4. The newly created class will look like the following screenshot:

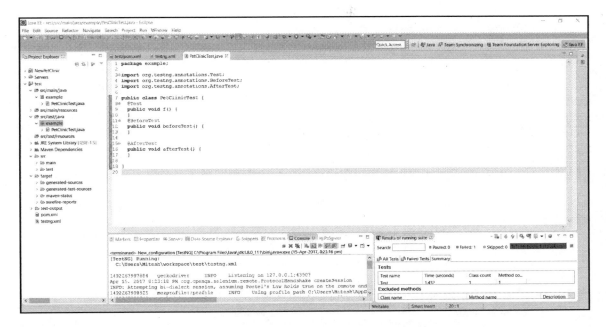

5. Right-click on the test file and click on **TestNG, convert to TestNG**.

6. It will create a `testing.xml` file that has details about the test suite.

7. Right-click on **Project** and click on **Run Configurations**.

8. Right-click on **TestNG** and click on **New**:

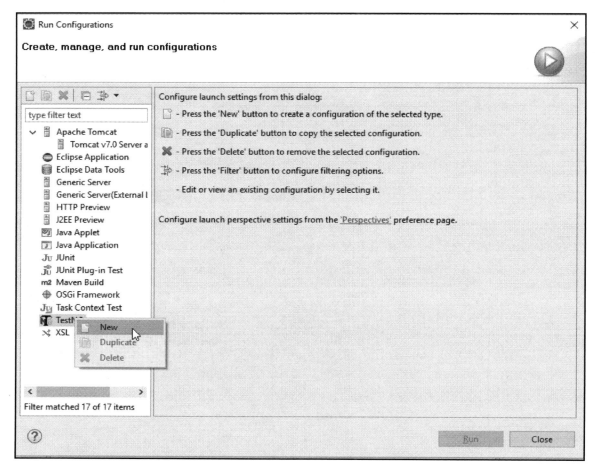

9. Provide the **Project** name and select `testing.xml` in the **Suite**.
10. Click **OK** and **Apply**.
11. Click on **Run**:

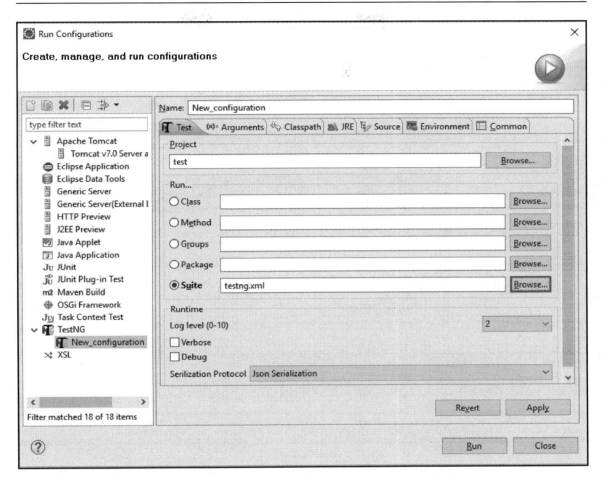

12. If Windows Firewall blocks it, then click on **Allow Access**.

There is no configuration available in testing.xml for execution, hence, even if the Maven execution runs successfully, no suite will be executed.

Generate the `TestNG` class under the `test` folder.

1. Select the `location`, `suite name`, and `class name`:

```xml
<?xml version="1.0" encoding="UTF-8"?>
<!DOCTYPE suite SYSTEM "http://testng.org/testng-1.0.dtd">
<suite name="Suite">
<test name="Test">
<classes>
<class name="example.PetClinicTest"/>
</classes>
</test><!-- Test -->
</suite><!-- Suite -->
```

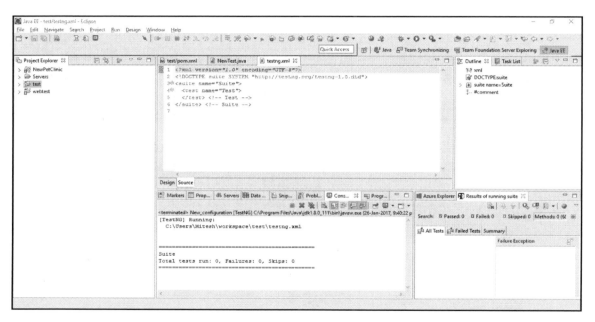

2. Go to `https://github.com/mozilla/geckodriver/releases` and download a version.
3. Extract the file available in the downloaded ZIP file based on the system configuration we have. In our case, we have downloaded `geckodriver-v0.13.0-win64`. Download the latest version available.
4. Click on it and verify the driver details.

5. Let's write some code as well. It will check whether the title of the web page contains a specific string or not. The result or the outcome of the following code is based on the title of the page. If it contains a given string, then the test case will pass; otherwise, it will fail the package example:

```
import java.io.File;
import org.openqa.selenium.WebDriver;
import org.openqa.selenium.firefox.FirefoxDriver;
import org.testng.Assert;
import org.testng.annotations.Test;
import org.testng.annotations.BeforeTest;
import org.testng.annotations.AfterTest;
public class PetClinicTest {
  private WebDriver driver;
    @Test
    public void testPetClinic() {
      driver.get("http://localhost:8090/petclinic/");
      String title = driver.getTitle();
      Assert.assertTrue(title.contains("a Spring Frameworkk"));
    }
    @BeforeTest
    public void beforeTest() {
      File file = new
File("F:\\##JenkinsEssentials\\geckodriver-v0.13.0-
win64\\geckodriver.exe");
      System.setProperty("webdriver.gecko.driver",
file.getAbsolutePath());
      driver = new FirefoxDriver();
    }
    @AfterTest
    public void afterTest() {
      driver.quit();
    }
}
```

6. The same file is available in the IDE, as shown in the following screenshot.

7. Let's run the Maven test again from Eclipse.

8. The following is the output when the test case is executed successfully:

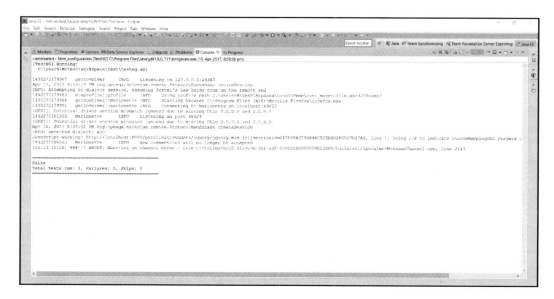

9. Verify the **All Tests** tab in the **Results of the running suite** section in Eclipse. We can see the successful execution here:

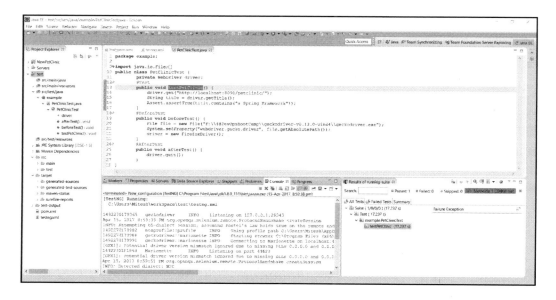

10. Verify the **Failed Tests** tab in the **Results of the running suite** section in Eclipse.
11. Verify the **Summary** tab in the **Results of the running suite** section in Eclipse in the successful scenario.
12. In the code, change the text available for title comparison so the test case fails.
13. Verify the output in the **Console**:

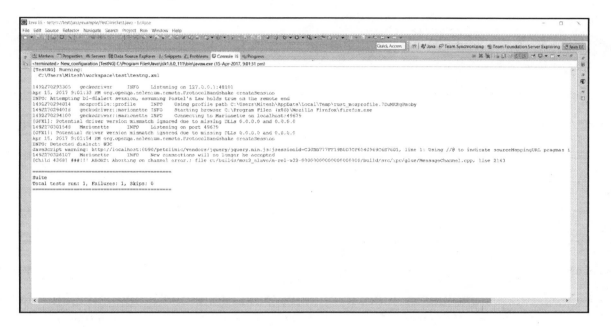

14. Verify the **All Tests** tab in the **Results of the running suite** section in Eclipse and notice the failure icon:

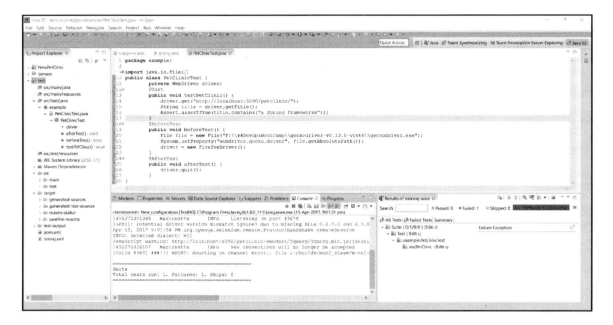

15. Verify the **Failed Tests** tab in the **Results of the running suite** section in Eclipse.
16. Click on **testPetClinic** and verify the **Failure Exception**.
17. Verify the **Summary** tab in the **Results of the running suite** section in Eclipse.

So, we have created a sample test case based on Selenium to verify the title of the PetClinic home page.

Integrating Jenkins and Selenium for functional testing

In this recipe, we will write a sample functional test using Selenium.

Getting ready

Install the **TestNG Results Plugin**:

Create a new project or build job in Jenkins.

How to do it...

Now let's try to execute the from Jenkins:

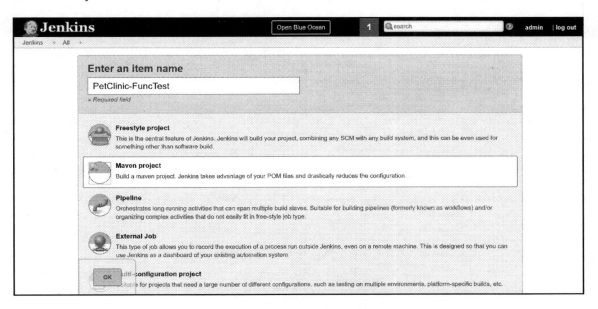

1. Check in the **Test Project** in **Repository**. Create a `PetClinic-FuncTest` freestyle job in Jenkins.

2. In the **Build** section, provide the **Root POM** location and **Goals and options** to execute:

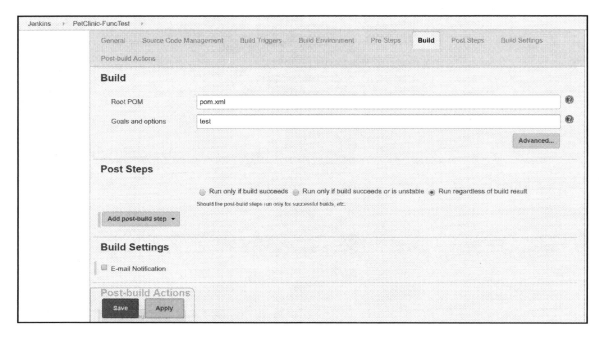

3. Save the build job and click on **Build now**.
4. Verify the execution of the build job in the **Console Output**.

5. It will open a Mozilla Firefox window and open a URL that is given in the code. This requires our PetClinic application to be deployed in a web server and running without any issues:

```
-------------------------------------------------------
 T E S T S
-------------------------------------------------------
Running TestSuite
1496574254522   geckodriver      INFO    Listening on 127.0.0.1:6486
Jun 04, 2017 4:34:14 PM org.openqa.selenium.remote.ProtocolHandshake createSession
INFO: Attempting bi-dialect session, assuming Postel's Law holds true on the remote end
1496574255134   mozprofile::profile      INFO    Using profile path
C:\Users\Mitesh\AppData\Local\Temp\rust_mozprofile.t3uOSiy56Onn
1496574255138   geckodriver::marionette INFO     Starting browser C:\Program Files (x86)\Mozilla Firefox\firefox.exe
1496574255175   geckodriver::marionette INFO     Connecting to Marionette on localhost:60430
[GFX1]: Potential driver version mismatch ignored due to missing DLLs 0.0.0.0 and 0.0.0.0
[GFX1]: Potential driver version mismatch ignored due to missing DLLs 0.0.0.0 and 0.0.0.0
1496574288578   Marionette       INFO    Listening on port 60430
Jun 04, 2017 4:34:49 PM org.openqa.selenium.remote.ProtocolHandshake createSession
INFO: Detected dialect: W3C
JavaScript warning:
http://localhost:8090/petclinic/vendors/jquery/jquery.min.js;jsessionid=884F4251137D820A5723530BAA688915, line 1:
Using //@ to indicate sourceMappingURL pragmas is deprecated. Use //# instead
>>>>>>PetClinic :: a Spring Framework demonstration
1496574305189   Marionette       INFO    New connections will no longer be accepted
Jun 04, 2017 4:35:12 PM org.openqa.selenium.os.UnixProcess destroy
SEVERE: Unable to kill process with PID 10376
Tests run: 1, Failures: 0, Errors: 0, Skipped: 0, Time elapsed: 69.499 sec - in TestSuite
Results :

Tests run: 1, Failures: 0, Errors: 0, Skipped: 0
```

6. Go to **Post-build Actions** and select **Publish TestNG Results**:

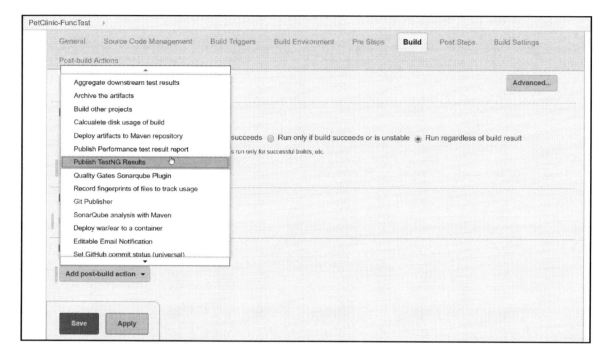

7. Provide the **TestNG XML report pattern**:

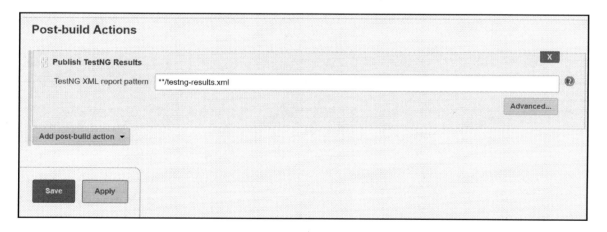

8. Click on **Build now**:

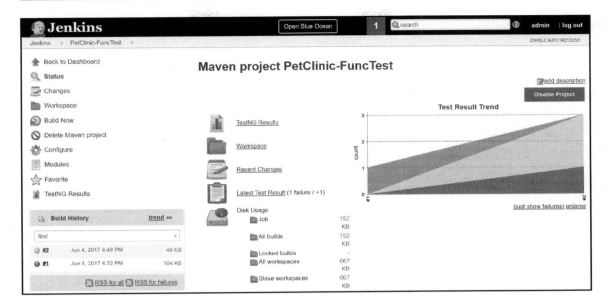

We have now seen how to execute Selenium-based test cases in Jenkins.

There's more

Go to the project dashboard and verify the graphs for TestNG results:

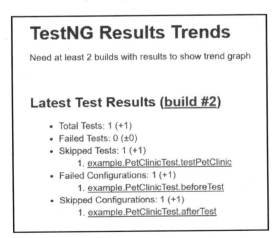

In the next section, we will see how to execute a load test using Jenkins.

Jenkins and Cucumber test reports

In this recipe, we will integrate Jenkins and Cucumber to publish Cucumber reports using Jenkins.

Getting ready

Go to the Jenkins dashboard | **Manage Jenkins** | **Manage Plugins** | **Available**.

Install the **Cucumber reports** plugin:

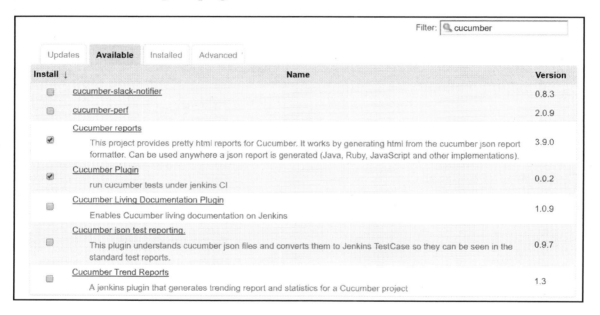

Click on **Install without restart**.

How to do it...

1. Create a **Maven Project** in Jenkins.
2. Select any GitHub project that has Cucumber integrated in it and which generates a .JSON file as a report:

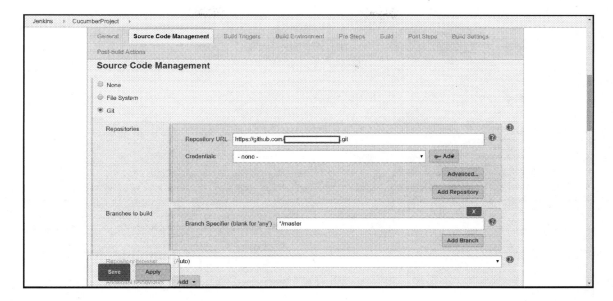

3. Configure **Root POM** and the test goal in the **Build** section:

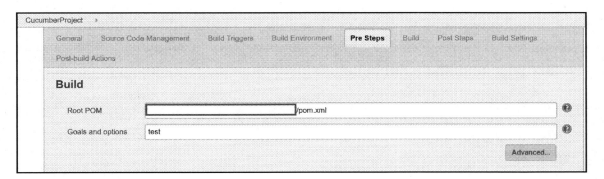

4. Select **Cucumber reports** from **Post-build Actions**.

5. Add the `*.json` file that will be generated after the test execution:

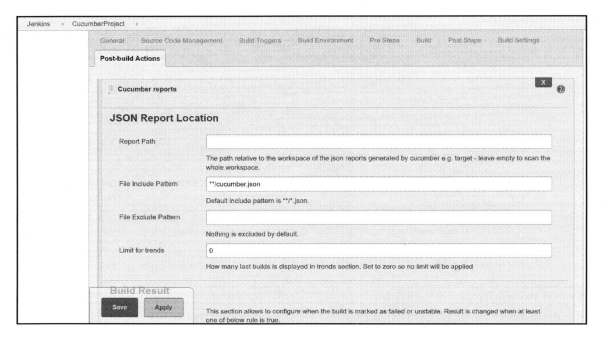

6. Save the build job.

7. Click on **Build now**.

8. Go to the **Console Output** and verify the test execution logs:

```
Tests run: 16, Failures: 2, Errors: 0, Skipped: 0

[ERROR] There are test failures.

Please refer to F:\1.DevOps2016\#JenkinsEssentials\FirstDraft\jenkinsHome\workspace\CucumberProject\[          ]
[                                        ]\target\surefire-reports for the individual test results.
[JENKINS] Recording test results
Started calculate disk usage of build
Finished Calculation of disk usage of build in 0 seconds
Started calculate disk usage of workspace
Finished Calculation of disk usage of workspace in 0 seconds
[INFO] ------------------------------------------------------------------------
[INFO] BUILD SUCCESS
[INFO] ------------------------------------------------------------------------
[INFO] Total time: 6.072 s
[INFO] Finished at: 2017-08-13T19:26:15+05:30
[INFO] Final Memory: 13M/130M
[INFO] ------------------------------------------------------------------------
[JENKINS] Archiving F:\1.DevOps2016\#JenkinsEssentials\FirstDraft\jenkinsHome\workspace\CucumberProject\[        ]
[                ]\pom.xml to [                                                        ]/0.0.1-
SNAPSHOT/[                                        ]-0.0.1-SNAPSHOT.pom
channel stopped
[CucumberReport] Preparing Cucumber Reports
[CucumberReport] JSON report directory is ""
[CucumberReport] Copied 5 json files from workspace
"F:\1.DevOps2016\#JenkinsEssentials\FirstDraft\jenkinsHome\workspace\CucumberProject" to reports directory
"F:\1.DevOps2016\#JenkinsEssentials\FirstDraft\jenkinsHome\jobs\CucumberProject\builds\6\cucumber-html-
reports\.cache"
[CucumberReport] Processing 1 json files:
[CucumberReport] F:\1.DevOps2016\#JenkinsEssentials\FirstDraft\jenkinsHome\jobs\CucumberProject\builds\6\cucumber-
html-reports\.cache\[                                        ]\target\cucumber.json
[CucumberReport] Found 1 failed steps, while expected not more than 0
[CucumberReport] Build status is left unchanged
Started calculate disk usage of build
Finished Calculation of disk usage of build in 0 seconds
Started calculate disk usage of workspace
Finished Calculation of disk usage of workspace in 0 seconds
```

9. On the **CucumberProject** dashboard, you will find **Test Result Trend** and the **Cucumber reports** link:

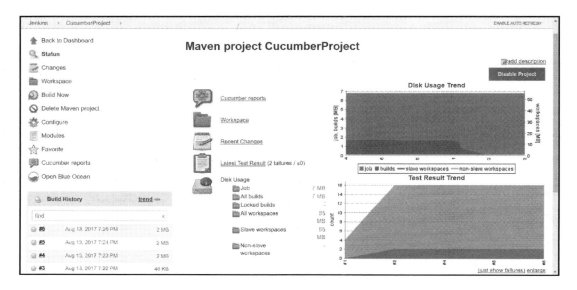

10. Click on the **Cucumber Reports** link:

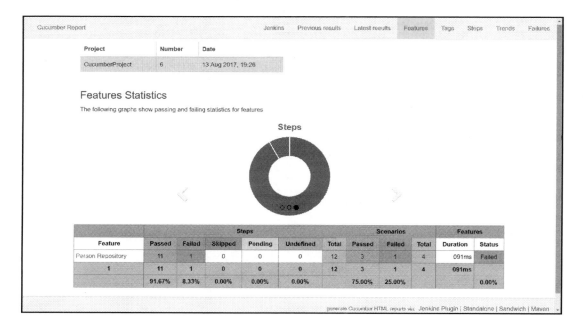

11. Check the steps, scenarios, and features-related graphs and data:

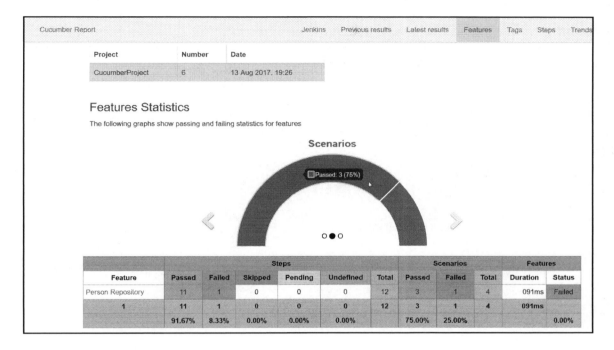

12. Verify the **Feature Report**:

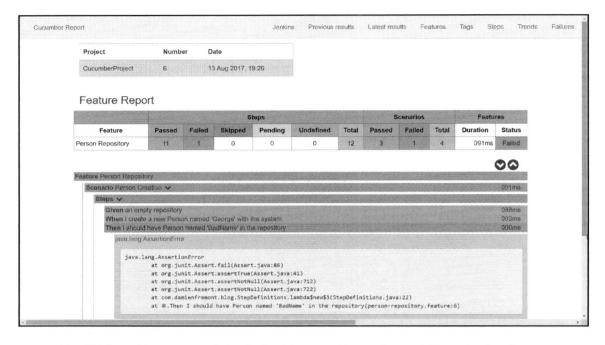

13. Click on **Features** and check the **Feature, Scenario,** and **Steps** in detail:

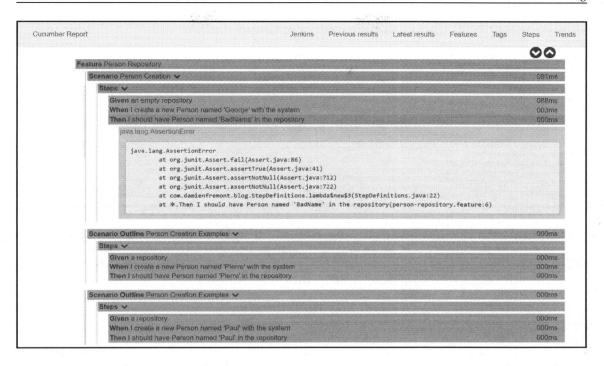

14. The following graph shows the **Steps Statistics** for this build. The following list is based on the results:

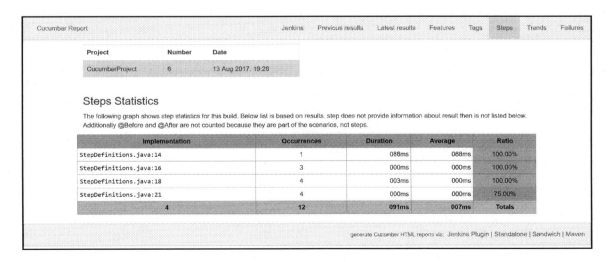

15. The **Trends Statistics** graph shows **Features**, **Scenarios**, and **Steps** for a period of time:

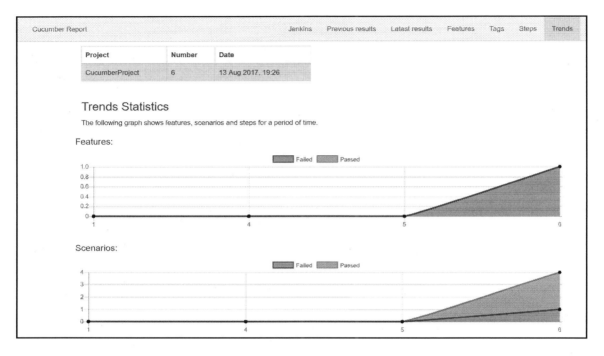

Try to find similar kinds of projects on GitHub and configure them in Jenkins to verify Cucumber reports in Jenkins.

Creating a load test in Apache JMeter

Apache JMeter is an open source Apache project. It is a pure Java application. Apache JMeter is used to load test, analyze, and measure the performance of services.

JMeter (http://jmeter.apache.org) is an open source tool for stress testing. It allows you to visually create a test plan and then hammer systems based on that plan.

JMeter can make many types of requests, known as samplers. It can sample HTTP, LDAP, and databases, use scripts, and much more. It can report back visually with listeners.

A beginner's book on JMeter is *Apache JMeter* by Emily H. Halili, published by Packt Publishing, ISBN 1847192955
(`http://www.packtpub.com/beginning-apache-jmeter`).

Two more advanced books from the same publisher are
`https://www.packtpub.com/application-development/performance-tes`
`ting-jmeter-29` and
`https://www.packtpub.com/application-development/jmeter-cookbook`
`-raw`.

In this recipe, you will write a test plan for hitting web pages whose URLs are defined in a text file. In the next recipe, *Reporting JMeter test plans*, you will configure Jenkins to run JMeter test plans.

Getting ready

Download Apache JMeter from `http://jmeter.apache.org/download_jmeter.cgi`. Extract the files and go to the `bin` directory. Execute `jmeter.bat` or `jmeter.sh`.

How to do it...

1. Jenkins' stable and recent versions are available in a `YUM` repository.
2. Open the Apache JMeter console and create a **Test Plan**.
3. Right-click on the **Test Plan** and click on **Add**; select **Threads (Users)**.
4. Select **Thread Group**.
5. Provide the **Thread Group name**.
6. In the **Thread Group** properties, provide the **Number of Threads**, **Ramp-up Period**, and **Loop Count**.
7. Right-click on **Thread Group**. Click on **Add**. Click on **Sampler**. Click on **HTTP Request**.
8. In **HTTP Request**, provide the **Server Name** or IP. In our case, it will be localhost or an IP address.
9. Give the **Port Number** where your web server is running.

10. Select the GET method and provide a path to the load test:

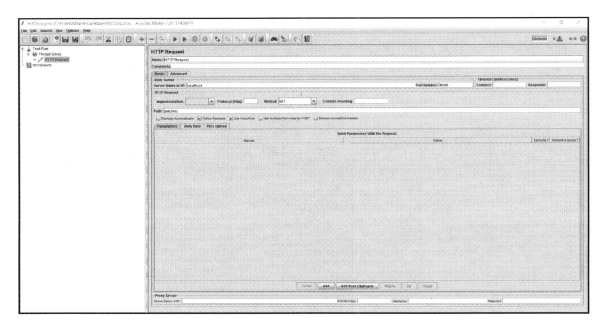

Apache JMeter HTTP Request Configuration

11. Save the .jmx file.
12. Run the test plan by pressing *Ctrl + R*.
13. Click on **View Results Tree**.

There's more

JMeter uses threads to run requests in parallel. Each thread is supposed to approximately simulate one user. In reality, a real user hits the system a lot less hard than a thread. Threads can hit the system many times a second, whereas, typically, a user clicks approximately once every 20 seconds.

The test plan uses a number of elements:

- **Thread Group**: This defines the number of threads that run.
- **Cookie manager**: This keeps the track of cookies per thread. This is important if you want to keep track of cookies between requests. For example, if a thread logs in to a Tomcat server, the unique JSESSIONID needs to be stored for each thread.
- **CSV Data Set Config**: This element parses the content of a CSV file, putting values in the **HOST**, **PORT**, and **URL** variables. A new line of the **CSV** file is read for each thread, once per iteration. The variables are expanded in the elements by using the `${variable_name}` notation.
- **View Results Tree**: This listener displays the results in the GUI as a tree of requests and responses. This is great for debugging but should be removed later.

A common mistake is to assume that a thread is equivalent to a user. The main difference is that threads can respond faster than an average user. If you do not add delay factors in the request, then you can really hammer your applications with a few threads. For example, a delay of 25 seconds per click is typical for the online systems at the University of Amsterdam.

If you are looking to coax out multithreading issues in your applications, then use a random delay element rather than a constant delay. This is also a better simulation of a typical user interaction.

Executing a load test from Jenkins

Now let's create a Jenkins job.

Getting ready

Create a **Freestyle project** in Jenkins:

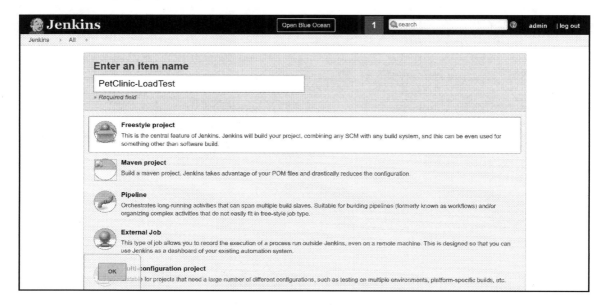

Add the build step **Execute Windows** `batch` command.

How to do it...

1. Add the following command. Replace the location of `jmeter.bat` based on the installation directory and the location of the `.jmx file` too:

   ```
   C:\apache-jmeter-3.0\bin\jmeter.bat -
   Jjmeter.save.saveservice.output_format=xml -n -t
   C:\Users\Mitesh\Desktop\PetClinic.jmx -l Test.jtl
   ```

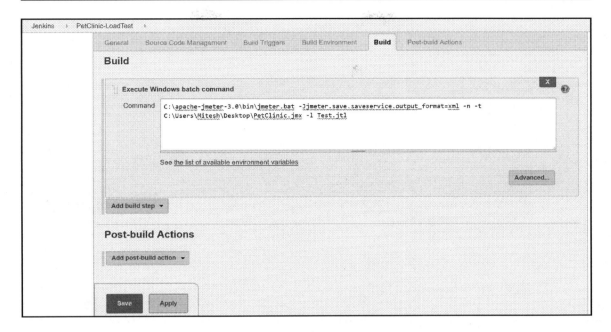

2. Add a **Post-build Actions**:

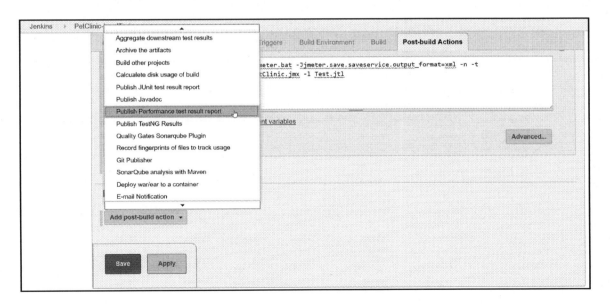

3. In the **Publish Performance test result report**, add `**/*.jtl` file:

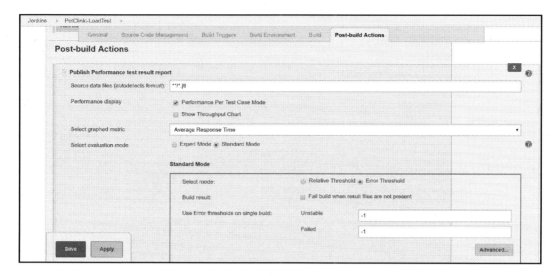

4. Click on **Build now**:

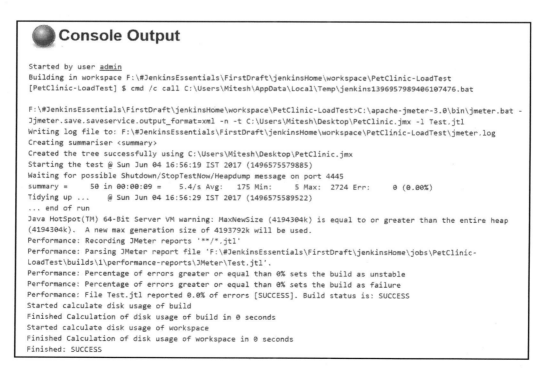

5. Verify the **Performance Trend** on the **Project** dashboard.

6. Click on **Performance Trend**:

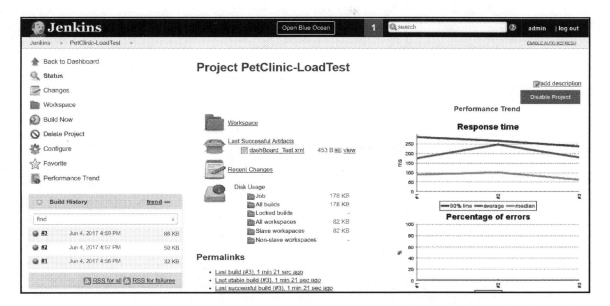

7. Verify performance breakdown:

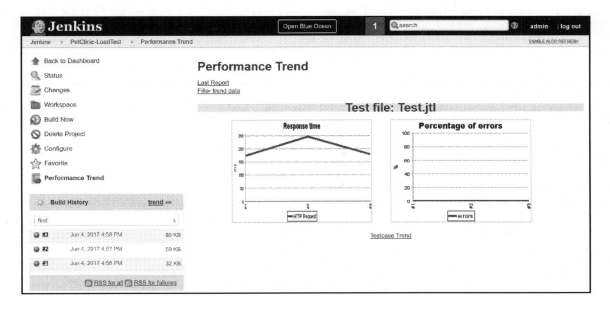

8. Click on the **Last Report** and get more details on the load test results:

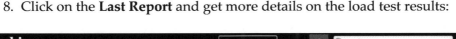

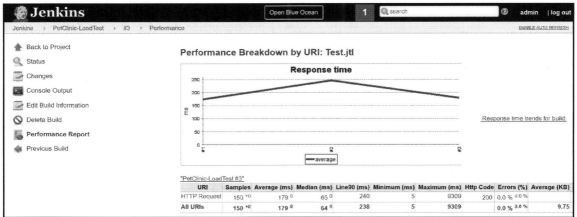

9. Done!

Reporting JMeter performance metrics

In this recipe, you will be shown how to configure Jenkins to run a JMeter test plan, and then collect and report the results. The passing of variables from an Ant script to JMeter will also be explained.

Getting ready

It is assumed that you have run through the last recipe creating the JMeter test plan. You will also need to install the Jenkins performance plugin (`https://wiki.jenkins-ci.org/display/JENKINS/Performance+Plugin`).

How to do it...

1. Open `./examples/jmeter_example.jmx` in JMeter and save as `./plans/URL_ping.jmx`.
2. Select **CSV Data Set Config** changing the filename to `${__property(csv)}`.
3. Under the **File** menu, select the **Save** option.

4. Create a **build.xml** file at the top level of your project with the following content:

```
<project default="jmeter.tests">
<property name="jmeter" location="/var/lib/jenkins/jmeter"
 />
<property name="target" location="${basedir}/target" />
<echo message="Running... Expecting variables [jvarg,desc]"
 />
<echo message="For help please read ${basedir}/README"/>
<echo message="[DESCRIPTION] ${desc}" />
<taskdef  name="jmeter"
 classname="org.programmerplanet.ant.taskdefs.jmeter.JMeterT
 ask" classpath="${jmeter}/extras/ant-jmeter-1.0.9.jar" />
    <target name="jmeter.init">
    <mkdir  dir="${basedir}/jmeter_results"/>
    <delete includeemptydirs="true">
    <fileset dir="${basedir}/jmeter_results"
includes="**/*" />
    </delete>
  </target>
    <target name="jmeter.tests" depends="jmeter.init"
description="launch jmeter load tests">
    <echo message="[Running] jmeter tests..." />
<jmeter jmeterhome="${jmeter}"
 resultlog="${basedir}/jmeter_results/LoadTestResults.jtl">
    <testplans dir="${basedir}/plans" includes="*.jmx"/>
    <jvmarg value="${jvarg}" />
    <property name="csv" value="${basedir}/data/URLS.csv"
 />
    </jmeter>
  </target>
</project>
```

5. Commit the updates to your subversion project.
6. Log in to Jenkins.
7. Create a new freestyle job with the name `ch6.remote.jmeter`.
8. Under **Source Code Management**, check **Subversion**, adding your subversion repository URL to the repository URL.
9. Within the **Build** section, add the build step, **Invoke Ant**.
10. Click on **Advanced** in the new **Invoke Ant** subsection, adding the following for properties:

```
jvarg=-Xmx512m
desc= This is the first iteration in a performance test
 environment - Driven by Jenkins
```

11. In the **Post-build Actions** section, check **Publish Performance test result report**. Add the input **jmeter_results/*.jtl** to **Report Files**.
12. Click on **Save**.
13. Run the job a couple of times and review the results found under the Performance trend link.

How it works...

The `build.xml` file is an Ant script that sets up the environment and then calls the JMeter Ant tasks defined in the library `/extras/ant-jmeter-1.0.9.jar`. The JAR file is installed as part of the standard JMeter distribution.

Any JMeter test plan found under the plans directory will be run. Moving the test plan from the `examples` directory to the `plans` directory activates it. The results are aggregated in `jmeter_results/LoadTestResults.jtl`.

The Ant script passes the `csv` variable to the JMeter test plan; the location of the `.csv` file, `${basedir}/data/URLS.csv`. `${basedir}`, is automatically defined by Ant. As the name suggests, it is the base directory of the Ant project.

You can call JMeter functions within its elements using the structure `${__functioncall(parameters)}`. You have added the function call `${__property(csv)}` to the test plan `CSV Data Set Config` element. The function pulls in the value of `.csv` that was defined in the Ant script.

The Jenkins job runs the Ant script, which in turn runs the JMeter test plans and aggregates the results. The Jenkins performance plugin then parses the results, creating a report.

There's more...

To build complex test plans speedily, consider using the transparent proxy (`http://jmeter.apache.org/usermanual/component_reference.html#HTTP_Proxy_Server`) built into JMeter. You can run it on a given port on your local machine, setting the proxy preferences in your web browser to match. The recorded JMeter elements will then give you a good idea of the parameters sent in the captured requests.

An alternative is Badboy (`http://www.badboysoftware.biz/docs/jmeter.html`), which has its own built-in web browser. It allows you to record your actions in a similar way to Selenium IDE and then save them to a JMeter plan.

Testing with FitNesse

FitNesse (http://fitnesse.org) is a fully integrated standalone wiki and acceptance-testing framework. You can write tests in tables and run them. Writing tests in a wiki language widens the audience of potential test writers and decreases the initial efforts required to learn a new framework.

If a test passes, the table row is displayed in green. If it fails, it is displayed in red. The tests can be surrounded by wiki content delivering context information, such as user stories, at the same location as the tests. You can also consider creating mock-ups of your web applications in FitNesse next to the tests, and pointing the tests at those mock-ups.

This recipe describes how to run FitNesse remotely and display the results within Jenkins.

Getting ready

Download the latest stable FitNesse JAR from http://fitnesse.org/FitNesseDownload. Install the FitNesse plugins for Jenkins from https://wiki.jenkins-ci.org/display/JENKINS/FitNesse+Plugin.

How to do it...

1. Create the fit/logs directories and place them in the fit directory, fitnesse-standalone.jar.
2. Run the FitNesse help from the command line and review the options:

```
java -jar fitnesse-standalone.jar -help
Usage: java -jar fitnesse.jar [-vpdrleoab]
-p <port number> {80}
-d <working directory> {.}
-r <page root directory> {FitNesseRoot}
-l <log directory> {no logging}
-f <config properties file> {plugins.properties}
-e <days> {14} Number of days before page versions expire
-o omit updates
-a {user:pwd | user-file-name} enable authentication.
-i Install only, then quit.
-c <command> execute single command.
-b <filename> redirect command output.
-v {off} Verbose logging
```

3. Run `FitNesse` from the command line and review the startup output:

```
java -jar fitnesse-standalone.jar -p 39996 -l logs -a
tester:test
Bootstrapping FitNesse, the fully integrated standalone wiki
and acceptance testing framework.
root page: fitnesse.wiki.fs.FileSystemPage at
./FitNesseRoot#latest
logger: /home/alan/Desktop/X/fitness/logs
authenticator: fitnesse.authentication.OneUserAuthenticator
page factory: fitnesse.html.template.PageFactory
page theme: fitnesse_straight
Starting FitNesse on port: 39996
```

4. Using a web browser, visit `http://localhost:39996`.
5. Click on the **Acceptance Test** link.
6. Click on the **Suite** link. This will activate a set of tests. Depending on your computer, the tests may take a few minutes to complete. The direct link is `http://localhost:39996/FitNesse.SuiteAcceptanceTests?suite`.
7. Click on the `Test History` link. You will need to log on as user `tester` with the password `test`.
8. Review the log in the `fit/logs` directory. After running the suite again, you will now see an entry similar to the following:

```
127.0.0.1 - tester [01/Oct/2014:11:14:59 +0100] "GET
/FitNesse.SuiteAcceptanceTests?suite HTTP/1.1" 200 6086667
```

9. Log in to Jenkins and create a freestyle software project named `ch6.remote.fitnesse`.
10. In the **Build** section, select the **Execute fitnesse tests** option from the **Add Build** step.
11. Check the option **FitNesse instance is already running**, adding:

- **Fitnesses Host**: `localhost`
- **Fitnesses Port**: `39996`
- **Target Page**: `FitNesse.SuiteAcceptanceTests?suite`
- Check the Is target a suite option
- HTTP Timeout (ms): `180000`
- `Path to fitnesse xml results` file: `fitnesse-results.xml`

12. In the **Post-build Actions** section, check the **Publish FitNesse results report** option.
13. Add the **fitnesse-results.xml** value to the input **Path to fitnesse xml results** file.
14. Click on **Save**.
15. Run the job.
16. Review the latest job by clicking on the link **FitNesse Results**.

How it works...

FitNesse has a built-in set of acceptance tests that it uses to check itself for regressions. The Jenkins plugin calls the test and asks for the results to be returned in XML format using an HTTP GET request with the URL: `http://localhost:39996/FitNesse.SuiteAcceptanceTests?suite&format=xml`. The results look similar to the following:

```
<testResults>
<FitNesseVersion>v20140901</FitNesseVersion>
<rootPath>FitNesse.SuiteAcceptanceTests</rootPath>
<result>
<counts><right>103</right>
<wrong>0</wrong>
<ignores>0</ignores>
<exceptions>0</exceptions>
</counts>
<runTimeInMillis>27</runTimeInMillis>
<relativePageName>CopyAndAppendLastRow</relativePageName>
<pageHistoryLink>
FitNesse.SuiteAcceptanceTests.SuiteFitDecoratorTests.CopyAndAppend
  LastRow?pageHistory&resultDate=20141101164526
</pageHistoryLink>
</result>
```

The Jenkins plugin then parses the XML and generates a report.

By default, there is no security enabled on FitNesse pages. In this recipe, a username and password were defined during startup. However, we did not take this further and define the security permissions on the page. To activate, you will need to go to the properties link on the left-hand side of the page and check the **security permission for secure-test**.

You can also authenticate through a list of users in a text file or Kerberos/Active Directory. For more details, review `http://fitnesse.org/FitNesse.FullReferenceGuide.UserGuide.AdministeringFitNesse.SecurityDescription`.

There is also a contributed plugin for LDAP authentication: `https://github.com/timander/fitnesse-ldap-authenticator`.

 Consider applying security in depth; adding IP restrictions through a firewall on the FitNesse server creates an extra layer of defense. For example, you can place an Apache server in front of the wiki, and enabling SSL/TLS ensures encrypted passwords. A thinner alternative to Apache is NGINX: `http://wiki.nginx.org`.

See also...

You will find the source code with information on building the newest version of FitNesse at its GitHub home: `https://github.com/unclebob/fitnesse`.

8
Orchestration

In this chapter, we will cover the following recipes:

- Introduction
- Understanding upstream and downstream jobs
- Configuring upstream and downstream jobs
- Configuring a build pipeline
- Creating a pipeline job
- Using a sample pipeline for execution
- Configuring a pipeline job for end-to-end automation
- Getting started with the Blue Ocean dashboard

Introduction

An orchestration or pipeline is all about defining a sequence of execution to manage an application life cycle based on requirements.

A simple example can be that you may want to perform a static code analysis first; if it complies to the defined quality gate, then it should only perform Continuous Integration and create an application package that can be deployed in a specific environment.

Once the package is ready, deploy it into a test environment for manual or automated testing based on the requirements and defined policies in the organization. Once it is promoted for UAT or the staging environment, then you may want to perform functional test execution and performance testing.

Once this flow is completed, you may want to deploy it in a production environment, but not without the approval of the specific stakeholder.

This is the orchestration of build jobs or the defined flow of execution.

Understanding upstream and downstream jobs

An upstream job is a configured project that triggers a project as part of its execution.

A downstream job is a configured project that is triggered as part of a execution of pipeline.

Upstream and downstream jobs help you to configure the sequence of execution for different operations and hence you can orchestrate the flow of execution. We can configure one or more projects as downstream jobs in Jenkins.

Getting ready

You need to divide the end-to-end automation of the application life cycle management process into multiple distinct projects.

The benefit of this strategy is that you can isolate automation tasks and execute independently on different agents.

How to do it...

Let's start with the first job for upstream and downstream jobs configuration. Keep a project that executes static code analysis as the first job:

1. Go to the **Post-build Actions** section in the configuration of the **PetClinic-Code** build job.
2. Select **Build other projects** from the available options:

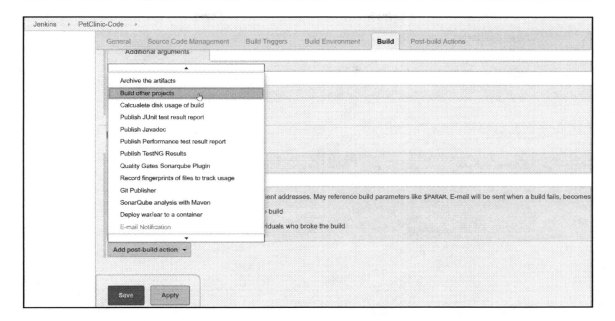

3. You should create the package after static code analysis is done, so you should select **PetClinic-Package** where Continuous Integration is configured for compilation of the source code, unit test execution, and package file creation.

4. Click **Save**.

Thus, for **PetClinic-Code**, **PetClinic-Package** is a downstream job while for **PetClinic-Package**, **PetClinic-Code** is an upstream job.

Configuring upstream and downstream jobs

Let's configure a complete flow using upstream and downstream jobs.

Getting ready

Make sure that you have all the build jobs available that you created in earlier chapters, such as the deployment of WAR files, functional testing, and load testing.

How to do it...

Once your package is ready, you should deploy it, so from the **PetClinic-Package** job, you will configure **PetClinic-Deploy** as a downstream job in **Post-build Actions**:

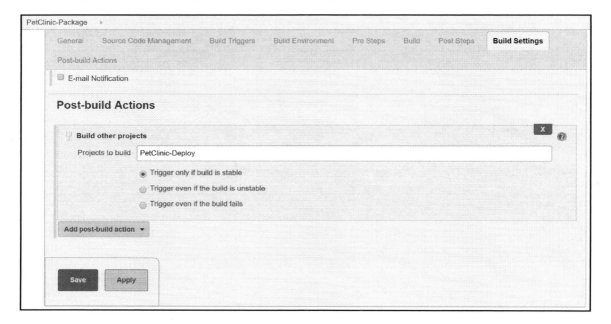

Once your application is deployed on the server, you should perform functional test cases, so from the `PetClinic-Deploy` job, you will configure `PetClinic-FuncTest` as a downstream job in **Post-build Actions**:

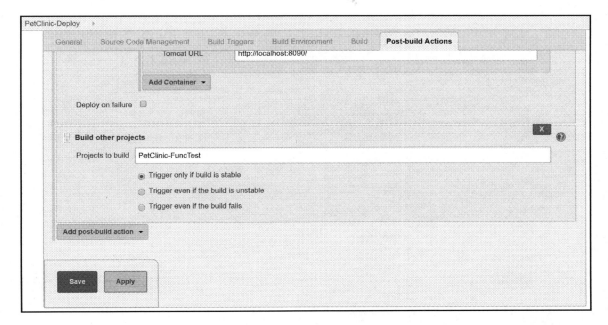

Once the functional test cases are executed successfully, you should perform load testing, so, from the `PetClinic-FuncTest` job, you will configure `PetClinic-LoadTest` as a downstream job in **Post-build Actions**:

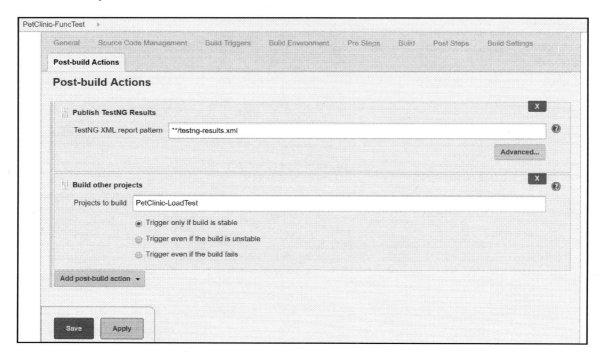

Once load testing is completed, you should deploy the application in the Prod environment, so from the PetClinic-LoadTest job, you will configure PetClinic-Prod as a downstream job in **Post-build Actions**:

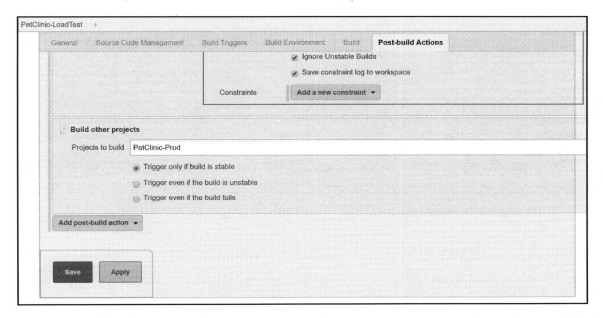

Configuring a build pipeline

Now you have configured all upstream and downstream jobs. You know the sequence so you can execute the first build and the rest of the builds will follow until any job fails in the sequence. You can configure to move ahead with unstable builds as well.

However, it is more useful if you have the visualization of the flow of execution you have configured as upstream and downstream jobs.

The build pipeline plugin provides visualization of the execution flow based on the upstream and downstream jobs configuration.

Getting ready

Install the plugin from **Manage Jenkins** | **Manage Plugins**:

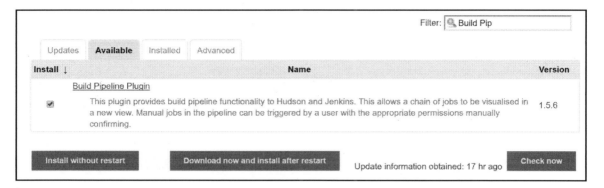

Verify the successful installation of the **Build Pipeline Plugin**:

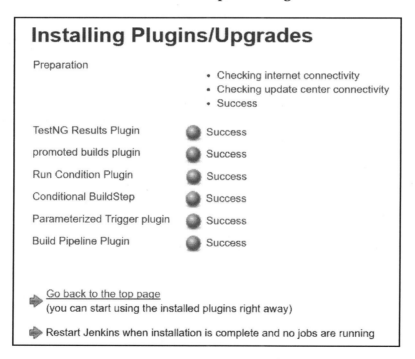

Now, you are ready to create a build pipeline and configure it with an initial job.

How to do it...

1. Go to the Jenkins dashboard and click on the **+** sign on the tabs available.
2. Provide the **View name** and select **Build Pipeline View**.
3. Click on **Save**:

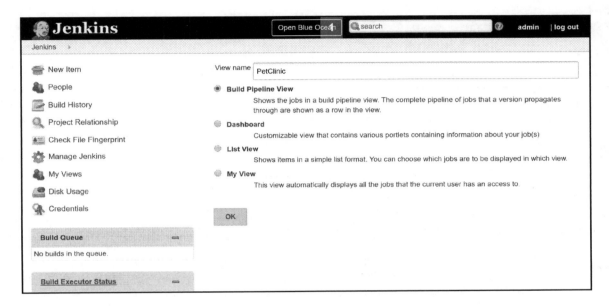

4. Verify that the **Layout** is configured as **Based on upstream/downstream relationship**.

5. You want to execute `PetClinic-Code` as a first job and you want to see the visualization from that job, so select it in the **Select Initial Job**:

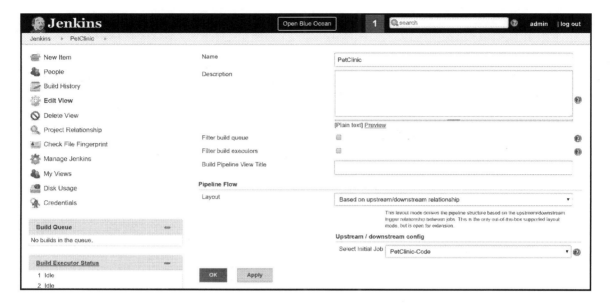

6. Select the rest of the configuration as per your requirements.
7. Change the **No Of Displayed Builds** from **1** to **3** so it will display the latest three build pipelines executed.
8. Click on **OK**:

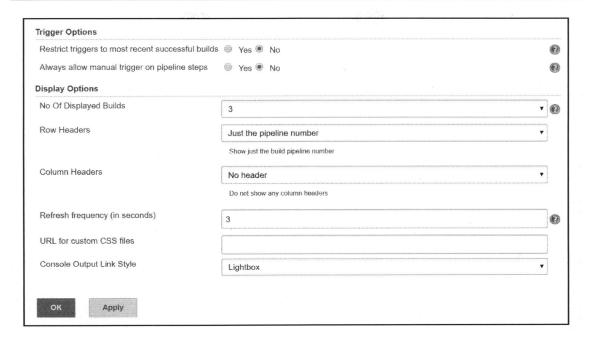

9. Verify the **Build Pipeline** view in the Jenkins dashboard:

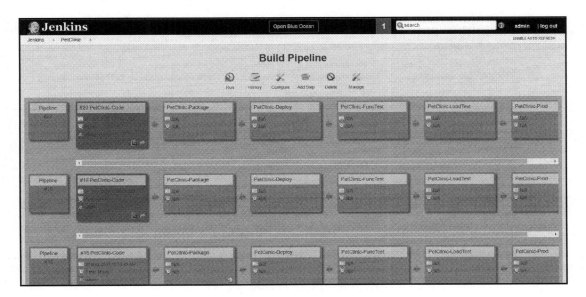

Build Pipeline in Initial Phase

10. What if you want to continue the execution of the pipeline even if some build is unstable? In such cases, you need to select **Trigger even if the build is unstable** option in **Post-build Actions**, as seen in the following screenshot:

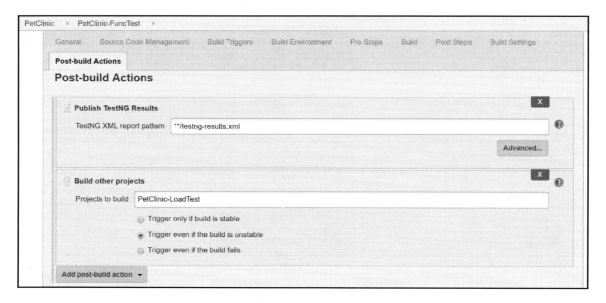

11. Click on the run in **Build Pipeline** view. Wait till the complete pipeline is executed:

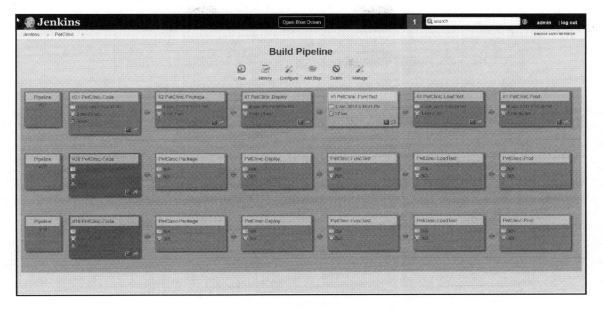

Successful Build Pipeline Execution

12. Done. This is how you can create a sequence of execution for different build jobs and achieve end-to-end automation for the application life cycle management. In the next recipe, you will achieve similar things using a the pipeline as a code feature.

Creating a pipeline job

In a pipeline, you model all related tasks to decide the sequence of execution. You will perform the same tasks you performed with the build pipeline, but with code.

Getting ready

Open the Jenkins dashboard.

How to do it...

1. Click on **New Item**. **Enter an item name** and select **Pipeline**.
2. Click **OK**:

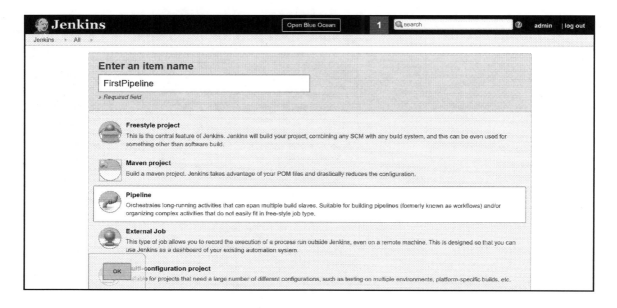

Using a sample pipeline for execution

Jenkins provides sample syntax to get a feel for how to configure a pipeline.

Getting ready

With Jenkins 2, the pipeline and other features are installed with the default installation with the suggested plugins.

How to do it...

1. Go to the Jenkins dashboard | **New item** | **Pipeline**.
2. It will open the configuration of a newly created pipeline job.
3. Go to the **Pipeline** section:

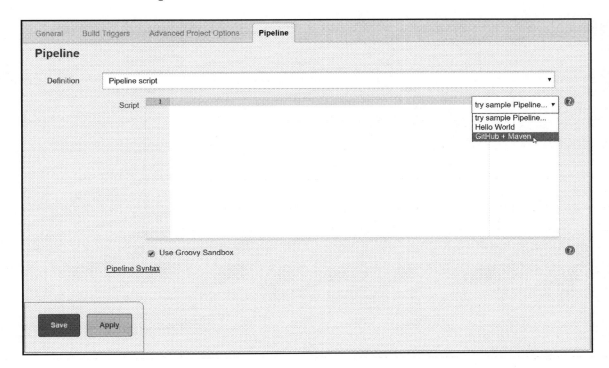

4. In the **try sample Pipeline...** dropdown, select **GitHub + Maven**. It will automatically generate the syntax for the sample code. Make sure that `mvnHome` has the proper value as per the path given for Maven in your system:

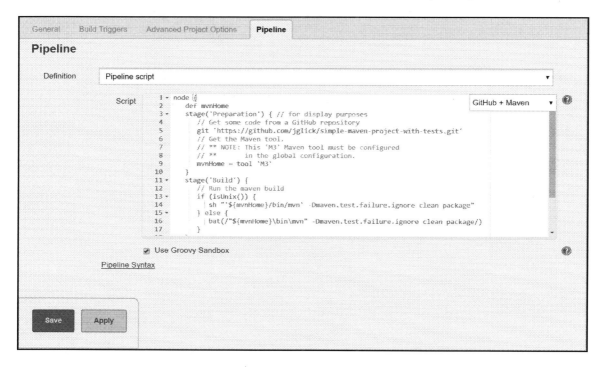

5. Click on **Save** and execute the build to verify it.
6. However, you will create your own pipeline with the same sequence you tried with the `Build Pipeline` plugin in the next recipe.

Configuring a pipeline job for end-to-end automation

In this recipe, you will create script to create a pipeline similar to what you configured with the `Build Pipeline` plugin.

Getting ready

Click on **Pipeline Syntax** to generate the syntax for specific tasks you want to execute.

You can select the steps and configure the required things, and then click on **Generate Pipeline Script** to get the syntax that you can directly utilize in your pipeline:

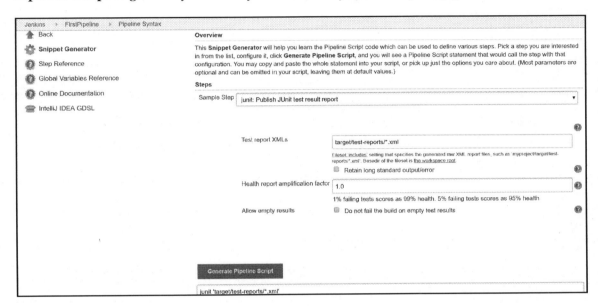

Before creating your first script for a pipeline, let's understand some important terms.

The `node` defines the node created in the context of the Jenkins' master agent architecture. It executes the step the moment the executor is available on node. It creates a workspace or a directory for the pipeline to keep files. The following is the sample syntax:

```
node {
    // execute the pipeline on Master node
}
node('windows') {
    // execute the pipeline on node labelled as Windows
}
```

The `stage` is a step that can be considered as a logically separate step, such as `Init`, `Build`, `Test`, `Deploy`, and so on.

A step or a build step is a task that can be executed to perform some activity such as copy artifact, archive artifact, checkout code from GitHub, and define an environment variable.

The script for the pipeline follows:

```
node {
def mvnHome
stage('Preparation') { // for display purposes
        // Get PetClinic code from a GitHub repository
git 'https://github.com/mitesh51/spring-
 petclinic.git'
        // Get the Maven tool.
        // ** NOTE: This 'apache-maven-3.3.1' Maven tool must
 be configured in the global configuration.
mvnHome = tool 'apache-maven-3.3.1'
    }
stage('SonarQube analysis') {
    // requires SonarQube Scanner 3.0+
def scannerHome = tool 'SonarQube Scanner 3.0.3';
// Sonarqube6.3 must be configured in the Jenkins
 Configuration -> Add SonarWube server
withSonarQubeEnv('Sonarqube6.3') {
//provide all required properties for Sonar
 execution
bat "${scannerHome}/bin/sonar-scanner -
 Dsonar.host.url=http://localhost:9000/ -
 Dsonar.login=1335c62cbfceab5
 954a5101ab7477cc974f58d56 -
 Dsonar.projectVersion=1.0
 -Dsonar.projectKey=petclinicKey -
 Dsonar.sources=src"
        }
    }


stage('Build') {
        // Run the maven build based on the Operating system
if (isUnix()) {
        sh "'${mvnHome}/bin/mvn' -
Dmaven.test.failure.ignore clean package"
  // Publish JUnit Report
junit '**/target/surefire-reports/TEST-*.xml'
        } else {
bat(/"${mvnHome}\bin\mvn" clean package/)
  // Publish JUnit Report
junit '**/target/surefire-reports/TEST-*.xml'


    }
    }


stage('Deploy') {
  // Archieve the artifact
```

```
archive 'target/*.war'
    // Execute the PetClinic-Deploy build to deploy war file into tomcat
    // Copy Artifact from this Pipeline Project into
  PetClinic-Deploy using Copy Artifact plugin
build 'PetClinic-Deploy'
    }

stage('Functional Test'){
// Checkout the code from Github to execute
  Functional test
git 'https://github.com/mitesh51/petclinic-
  func.git'
// Go to GitHub Directory and Fork it ... Change the URL in petclinic-
func/src/test/java/example/NewTest.java
//driver.get("http://localhost:8090/petclinic/");
//In the same file Change location of Gecko driver, you have used Firefox
here on Windows... File = new
File("C:\\Users\\Mitesh\\Downloads\\geckodriver-v0.13.0-
win64\\geckodriver.exe");
// Run the maven build with test goal to execute
  functional test
bat(/"${mvnHome}\bin\mvn" test/)
    }

// This stage can be optional based on the requirements
stage('Load Test'){
// Execute command to perform load testing with the
  use of Apache JMeter. In our case we are using the JMeter that is already
installed on Windows hence the bat file is used. Make sure to change this
location based on the Apache JMeter installation directory available on
your system.
bat "C:/apache-jmeter-3.0/bin/jmeter.bat -
  Jjmeter.save.saveservice.output_format=xml -n -t
  C:/Users/Mitesh/Desktop/PetClinic.jmx -l Test.jtl"
// Publish Apache JMeter results
perfReport errorFailedThreshold: 50,
  errorUnstableThreshold: 30, ignoreFailedBuilds:
  true, ignoreUnstableBuilds: true,
  persistConstraintLog: true, sourceDataFiles:
  'Test.jtl'
    }
    //Done!
}
```

How to do it...

Let's see how to execute the **Pipeline as a Code** feature in Jenkins:

1. Click on **Build now** for the pipeline execution:

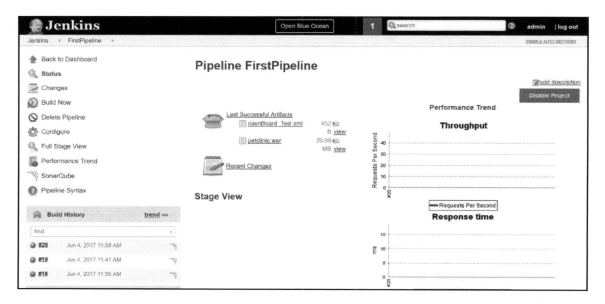

2. Verify the stage view of the pipeline you have created by clicking on **Full Stage View** on the Jenkins dashboard:

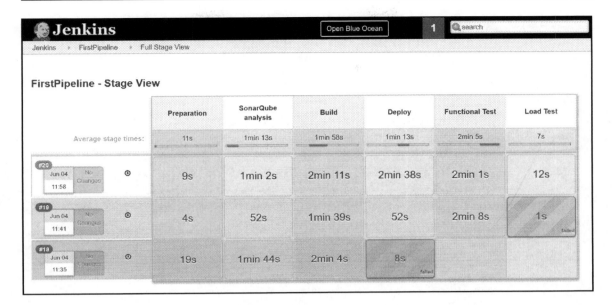

3. Mouse over the specific stage and click on **Logs**:

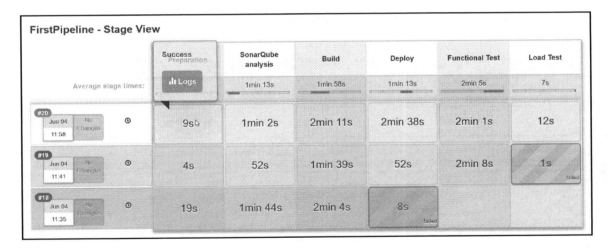

4. You can see and verify the stage logs directly from the stage view:

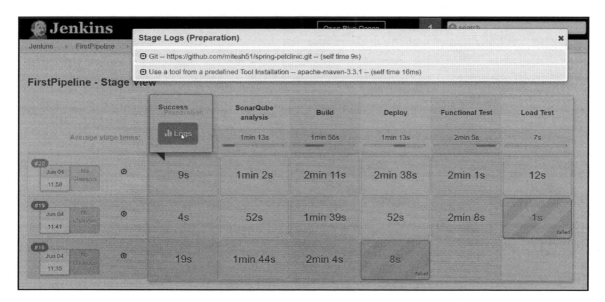

5. Click on the dropdown to get more details on the log:

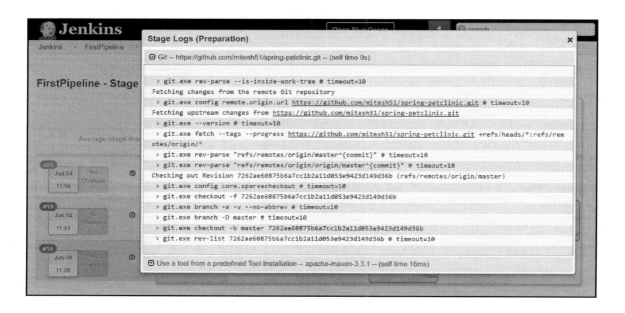

6. Let's go to the individual stage logs in the **Console Output**.
7. Look at the log for the preparation stage:

 Console Output

```
Started by user admin
[Pipeline] node
Running on master in F:\#JenkinsEssentials\FirstDraft\jenkinsHome\workspace\FirstPipeline
[Pipeline] {
[Pipeline] stage
[Pipeline] { (Preparation)
[Pipeline] git
 > git.exe rev-parse --is-inside-work-tree # timeout=10
Fetching changes from the remote Git repository
 > git.exe config remote.origin.url https://github.com/mitesh51/spring-petclinic.git # timeout=10
Fetching upstream changes from https://github.com/mitesh51/spring-petclinic.git
 > git.exe --version # timeout=10
 > git.exe fetch --tags --progress https://github.com/mitesh51/spring-petclinic.git
+refs/heads/*:refs/remotes/origin/*
 > git.exe rev-parse "refs/remotes/origin/master^{commit}" # timeout=10
 > git.exe rev-parse "refs/remotes/origin/origin/master^{commit}" # timeout=10
Checking out Revision 7262ae60875b6a7cc1b2a11d053e9423d149d36b (refs/remotes/origin/master)
 > git.exe config core.sparsecheckout # timeout=10
 > git.exe checkout -f 7262ae60875b6a7cc1b2a11d053e9423d149d36b
 > git.exe branch -a -v --no-abbrev # timeout=10
 > git.exe branch -D master # timeout=10
 > git.exe checkout -b master 7262ae60875b6a7cc1b2a11d053e9423d149d36b
 > git.exe rev-list 7262ae60875b6a7cc1b2a11d053e9423d149d36b # timeout=10
[Pipeline] tool
```

8. **Look at the log for** Sonarqube Analysis Stage:

```
[Pipeline] stage
[Pipeline] { (SonarQube analysis)
[Pipeline] tool
[Pipeline] wrap
Injecting SonarQube environment variables using the configuration: Sonarqube6.3
[Pipeline] {
[Pipeline] bat
[FirstPipeline] Running batch script

F:\#JenkinsEssentials\FirstDraft\jenkinsHome\workspace\FirstPipeline>F:\#JenkinsEssentials\FirstDraft\jenkinsHome\t
ools\hudson.plugins.sonar.SonarRunnerInstallation\SonarQube_Scanner_3.0.3/bin/sonar-scanner -
Dsonar.host.url=http://localhost:9000/ -Dsonar.login=****** -Dsonar.projectVersion=1.0 -
Dsonar.projectKey=petclinicKey -Dsonar.sources=src
INFO: Scanner configuration file:
F:\#JenkinsEssentials\FirstDraft\jenkinsHome\tools\hudson.plugins.sonar.SonarRunnerInstallation\SonarQube_Scanner_3
.0.3\bin\..\conf\sonar-scanner.properties
INFO: Project root configuration file: F:\#JenkinsEssentials\FirstDraft\jenkinsHome\workspace\FirstPipeline\sonar-
project.properties
INFO: SonarQube Scanner 3.0.3.778
INFO: Java 1.8.0_111 Oracle Corporation (64-bit)
INFO: Windows 10 10.0 amd64
INFO: User cache: C:\Users\Mitesh\.sonar\cache
INFO: Load global settings
INFO: Load global settings (done) | time=3968ms
INFO: User cache: C:\Users\Mitesh\.sonar\cache
INFO: Load plugins index
INFO: Load plugins index (done) | time=138ms
INFO: SonarQube server 6.3.1
```

9. Look at the log for Build Stage:

```
[Pipeline] stage
[Pipeline] { (Build)
[Pipeline] isUnix
[Pipeline] bat
[FirstPipeline] Running batch script

F:\#JenkinsEssentials\FirstDraft\jenkinsHome\workspace\FirstPipeline>"C:\apache-maven-3.3.1\bin\mvn" clean package
[INFO] Scanning for projects...
[INFO]
[INFO] ------------------------------------------------------------------------
[INFO] Building petclinic 4.2.5-SNAPSHOT
[INFO] ------------------------------------------------------------------------
[INFO]
[INFO] --- maven-clean-plugin:2.5:clean (default-clean) @ spring-petclinic ---
[INFO] Deleting F:\#JenkinsEssentials\FirstDraft\jenkinsHome\workspace\FirstPipeline\target
[INFO]
[INFO] --- cobertura-maven-plugin:2.7:clean (default) @ spring-petclinic ---
[INFO]
[INFO] --- maven-resources-plugin:2.6:resources (default-resources) @ spring-petclinic ---
[INFO] Using 'UTF-8' encoding to copy filtered resources.
[INFO] Copying 18 resources
[INFO]
[INFO] --- maven-compiler-plugin:3.0:compile (default-compile) @ spring-petclinic ---
[INFO] Changes detected - recompiling the module!
[INFO] Compiling 45 source files to
F:\#JenkinsEssentials\FirstDraft\jenkinsHome\workspace\FirstPipeline\target\classes
[parsing started
RegularFileObject[F:\#JenkinsEssentials\FirstDraft\jenkinsHome\workspace\FirstPipeline\src\main\java\org\springfram
ework\samples\petclinic\web\PetValidator.java]]
[parsing completed 219ms]
```

10. Look at the log for deploy and functional test stage:

```
[INFO] Building war: F:\#JenkinsEssentials\FirstDraft\jenkinsHome\workspace\FirstPipeline\target\petclinic.war
[INFO] ------------------------------------------------------------------------
[INFO] BUILD SUCCESS
[INFO] ------------------------------------------------------------------------
[INFO] Total time: 02:03 min
[INFO] Finished at: 2017-06-04T12:01:43+05:30
[INFO] Final Memory: 27M/88M
[INFO] ------------------------------------------------------------------------
[Pipeline] }
[Pipeline] // stage
[Pipeline] stage
[Pipeline] { (Deploy)
[Pipeline] step
Recording test results
[Pipeline] archive
[Pipeline] build (Building PetClinic-Deploy)
Scheduling project: PetClinic-Deploy
Starting building: PetClinic-Deploy #6
[Pipeline] }
[Pipeline] // stage
[Pipeline] stage
[Pipeline] { (Functional Test)
[Pipeline] git
 > git.exe rev-parse --is-inside-work-tree # timeout=10
Fetching changes from the remote Git repository
 > git.exe config remote.origin.url https://github.com/mitesh51/petclinic-func.git # timeout=10
Fetching upstream changes from https://github.com/mitesh51/petclinic-func.git
 > git.exe --version # timeout=10
 > git.exe fetch --tags --progress https://github.com/mitesh51/petclinic-func.git
+refs/heads/*:refs/remotes/origin/*
```

11. Look at the log for load test stage:

```
Results :

Tests run: 1, Failures: 0, Errors: 0, Skipped: 0

[INFO] ------------------------------------------------------------------------
[INFO] BUILD SUCCESS
[INFO] ------------------------------------------------------------------------
[INFO] Total time: 01:42 min
[INFO] Finished at: 2017-06-04T12:06:24+05:30
[INFO] Final Memory: 18M/80M
[INFO] ------------------------------------------------------------------------
[Pipeline] }
[Pipeline] // stage
[Pipeline] stage
[Pipeline] { (Load Test)
[Pipeline] bat
[FirstPipeline] Running batch script

F:\#JenkinsEssentials\FirstDraft\jenkinsHome\workspace\FirstPipeline>C:/apache-jmeter-3.0/bin/jmeter.bat -
Jjmeter.save.saveservice.output_format=xml -n -t C:/Users/Mitesh/Desktop/PetClinic.jmx -l Test.jtl
Writing log file to: F:\#JenkinsEssentials\FirstDraft\jenkinsHome\workspace\FirstPipeline\jmeter.log
Creating summariser <summary>
Created the tree successfully using C:/Users/Mitesh/Desktop/PetClinic.jmx
Starting the test @ Sun Jun 04 12:06:32 IST 2017 (1496558192833)
Waiting for possible Shutdown/StopTestNow/Heapdump message on port 4445
summary +      1 in 00:00:01 =    1.0/s Avg:   270 Min:   270 Max:   270 Err:     0 (0.00%) Active: 1 Started: 1
Finished: 0
summary +     49 in 00:00:01 =   61.1/s Avg:    13 Min:     4 Max:   157 Err:     0 (0.00%) Active: 0 Started: 1
Finished: 1
summary =     50 in 00:00:02 =   27.0/s Avg:    18 Min:     4 Max:   270 Err:     0 (0.00%)
```

12. On the project dashboard, look at the stage view at the bottom:

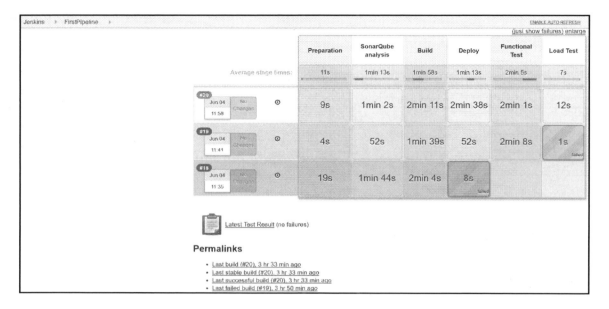

Getting started with the Blue Ocean dashboard

Blue Ocean is a new user interface for Jenkins. The idea of introducing Blue Ocean is to make Jenkins and Continuous Delivery approachable to all team members.

Getting ready

You will use Blue Ocean later in the chapter but you will install it here:

Install ↓	Name	Version
☑	**Blue Ocean** Blue Ocean is a new project that rethinks the user experience of Jenkins. Designed from the ground up for Jenkins Pipeline and compatible with Freestyle jobs, Blue Ocean reduces clutter and increases clarity for every member of your team.	1.0.1
☐	Common API for Blue Ocean	1.0.1
☐	Config API for Blue Ocean	1.0.1
☐	Dashboard for Blue Ocean	1.0.1
☐	Events API for Blue Ocean	1.0.1
☐	Git Pipeline for Blue Ocean	1.0.1
☐	GitHub Pipeline for Blue Ocean	1.0.1
☐	i18n for Blue Ocean	1.0.1
☐	JWT for Blue Ocean	1.0.1
☐	Personalization for Blue Ocean	1.0.1

Tabs: Updates | **Available** | Installed | Advanced

Verify in the Jenkins dashboard regarding the successful installation of the plugin:

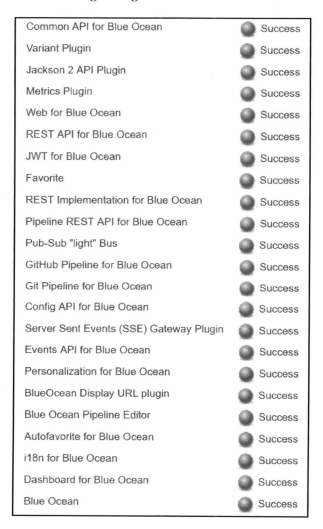

Now you will create your first pipeline in Jenkins.

How to do it...

Now let's see how your pipeline looks in the Blue Ocean user interface. Go to the **FirstPipeline** pipeline job that you have created. Click on the Blue Ocean link in the top bar on the Jenkins dashboard.

Click on **Successful pipeline 20**:

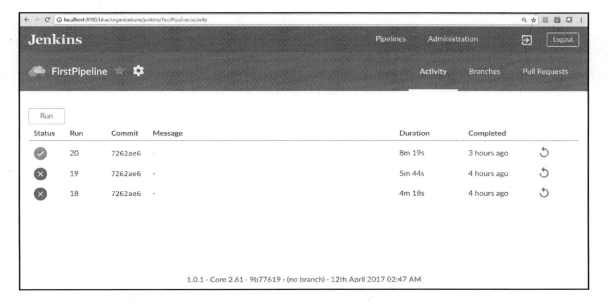

It will give details of the execution status of each stage in the Blue Ocean dashboard. Logs are available on the same page:

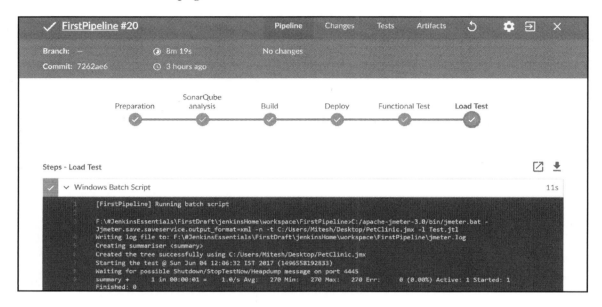

Select any stage and check the logs for the stage on the same page:

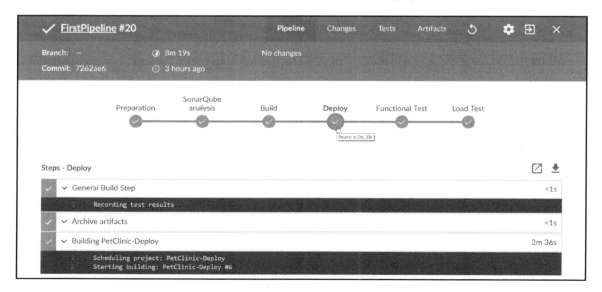

Click on the **Tests** link on the top bar to verify the status of the **Junit** test cases executed in the pipeline:

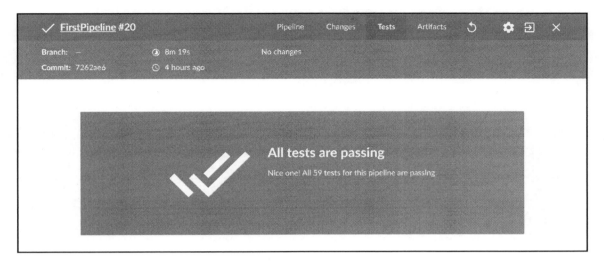

Click on the **Artifacts** link on the top bar to verify all the artifacts available in this pipeline:

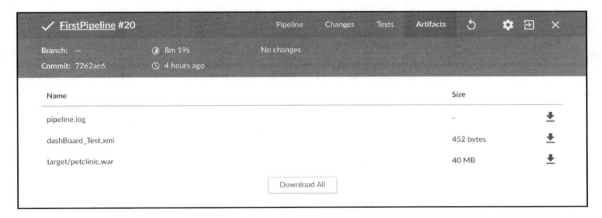

In this chapter, you have created a pipeline using the `Build Pipeline` plugin and `pipeline as a code` feature available in Jenkins 2 and later.

9
Jenkins UI Customization

In this chapter, we will cover the following recipes:

- Skinning Jenkins with the simple themes plugin
- Skinning and provisioning Jenkins using a WAR overlay
- Generating a home page
- Creating HTML reports
- Efficient use of views
- Saving screen space with the Dashboard View plugin
- Making noise with HTML5 browsers
- An extreme view for reception areas

Introduction

This chapter explores communication through Jenkins, recognizing that there are different target audiences.

Jenkins is a talented communicator. Its home page displays the status of all jobs, allowing you to make quick decisions. You can easily set up multiple views, prioritizing information naturally. Jenkins, with its hordes of plugins, notifies you by email, dashboards, and Google services. It shouts at you through mobile devices, radiates information as you walk past big screens, and fires at you with USB sponge missile launchers.

Its primary audience is developers, but don't forget the wider audience that wants to use the software being developed. Seeing Jenkins regularly building with consistent views and a corporate look and feel builds confidence in the software's roadmap. This chapter includes recipes to help you reach this wider audience.

When creating a coherent communication strategy, there are many Jenkins-specific details to configure. Here are a few that will be considered in this chapter:

- **Notifications**: Developers need to know quickly when something is broken. Jenkins has many plugins; you should select a few that suit the team's ethos.

- **Page decoration**: A page decorator is a plugin that adds content to each page. You can cheaply generate a corporate look and feel by adding your own style sheets and JavaScript.

- **Overlaying Jenkins**: Using the Maven WAR plugin, you can overlay your own content on top of Jenkins. You can use this to add custom content and provision resources such as home pages, which will enhance the corporate look and feel.

- **Optimize the views**: Front page views are lists of jobs that are displayed in a tab. The front page is used by the audience to quickly decide which job to select for review. Plugins expand the choice of view types and optimize information digestion. This potentially avoids the need to look further, saving precious time.

- **Drive by notification**: Extreme views that radiate information visually look great on large monitors. If you place a monitor by watering holes such as receptions or coffee machines, then passers-by will absorb the ebb and flow of job status changes. The view sublimely hints at the professionalism of your company and the stability of your product's roadmap.

- **Keeping track of your audience**: If you are openly communicating, then you should track usage patterns so that you can improve services. Consider connecting your Jenkins pages to Google Analytics or Piwik, an open source analytics application.

Skinning Jenkins with the simple themes plugin

This recipe modifies the Jenkins look and feel through the themes plugin.

The themes plugin is a page decorator; it decorates each page with extra HTML tags. The plugin allows you to upload a style sheet and JavaScript file. The files are then reachable through a local URL. Each Jenkins page is then decorated with HTML tags that use the URLs to pull in your uploaded files. Although straightforward, when properly crafted, the visual effects are powerful.

Getting ready

1. Install the themes plugin
   (`https://wiki.jenkins-ci.org/display/JENKINS/Simple+Theme+Plugin`).

2. Click on **Install without restart**:

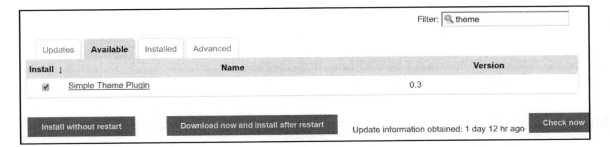

3. Wait until the plugin is installed successfully:

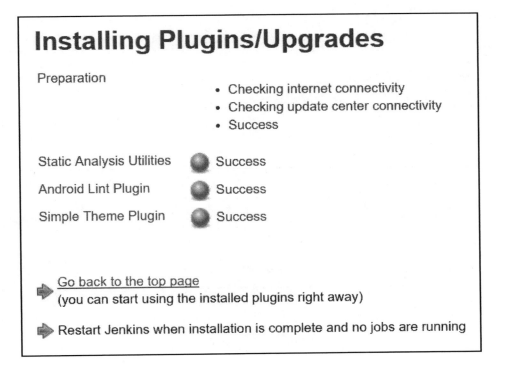

4. Go to the Jenkins dashboard and **Manage Jenkins** | **Configure System** | **Theme:**

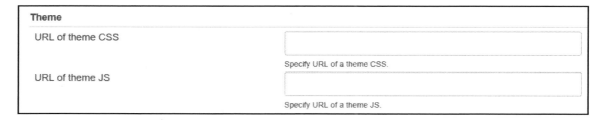

You need to provide custom CSS and custom JS files here to change the look and feel of the Jenkins dashboard.

How to do it...

1. Under the Jenkins userContent directory, create a file named my.js with the following line of code:

```
document.write("<h1 id='test'>Example Location</h1>")
```

2. Create a mycss.css file in the Jenkins userContent directory with the following lines of code:

```
@charset "utf-8";
#test {
background-image: url(/userContent/camera.png);
}
#main-table{
background-image: url(/userContent/camera.png)
 !important;
```

3. Download and unpack the icon archive from
http://sourceforge.net/projects/openiconlibrary/files/0.11/open_icon_l
ibrary-standard-0.11.tar.bz2/download and review the available icons.
Alternatively, you can use the icon included in the download from the book's
website (www.packtpub.com/support). Add an icon to the userContent directory
renaming it to camera.png.

4. Visit the Jenkins main configuration page: `/configure`. Under the **Theme** section, fill in the location of the CSS and JavaScript files:

- **URL of theme CSS**: `/userContent/mycss.css`
- **URL of theme JS**: `/userContent/myjavascript.js`

5. Click on **Save**.
6. Return to the Jenkins home page and review your work, as shown in the following screenshot:

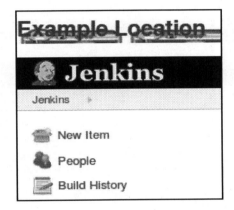

Another way to change the Jenkins theme is to use any one of the following URLs in the CSS field to change the look and feel:

- `https://jenkins-contrib-themes.github.io/jenkins-material-theme/dist/material-red.css`
- `https://jenkins-contrib-themes.github.io/jenkins-material-theme/dist/material-pink.css`
- `https://jenkins-contrib-themes.github.io/jenkins-material-theme/dist/material-purple.css`

- https://jenkins-contrib-themes.github.io/jenkins-material-theme/dist/material-deep-purple.css
- https://jenkins-contrib-themes.github.io/jenkins-material-theme/dist/material-indigo.css
- https://jenkins-contrib-themes.github.io/jenkins-material-theme/dist/material-blue.css
- https://jenkins-contrib-themes.github.io/jenkins-material-theme/dist/material-light-blue.css

- https://jenkins-contrib-themes.github.io/jenkins-material-theme/dist/material-cyan.css
- https://jenkins-contrib-themes.github.io/jenkins-material-theme/dist/material-teal.css
- https://jenkins-contrib-themes.github.io/jenkins-material-theme/dist/material-green.css
- https://jenkins-contrib-themes.github.io/jenkins-material-theme/dist/material-light-green.css
- https://jenkins-contrib-themes.github.io/jenkins-material-theme/dist/material-lime.css
- https://jenkins-contrib-themes.github.io/jenkins-material-theme/dist/material-yellow.css
- https://jenkins-contrib-themes.github.io/jenkins-material-theme/dist/material-amber.css
- https://jenkins-contrib-themes.github.io/jenkins-material-theme/dist/material-orange.css
- https://jenkins-contrib-themes.github.io/jenkins-material-theme/dist/material-deep-orange.css
- https://jenkins-contrib-themes.github.io/jenkins-material-theme/dist/material-brown.css
- https://jenkins-contrib-themes.github.io/jenkins-material-theme/dist/material-grey.css
- https://jenkins-contrib-themes.github.io/jenkins-material-theme/dist/material-blue-grey.css

You can also go to the mentioned location and copy the content of the file and paste it in `/userContent/mycss.css`:

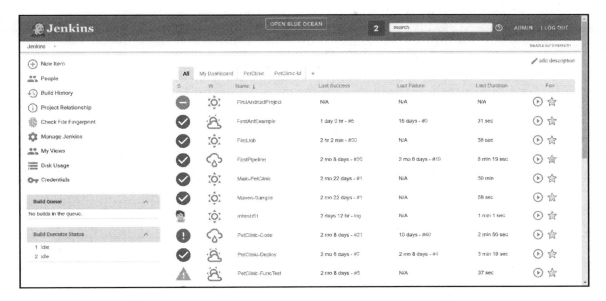

You can make changes to CSS and customize based on your needs.

How it works...

The simple themes plugin is a page decorator. It adds the following information to every page:

```
<script>
<link rel="stylesheet" type="text/css"
 href="/userContent/mycss.css" /><script
 src="/userContent/myjavascript.js" type="text/javascript">
</script>
```

The JavaScript writes a heading near the top of the generated pages with `id="test"`. Triggering the cascading style sheet rule through the CSS locator `#test` adds the camera icon to the background.

The picture dimensions are not properly tailored for the top of the screen; they are trimmed by the browser. This is a problem you can solve later by experimenting.

The second CSS rule is triggered for `main-table`, which is part of the standard front page generated by Jenkins. The full camera icon is displayed there.

On visiting other parts of Jenkins, you will notice that the camera icon looks out of context and is oversized. You will need time to modify the CSS and JavaScript to generate better effects. With care and custom code, you can skin Jenkins to fit your corporate image.

CSS 3 quirks:

There are quirks in the support for the various CSS standards between browser types and versions. For an overview, please visit `http://www.quirksmode.org/css/contents.html`.

There's more...

Here are a few more things for you to consider.

CSS 3

CSS 3 has a number of features. To draw a button around the header generated by JavaScript, change the `#test` section of the CSS file to the following code:

```
#test {
width: 180px; height: 60px;
background: red; color: yellow;
text-align: center;
  -moz-border-radius: 40px; -webkit-border-radius: 40px;
}
```

Using Firefox, the CSS rule generates the following button:

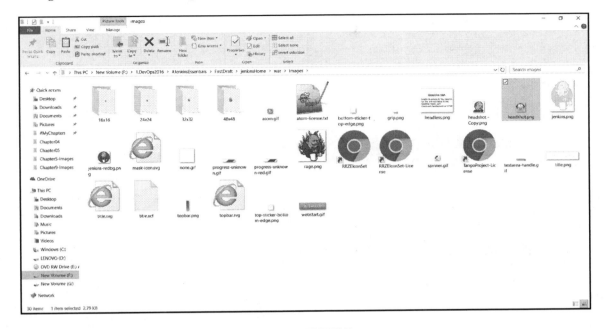

Images in JENKINS_HOME

For the impatient, you can download a CSS 3 cheat sheet at the Smashing Magazine website: `http://coding.smashingmagazine.com/wp-content/uploads/images/css3-cheat-sheet/css3-cheat-sheet.pdf`.

Included JavaScript library frameworks

Jenkins uses the `YUI` library: `http://yuilibrary.com/`. Decorated in each HTML page, the core `YUI` library (`/scripts/yui/yahoo/yahoo-min.js`) is pulled in ready for reuse. However, many web developers are used to jQuery. You can include this library as well by installing the `jQuery` plugin (`https://wiki.jenkins-ci.org/display/JENKINS/jQuery+Plugin`). You can also consider adding your favorite JavaScript library to the `Jenkins/scripts` directory through a WAR overlay (refer to the next recipe).

Trust but verify

With great power comes great responsibility. If only a few administrators maintain your Jenkins deployment, then you can most likely trust everyone to add JavaScript with no harmful side effects. However, if you have a large set of administrators who use a wide range of Java libraries, then your maintenance and security risks increase rapidly. Consider your security policy and at least add the audit trail plugin (`https://wiki.jenkins-ci.org/display/JENKINS/Audit+Trail+Plugin`) to keep track of the actions.

This plugin adds an **Audit Trail** section in the main Jenkins configuration page. Here you can configure log location and settings (file size and number of rotating log files), and a URI pattern for requests to be logged. The default options select most actions with significant effect such as creating/configuring/deleting jobs and views or delete/save-forever/start a build. The log is written to disk as configured and recent entries can also be viewed in the **Manage/System Log** section.

Also, see the JobConfigHistory plugin for recording actual changes made to job configurations:

There's more

- To directly change any images or icon, you can go to **JENKINS_HOME** | **war** | **images:**

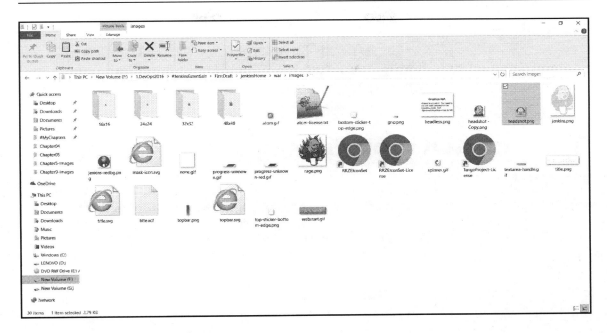

- Restart Jenkins and verify the changes:

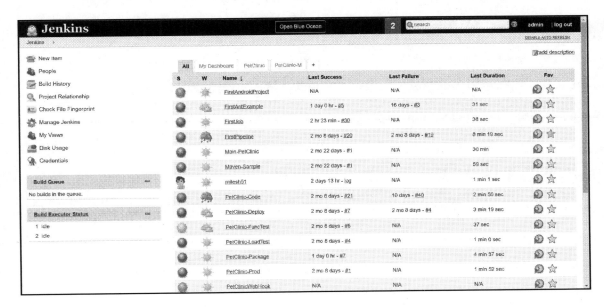

See also

- The *Skinning and provisioning Jenkins using a WAR overlay* recipe
- The *Generating a home page* recipe

Skinning and provisioning Jenkins using a WAR overlay

This recipe describes how to overlay content onto the Jenkins WAR file. With a WAR overlay, you can change the Jenkins look and feel ready for corporate branding and content provisioning of home pages. The basic example of adding your own custom favicon.ico (the icon in your web browser's address bar) is used. It requires little effort to include more content.

Jenkins keeps its versions as dependencies in a Maven repository. You can use Maven to pull in the WAR file, expand it, add content, and then repackage. This enables you to provision resources such as images, home pages, the icon in the address bar called a fav icon, and `robots.txt` that affects how search engines look through your content.

Be careful, using a WAR overlay will be cheap if the structure and the graphical content of Jenkins do not radically change over time. However, if the overlay does break the structure, then you might not spot this until you perform detailed functional tests.

You can also consider minimal changes through a WAR overlay, perhaps only changing `favicon.ico`, adding images and `userContent`, then using the simple theme plugin (see the preceding recipe) to do the styling.

Getting ready

Create the directory named `CH9.communicating/war_overlay` for the files in this recipe.

How to do it...

1. Browse to the `Maven` repository at `http://repo.jenkins-ci.org/releases/org/jenkins-ci/main/jenkins-war/` and review the Jenkins dependencies.

2. Create the following `pom.xml` file. Feel free to update to a newer Jenkins version:

```
<project xmlns="http://maven.apache.org/POM/4.0.0"
xmlns:xsi="http://www.w3.org/2001/XMLSchema-instance"
xsi:schemaLocation="http://maven.apache.org/POM/4.0.0
 http://maven.apache.org/maven-v4_0_0.xsd">
<modelVersion>4.0.0</modelVersion>
<groupId>nl.uva.berg</groupId>
<artifactId>overlay</artifactId>
<packaging>war</packaging>
<!-- Keep version the same as Jenkins as a hint -->
<version>1.437</version>
<name>overlay Maven Webapp</name>
<url>http://maven.apache.org</url>
<dependencies>
<dependency>
<groupId>org.jenkins-ci.main</groupId>
<artifactId>jenkins-war</artifactId>
<version>1.437</version>
<type>war</type>
<scope>runtime</scope>
</dependency>
</dependencies>
<repositories>
<repository>
 <id>Jenkins</id>
 <url>http://repo.jenkins-ci.org/releases</url>
 </repository>
</repositories>
</project>
```

3. Visit a `favicon.ico` generation website such as `http://www.favicon.cc/`. Following their instructions, create your own `favicon.ico`. Alternatively, use the example provided.

4. Add `favicon.ico` to the `src/main/webapp` location.

5. Create the directory `src/main/webapp/META-INF` and add a file named `context.xml` with the following line of code:

```
<Context logEffectiveWebXml="true" path="/"></Context>
```

6. In your top-level directory, run the following command:

mvnpackage

7. In the newly-generated target directory, you will see the WAR file `overlay-1.437.war`. Review the content verifying that you have modified `favicon.ico`.

8. (Optional) Deploy the WAR file to a local Tomcat server, verify, and browse the updated Jenkins server:

How it works...

Jenkins has its WAR files exposed through a central Maven repository. This allows you to pull in specific versions of Jenkins through standard Maven dependency management.

Maven uses conventions. It expects to find the content to overlay at `src/main/webapp` or `src/main/resources`.

The `context.xml` file defines certain behaviors for a web application such as database settings. In this example, the `logEffectiveWebXML` setting is asking Tomcat to log specific information on startup of the application (`http://tomcat.apache.org/tomcat-7.0-doc/config/context.html`). The setting was recommended in the Jenkins Wiki (`https://wiki.jenkins-ci.org/display/JENKINS/Installation+via+Maven+WAR+Overlay`). The file is placed in the `META-INF` directory as Tomcat picks up the settings here without the need for a server restart.

The `<packaging>war</packaging>` tag tells Maven to use the WAR plugin for packaging.

You used the same version number in the name of the final overlayed WAR as the original Jenkins WAR version. It makes it easier to spot if the Jenkins version changes. This again highlights that using conventions aids readability and decreases the opportunity for mistakes. When deploying from your acceptance environment to production, you should remove the version number.

In the `pom.xml` file, you defined `http://repo.jenkins-ci.org/` as the repository in which to find Jenkins.

The Jenkins WAR file is pulled in as a dependency of type war and scope runtime. The runtime scope indicates that the dependency is not required for compilation, but is for execution. For more detailed information on scoping, review
`http://maven.apache.org/guides/introduction/introduction-to-dependency-mechanism.html#Dependency_Scope`.

For further details about WAR overlays, review
`http://maven.apache.org/plugins/maven-war-plugin/index.html`.

Avoiding work:

To limit maintenance effort, it is better to install extra content rather than replacing content that might be used elsewhere or by third-party plugins.

There's more...

There are a lot of details that you need to cover if you wish to fully modify the look and feel of Jenkins. The following sections mention some of the details.

Which types of content can you replace?

The Jenkins server deploys to two main locations. The first location is the core application and the second is the workspace, which stores information that changes. To gain a fuller understanding of the content, review the directory structure. A useful command in Linux is the tree command, which displays the directory structure. To install under Ubuntu, use the following command:

```
apt-get install tree
```

In Windows OS it's available by default in the Command Prompt.

For the Jenkins Ubuntu workspace, using the following command helps you to generate a tree view of the workspace:

```
tree -d -L 1 /var/lib/Jenkins
```

- fingerprints: This is the directory that is used to store checksums to uniquely identify files
- jobs: This stores job configuration and build results
- plugins: This is where plugins are deployed and usually configured
- tools: This is where tools such as Maven and Ant are deployed

- `updates`: This is used for updates
- `userContent`: The content is made available under the URL `/userContent`
- `users`: This is the user information displayed under the `/me` URL

The default Ubuntu location of the web app is `/var/run/jenkins/war`. If you are running Jenkins from the command line, then the option for placing the web app is as follows:

-webroot

- `css`: This is the location of Jenkins style sheets
- `executable`: This is used for running Jenkins from the command line
- `favicon.ico`: This is the icon we replaced in this recipe
- `help`: This is the directory with help content
- `images`: This includes the graphics in different sizes
- `META-INF`: This is the location for the manifest file and the `pom.xml` file that generated the WAR
- `robots.txt`: This is used to tell search engines where they are allowed to crawl
- `scripts`: This is the location of the JavaScript library
- `WEB-INF`: This is the main location for the servlet part of the web application
- `winstone.jar`: This is the servlet container available at `http://winstone.sourceforge.net/`

Search engines and robots.txt

If you are adding your own custom content, such as user home pages, company contact information, or product details, then consider modifying the top-level `robots.txt` file. At present, it excludes search engines from all content:

```
# we don't want robots to click "build" links
User-agent: *
Disallow: /
```

You can find the full details of the structure of the `robots.txt` at `http://www.w3.org/TR/html4/appendix/notes.html#h-B.4.1.1`.

Google uses richer structures that allow as well as disallow; refer to `https://developers.google.com/webmasters/control-crawl-index/docs/robots_txt?csw=1`.

The following `robots.txt` allows access by the Google crawler to the directory `/userContent/corporate/`. It is an open question whether all web crawlers will honor the intent.

```
User-agent: *
Disallow: /
User-agent: Googlebot
Allow: /userContent/corporate/
```

> To help secure your Jenkins infrastructure, refer to the recipes in `Chapter 3`, *Managing Security*.

See also

- The *Skinning Jenkins with the simple themes plugin* recipe
- The *Generating a home page* recipe

Generating a home page

The user's home page is a great place to express your organization's identity. You can create a consistent look and feel that expresses your team's spirit.

This recipe will explore the manipulation of home pages found under the `/user/userid` directory and configured by the user through the `Jenkins/me` URL.

> A similar plugin worth reviewing is the Gravatar plugin. You can find the plugin's home page at `https://wiki.jenkins-ci.org/display/JENKINS/Gravatar+plugin`.

Getting ready

Install the `Avatar` plugin
(`https://wiki.jenkins-ci.org/display/JENKINS/Avatar+Plugin`):

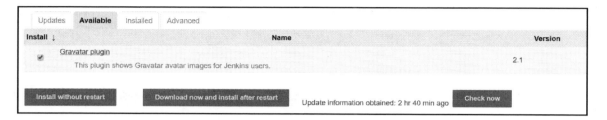

How to do it...

1. Install the plugin on a Jenkins and it will automatically show Gravatars for the users that has an email and a Gravatar. No configuration is required except installing the plugin.

Creating HTML reports

The left-hand side menu of a job's dashboard is valuable real estate. The developer's eyes naturally scan this area. This recipe describes how you can add a link from a custom HTML report to the menu, getting the report noticed more quickly.

Getting ready

Install the HTML publisher plugin
(`https://wiki.jenkins-ci.org/display/JENKINS/HTML+Publisher+Plugin`). We assume that you have a subversion repository with the Packt code committed.

How to do it...

1. Create a free-style software project and name it CH9.html_report.
2. Under the **Source Code Management** section, click on **Subversion**.
3. Under the **Modules** section, add Repo/CH9.communicating/html_report to **Repository URL**, where Repo is the URL to your subversion repository.
4. Under the **Post-build Actions** section, check **Publish HTML reports**. Add the following details:

   - **HTML directory to archive**: target/custom_report
   - **Index pages[s]**: index.html
   - **Report title**: My HTML Report
   - Tick the **Keep past HTML reports** checkbox

5. Click on **Save**.
6. Run the job and review the left-hand side menu. You will now see a link to your report, as shown in the following screenshot:

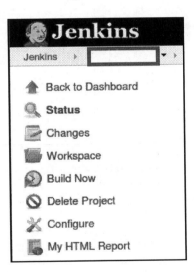

How it works...

Your subversion repo contains an `index.html` file that is pulled into the workspace of the job. The plugin works as advertised and adds a link pointing to the HTML report. This allows your audience to efficiently find your custom-generated information.

There's more...

The example report is shown as follows:

```
<html><head><title>Example Report</title>
<link rel="stylesheet" type="text/css" href="/css/style.css" /></head>
<body>
<h2>Generated Report</h2>
Example icon: <img title="A Jenkins Icon" alt="Schedule a build"
src="/images/24x24/clock.png" />
</body></html>
```

It pulls in the main Jenkins style sheet `/css/style.css`.

It is possible that when you update a style sheet in an application, you do not see the changes in your browser until you have cleaned your browser cache. Jenkins gets around this latency issue in a clever way. It uses a URL with a unique number that changes with each Jenkins version. For example, for the `css` directory, you have two URLs:

- `/css`
- `/static/uniquenumber/css`

Most Jenkins URLs use the latter form. Consider doing so for your style sheets.

 The unique number changes per version, so you will need to update the URL for each upgrade

When running the site goal in a Maven build, a local website is generated (http://maven.apache.org/plugins/maven-site-plugin). This website has a fixed URL inside the Jenkins job that you can point at with the **My HTML Report** link. This brings documentation such as test results within easy reach.

See also

- The *Efficient use of views* recipe
- The *Saving screen space with the Dashboard View plugin* recipe

Efficient use of views

Jenkins' addictive ease of configuration lends itself to creating a large number of jobs. This increases the volume of information exposed to developers. Jenkins needs to avoid chaos by utilizing browser space efficiently. One approach is to define minimal views. In this recipe, you will use the `DropDownViewsTabBar` plugin. It removes views as tabs and replaces the tabs with one select box. This aids in quicker navigation. You will also be shown how to provision lots of jobs quickly using a simple HTML form generated by a script.

 In this recipe, you will be creating a large number of views that you may want to delete later. If you are using a virtual box image, consider cloning the image and deleting it after you have finished.

Getting ready

Install the `DropDownViewsTabBar` plugin (https://wiki.jenkins-ci.org/display/JENKINS/DropDown+ViewsTabBar+Plugin).

How to do it...

1. Copy and paste the following Perl script into an executable file named `create.pl`:

```
#!/usr/bin/perl
$counter=0;
$end=20;
$host='http://localhost:8080';
while($end > $counter){
  $counter++;
print "<form action=$host/createItem?mode=copy
 method=POST>\n";print "<input type=text name=name
 value=CH9.fake.$counter>\n";
```

```
print "<input type=text name=from value=Template1 >\n";
print "<input type=submit value='Create
  CH9.fake.$counter'>\n";
print "</form><br>\n";
print "<form action=$host/job/CH9.fake.$counter/doDelete
  method=POST>\n";print "<input type=submit value='Delete
  CH9.fake.$counter'>\n";
print "</form><br>\n";
}
```

2. Create an HTML file from the output of the Perl script, for example:

```
perl create.pl > form.html
```

3. In a web browser, as an administrator, log in to Jenkins.

4. Create the `Template1` job, adding any details you wish. This is your template job that will be copied into many other jobs.

5. Load `form.html` into the same browser.

6. Click on one of the **Create CH9.fake** buttons. Jenkins returns an error message:

```
HTTP ERROR 403
 Problem accessing /createItem. Reason:
No valid crumb was included in the request
```

7. Visit **Configure Global Security** on `http://localhost:8080/configureSecurity` and uncheck the **Prevent Cross Site Request Forgery exploits** box.

8. Click on **Save**.

9. Click on all of the **Create CH9.fake** buttons.

10. Visit the front page of Jenkins and verify that the jobs have been created and are based on the `Template1` job.

11. Create a large number of views with a random selection of jobs. Review the front page, noting the chaos.

12. Visit the **configuration screen /configure**; selecting **DropDownViewsTabBar** provides a drop-down menu for selecting views in the **View Tab Bar** select box. In the **DropDown ViewsTabBar** subsection, check the **Show Job Counts** box, as shown in the following screenshot:

SCM checkout retry count	0
Views Tab Bar	DropDownViewsTabBar provides a drop down menu for selecting views.
	DropDown ViewsTabBar
	Show Job Counts ☑

13. Click on the **Save** button:
14. In Jenkins, visit **Configure Global Security** at `http://localhost:8080/configureSecurity` and check the **Prevent Cross Site Request Forgery exploits** box.
15. Click on **Save**.

How it works...

The form works as long as the bread crumbing security feature in Jenkins is turned off. The feature, when turned on, generates a random number that the form has to return when you submit. This allows Jenkins to know that the form is part of a valid conversation with the server. The HTTP status error generated is in the 4xx range, which implies that the client input is invalid. If Jenkins returned a 5xx error, then that would imply a server error. We therefore had to turn the feature off when submitting our own data. We do not recommend this in a production environment.

Once you have logged in to Jenkins as an administrator, you can create jobs. You can do this through the GUI or by sending POST information. In this recipe, we copied a job named Template1 to new jobs starting with the name CH9.fake, as shown in the following code:

```
<form action=http://localhost:8080/createItem?mode=copy
 method=POST>
<input type=text name=name value=CH9.fake.1>
<input type=text name=from value=Template1 >
<input type=submit value='Create CH9.fake.1'>
</form>
```

The POST variables you used were name for the name of the new job, and from for the name of your template job. The URL for the POST action is /createItem?mode=copy.

To change the hostname and port number, you will have to update the $host variable found in the Perl script.

To delete a job, the Perl script generated forms with actions pointing to `/job/Jobname/doDelete` (for example, `/job/CH9.fake.1/doDelete`). No extra variables were needed.

To increase the number of form entries, you can change the variable `$end` from `20`.

There's more...

Jenkins uses a standard library, Stapler (`http://stapler.kohsuke.org/what-is.html`), to bind services to URLs. Plugins also use Stapler. When you install plugins, the number of potential actions also increases. This means that you can activate a lot of actions through HTML forms similar to this recipe. You will learn in `Chapter 7`, *Exploring Plugins*, that writing binding code to Stapler requires minimal effort.

See also

- The *Saving screen space with the Dashboard View plugin* recipe

Saving screen space with the Dashboard View plugin

In the *Efficient use of views* recipe, you discovered that you can save horizontal tab space using the `Views` plugin. In this recipe, you will use the `Dashboard View` plugin to condense the use of the horizontal space. Condensing the horizontal space aids in assimilating information efficiently.

The `Dashboard View` plugin allows you to configure areas of a view to display specific functionality, for example, a grid view of the jobs or an area of the view that shows the subset of jobs failing. The user can drag and drop the areas around the screen.

 The developers have made the dashboard easily extensible, so expect more choices later.

Getting ready

Install the `Dashboard View` plugin
(`https://wiki.jenkins-ci.org/display/JENKINS/Dashboard+View`). Either create a few
jobs by hand or use the HTML form that provisioned jobs in the last recipe.

How to do it...

1. The `Dashboard View` plugin divides up the screen into areas. During dashboard
   configuration, you choose the jobs grid and the unstable job portlets. Other
   dashboard portlets include a jobs list, latest builds, slave statistics, test statistics
   chart or grid, and the test trend chart. There will be more choices as the plugin
   matures.
2. As a Jenkins administrator, log in to the home page of your Jenkins instance.
3. Create a new view by clicking on the plus sign in the second tab at the top of the
   screen.
4. Choose the **Dashboard** view.
5. Click on **OK**:

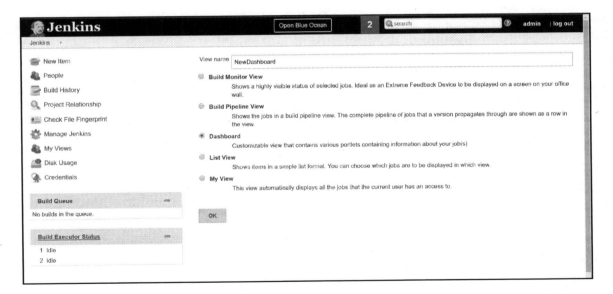

6. Select **Jobs** in **Job Filters**:

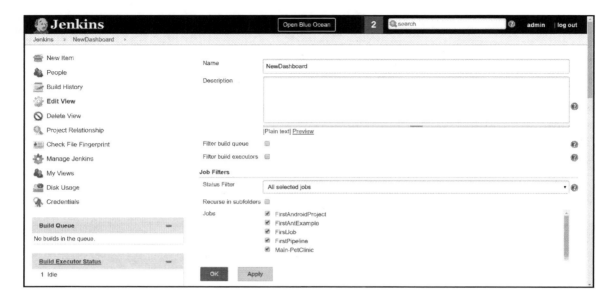

7. Select the **Dashboard Portlets**:

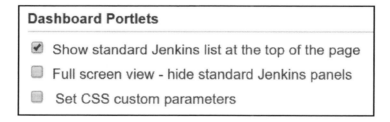

8. Add or remove columns to keep in Dashboard view:

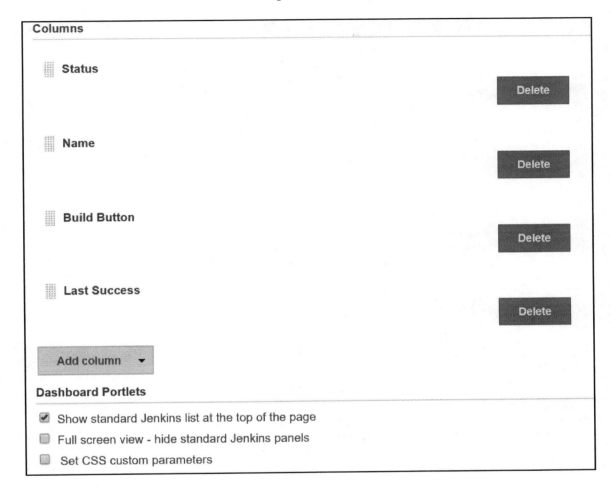

9. Click on **Save** and verify the **New Dashboard** view:

10. You can add **Dashboard Portlets** in different sections of the page:

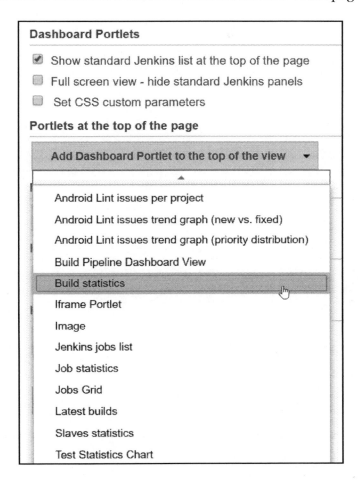

11. Select the **Build statistics** portlet and **Save**:

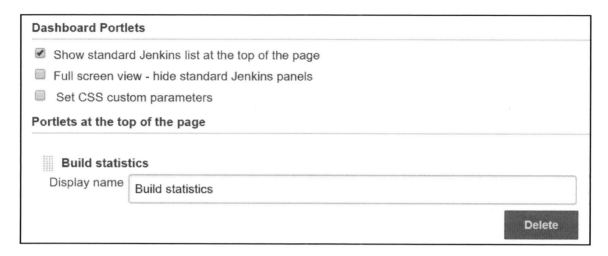

12. Verify the new portlet after saving the configuration in the Jenkins dashboard:

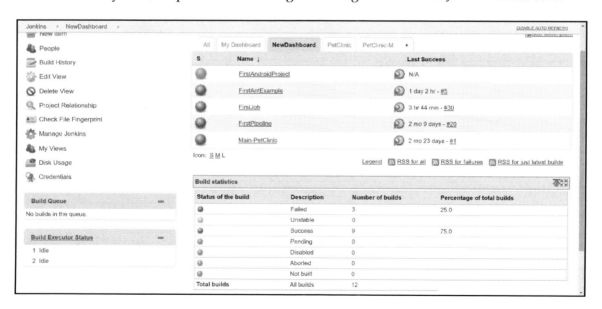

The **Job grid** portlet saves space compared to other views, as the density of jobs displayed is high.

If you are also using the **Many Views** tab (see the preceding recipe) there is a little glitch. When you click on the dashboard tag, the original set of views is displayed rather than the select box.

There's more...

The Dashboard plugin provides a framework for other plugin developers to create dashboard views. One example of this type of usage is the Project Statistics plugin (https://wiki.jenkins-ci.org/display/JENKINS/Project+Statistics+Plugin).

See also

- The *Creating HTML reports* recipe
- The *Efficient use of views* recipe

Making noise with HTML5 browsers

This recipe describes how to send a custom sound to a Jenkins user's browser when an event occurs, such as a successful build. You can also send sound messages at arbitrary times. Not only is this good for developers who enjoy being shouted at, sang at by famous actors, and so on, but also for system administrators who are looking for a computer in a large server farm.

Getting ready

Install the Jenkins sounds plugin (https://wiki.jenkins-ci.org/display/JENKINS/Jenkins+Sounds+plugin). Make sure that you have a compliant web browser installed, such as a current version of Firefox or Chrome.

 For more details of HTML5 compliancy in browsers, consider reviewing: http://en.wikipedia.org/wiki/Comparison_of_layout_engines_%28HTML5%29.

How to do it...

1. Log in as a Jenkins administrator and visit the **Configure System** screen `/configure`.

2. Under the **Jenkins Sound** section, check **Play through HTML5 Audio enabled Browser**.

> If Jenkins has problems finding the sound archive with an error message such as `File not found 'file:/C:/Users/Alan/.jenkins/jar:file:/C:/Users/Alan/.jenkins/plugins/sounds/WEB-INF/lib/classes.jar/sound-archive.zip'`, then unzip the `classes.jar` file and move the `sounds-archive.zip` file to the same directory mentioned in the error message. Finally, point the configuration to the archive, for example, `file:/C:/Users/Alan/.jenkins/plugins/sounds/WEB-INF/lib/sound-archive.zip`.

3. Click on the **Save** button.
4. Select the **Job creation** link found on the Jenkins home page.
5. Create a **New Job** with the **Job name** `ch4.sound`.
6. Select **Build a free-style software project**.
7. Click on **OK**.
8. In the **Post-build Actions** section, check the **Jenkins Sounds** option.
9. Add two sounds: **EXPLODE** and **doh**.
10. Click on **Save**.
11. Click on the **Build now** link.
12. On success, your browser will play the `EXPLODE` wav file.
13. Edit your job so that it fails, for example, by adding a non-existent source code repository.
14. Build the job again. On failure, your web browser will play the `doh` wav file.

How it works...

You have successfully configured your job to play different sounds based on the success or failure of the build.

You can refine how the plugin reacts further by configuring which event transitions will trigger a sound, for example, if the previous build result was a failure and the current build result is a success. This is defined in the **For previous build result** set of checkboxes.

The plugin works as a page decorator. It adds the following JavaScript that asynchronously polls for new sounds. Your browser is doing the majority of the work, freeing server resources:

```
<script src="/sounds/script"
 type="text/javascript"></script><script type="text/javascript"
 defer="defer">function _sounds_ajaxJsonFetcherFactory(onSuccess,
 onFailure) {
return function() {
newAjax.Request("/sounds/getSounds", {
parameters: { version: VERSION },
onSuccess: function(rsp) {
onSuccess(eval('x='+rsp.responseText))
        },
onFailure: onFailure
    });
  }
}
if (AUDIO_CAPABLE) {
    _sounds_pollForSounds(_sounds_ajaxJsonFetcherFactory);
}</script>
```

There's more...

The sound plugin also allows you to stream arbitrary sounds to connected web browsers. Not only is this useful for practical jokes and motivational speeches directed at your distributed team, you can also perform useful actions such as a 10-minute warning alert before restarting a server.

You can find some decent sound collections at
`http://www.archive.org/details/opensource_audio`.

For example, you can find a copy of the One Laptop per Child music library at `http://www.archive.org/details/OpenPathMusic44V2`. Within the collection, you will discover `shenai.wav`. First, add the sound somewhere on the internet where it can be found. A good place is the Jenkins `userContent` directory. To play the sound on any connected web browser, you will need to visit the trigger address (replacing `localhost:8080` with your own address):

```
http://localhost:8080/sounds/playSound?src=http://localhost:8080/userContent/shenai.wav
```

See also

- The *Keeping in contact with Jenkins through Firefox* recipe in `Chapter 1`, *Getting Started with Jenkins*

An extreme view for reception areas

Agile projects emphasize the role of communication over the need to document. Information radiators aid in returning feedback quickly. Information radiators have two main characteristics: they change over time and the data presented is easy to digest.

The `eXtreme Feedback Panel` plugin is one example of an information radiator. It is a highly visual Jenkins view. If the layout is formatted consistently and displayed on a large monitor, it is ideal for the task. Consider this also as a positive advertisement of your development process. You can display it behind your reception desk or in a well-visited social area such as near the coffee machine or project room.

In this recipe, you will add the `eXtreme Feedback Panel` plugin and modify its appearance through HTML tags in the description.

Getting ready

Install the eXtreme Feedback Panel plugin
(https://wiki.jenkins-ci.org/display/JENKINS/eXtreme+Feedback+Panel+Plugin).

How to do it...

1. Create a job with a descriptive name such as Blackboard Report Pro Access and add the following description:

   ```
   <center>
   <p>Writes Blackboard sanity reports<br>
   and sends them to a list.
   <table border="1" class="myclass"><tr><td>More
   Details</td></tr></table>
   </center>
   ```

2. Create a new view (/newView) named eXtreme. Check the **eXtremeFeedBack Panel** and then click on **OK**.

3. Select 6-24 already created jobs, including the one previously created in this recipe.

4. Set the number of columns as **2**.

5. Select the refresh time in seconds as **20**.

6. Click on **Show Job descriptions**.

7. Click on **OK**.

8. Experiment with the settings (especially the pixel size of the fonts). Optimizing the view depends on the monitors used and the distance from the monitor that the audience view at, as shown in the following screenshot:

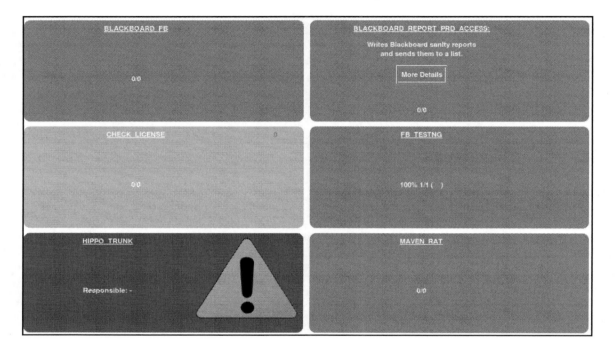

How it works...

Setting up and running this information radiator was easy. The results deliver a beautifully rendered view of the dynamics of your software process.

Setting the refresh rate to 20 seconds is debatable. A long delay between updates dulls the viewer's interest.

You have written one description that is partially formatted in the extreme view, but HTML escaped in the jobs configuration page and elsewhere in Jenkins. You can see that the information area is easier to digest than the other projects. This highlights the need to write consistent descriptions that follow in-house conventions, following a certain length to fit naturally on the screen. A longer, more descriptive name for a job helps the viewer understand the job's context better.

A shortcut to configuring views is through the URL
`http://localhost:8080/view/Jobname/configure`, replacing any
spaces in `Jobname` with `%20`.

There's more...

Information radiators are fun and take a rich variety of shapes and forms. From different views displayed in large monitors, to USB sponge missile firing and abuse from the voices of famous actors (see the *Making noise with HTML5 browsers* recipe).

A number of example electronic projects worth exploring in Jenkins are given as follows:

- **Lava Lamps**:
  `https://wiki.jenkins-ci.org/display/JENKINS/Lava+Lamp+Notifier`
- **USB missile launcher**: `https://github.com/codedance/Retaliation`
- **Traffic lights**: `http://code.google.com/p/hudsontrafficlights/`

Remember, let's be careful out there.

See also

- The *Saving screen space with the Dashboard View plugin* recipe
- The *Making noise with HTML5 browsers* recipe

Processes that Improve Quality

Quality assurance requires that the experts pay attention to a wide range of details. Rather than being purely technical, many of these details relate to human behavior. This chapter mentions both the soft skills needed to run successful projects and the configuration skills codified in the recipes of this book. Here are a few hard-learned observations.

Culture and collaboration

- DevOps is a cultural movement and it is all about changing the culture of an organization to make the processes more effective and to make people more productive with the use of tools.
- Culture of an organization is the key to success. Over the years, templates, best practices, and patterns are created in the organizations considering the resource capabilities, environment, and many other factors. If the culture of an organization can adapt to change, then it is a blessing in a dynamic environment of today's day and age.
- If the culture of an organization supports knowledge sharing and collaboration, then it not only creates robust assets that can be utilized over and over, but it also creates scopes of innovation and applies them across different business units.
- Planning for processes to setup Continuous Development, Continuous Integration, Continuous Testing, and Continuous Deployment require collaboration across different stakeholders for better implementation and effective results.

Fail early or fail faster

It is always better to avoid or prevent problems rather than solving them later in a situation where lot of things are at stake and the cost interms of price, reputation, and market scenario is much harder to deal with. The later in the software life cycle you correct a problem, the costlier it will prove to be. Failing early is significantly cheaper than failing later. Continuous Integration allows you to automatically fail software early. Adding extra tests through plugins or connected cloud services gives greater opportunity to face your issues early, improving quality and decreasing costs. Embrace acknowledging issues because you are saving time and money. Failing later in the project creates a situation of no point of return. Even in case of infrastructure provisioning, cloud computing has changed a scenario. Because of pay-as-you-go billing models, organizations and SMBs can also afford resources that they wouldn't have dreamt of earlier. You can use the same type of resources in Dev and Test environments for a specific amount of time and you know exactly what kind of issues will take place and how to solve them. Environment is going to be same in production as well, and hence you won't have to deal with any major issues later in the application development life cycle because you have already faced these issues and you are very well aware how to deal with them quickly.

Often, the experience of failing early helps to create a framework or best practices that not only solves the issues but also makes the overall scenario more robust and leads to the creation of design patterns of specific solutions.

Data-driven testing

You can efficiently cover your testing surface if you use a data-driven testing approach. For example, when writing JMeter test plans, you can use the CSV configuration element to read in variables from text files. This allows JMeter to read out parameters from your CSV files, such as hostname, and transverse your infrastructure. This enables one test plan to attack many servers. The same is true for SoapUI; by adding an Excel data source and looping through the rows, you can test an application with many different test users who each have a range of roles. Data-driven testing has a tendency to be maintainable. During refactoring, instead of changing your test plan as the URLs in your application change, you can factor the URLs out into CSV files.

Learning from history

Teams tend to have their own coding habits and this varies from organization to organization because of the tools they use and coding standards they follow. If a project fails because of the quality of the code, try to work out which code metrics would have stopped the code reaching production. Which mistakes are seen repeatedly? Take a look at the following examples:

- **Friday afternoon code failure**: We all are human and have secondary agendas. By the end of the week, programmers may have their minds focused elsewhere other than on the code. A small subset of programmers have their code quality affected, consistently injecting more defects toward the tail end of their roster. Consider scheduling a weekly Jenkins job that has harsher thresholds for quality metrics near the time of least attention.

- **Code churn**: A sudden surge in code commits just before a product is being moved from an acceptance environment to product indicates that there is a last-minute rush. For some teams with a strong sense of code quality, this is also a sign of extra vigilance. For other less-disciplined teams, this could be a naïve push toward destruction. If a project fails and QA is overwhelmed due to a surge of code changes, look at setting up a warning Jenkins job based on commit velocity. If necessary, you can display your own custom metrics.

- **A rogue coder**: Not all developers create code of the same uniform high quality. It is possible that there is consistent underachievement within a project. Rogue coders are caught by human code review. However, for a secondary defense, consider setting thresholds on static code review reports from SonarQube, FindBugs, and PMD. If a particular developer is not following accepted practice, builds will fail with great regularity.

- **The GUI does not make sense**: Isn't it painful when you build a web application only to be told at the last moment that the GUI does not quite interact in the way that the product owner expected? One solution is to write a mockup in FitNesse and surround it with automatic functional tests, using fixtures. When the GUI diverges from the planned workflow, then Jenkins will start shouting.

- **Tracking responsibility**: Mistakes are made and lessons need to be learned. However, if there is no clear chain of documented responsibility, it is difficult to pin down who needs the learning opportunity. One approach is to structure the workflow in Jenkins through a series of connected jobs and use the promoted builds plugin to make sure the right group verifies at the right point. This methodology is also good for reminding the team of the short-term tasks.

For better code quality, you can create a Jenkins build that takes the code from the central repository every night, performs static code analysis using SonarQube, and sends the results to stakeholders daily. By doing this, we are not only communicating issues daily, but we are also creating a culture for Continuous Improvement by cultivating habits. There may come a time when programmers will know exactly what kind of programming they need to avoid and hence the quality of the code will start getting better.

Considering test automation as a software project

If you see automated testing as a software project and apply well-known principles, then you will save on maintenance costs and increase the reliability of tests.

The **Don't Repeat Yourself (DRY)** principle is a great example. Under time pressure, it is tempting to cut and paste similar tests from one area of the code base to another, don't. Projects evolve bending the shape of the code base; the tests need to be reusable to adapt to that change. Fragile tests push up maintenance costs. If you separate the code into pages, then when the workflow between pages changes, most of the testing code remains intact.

The **Keep It Simple Stupid (KISS)** principle implies keeping every aspect of the project as simple as possible. For example, it is possible to use real browsers for automated functional tests or the HtmlUnit framework to simulate a browser. The second choice avoids the need to set up an in-memory X server or VNC (`http://en.wikipedia.org/wiki/Virtual_Network_Computing`) and will also keep track of browser versioning. These extra chores decrease the reliability of running a Jenkins job, but do increase the value of the tests. Therefore, for small projects, consider starting with `HtmlUnit`. For larger projects, the extra effort is worth the cost.

Consider if you need a standalone integration server or if you can get away with using a Jetty server called during the integration goal in Maven.

Visualize, visualize, and visualize!

There is a popular phrase in India called *entertainment, entertainment, and entertainment.* Visualization is extremely effective to keep things robust. When you have many projects scattered across multiple servers developed by different teams and individuals, it is difficult to understand the key metrics and emerging issues.

With 80 percent of information going through to your brain being visual and your brain being an excellent pattern recognizer, one of the tricks to understand the underlying complexity is to visualize the results of your Jenkins jobs.

SonarQube is an excellent starting point to visualize and gain an overview of the overall quality of projects and for delving into relationships and couplings between different areas of the code.

However, if you have specialized requirements, you will need to build graph generation. Test results are usually stored in XML or CSV format. Once you have accumulated the results, you can easily transform them with your language of choice.

You can also create a monitoring view or build pipeline to have visualization of different jobs running in Jenkins.

Conventions are good

By following conventions, you decrease the amount of maintenance and lower the number of defects hidden in your code. Coding conventions are particularly important when more than one developer is involved in writing the code. Conventions aid readability. Consistently indented code focuses the eye on poorly-written sections. Well-structured variable names help avoid naming collisions between code written in different parts of the organization. Structure in naming highlights the data that you can later move to configuration files and it also increases the opportunity for semi-automatic refactoring using regular expressions, for example, you can write a short piece of R code to visualize the number of global variables you have per module. The more global variables you have, the greater the risk of using the same variable for multiple purposes. Hence, the plot is a rough indicator of smelly code.

Properly followed conventions help to minimize the issues and also help in troubleshooting. It creates a unique culture in the organization.

Test frameworks and commercial choices are increasing

Test frameworks and commercial choices are increasing. In the past few years, there has been a lot of improvement in test automation. One example is that static code review is being used more thoroughly for security checks. SonarQube is an all-encompassing reporter of project quality and new frameworks are emerging to improve on the old. Here are a few implications:

- **SonarQube**: This measures the project quality. Its community is active. SonarQube will evolve faster than the full range of Jenkins quality metrics plugins. Consider using Jenkins plugins for early warnings of negative quality changes and SonarQube for in-depth reporting.
- You can find the SonarQube Jenkins plugin at: `https://wiki.jenkins.io/display/JENKINS/SonarQube+plugin`:

- **Static code review tools**: These are improving. FindBugs has moved comment-making into the cloud. More bug pattern detectors are being developed. Static code review tools are getting better at finding security defects. Expect significantly improved tools over time, possibly just by updating the version of your current tools.
- **Code search**: Wouldn't it be great if code search engines ranked the position in their search results of a particular piece of code, based on the defect density or coding practice? You could then search a wide range of open source products for best practices. You could search for defects to remove and then send patches back to the code's communities.

- **The cloud**: CloudBees allows you to create on-demand slave nodes in the cloud. Expect more kinds of cloud-like integrations around Jenkins.

For more information about SonarQube's features and the CloudBees cloud service, visit `http://www.sonarqube.org/features/` and `http://www.CloudBees.com/products/dev`.

Offsetting work to Jenkins nodes

Thanks to its wealth of plugins, Jenkins can easily connect many types of systems. Therefore, Jenkins' usage can grow virally in an organization. Testing and Javadoc generation takes up system resources. A master Jenkins is best used to report back quickly on the jobs distributed across a range of Jenkins nodes. This approach makes it easier to analyze where the failure lies in the infrastructure.

If you are using JMeter for your performance tests at scale, consider offloading from Jenkins to a cloud service such as BlazeMeter (`http://blazemeter.com/`).

For functional testing with Selenium, there is also a wide range of cloud services. Consider using them not only because of load, but also because of the use of a wide range of browser types and versions offered. One example of a commercial service is Sauce Labs (`https://saucelabs.com/`). It is worth periodically reviewing the market for new cloud services.

There are other scenarios as well where you can utilize distributed architecture in Jenkins. For example, to keep Android and iOS agents and bind them with the Jenkins master so all jobs related to Android and iOS apps are offloaded from the master Jenkins.

Starving QA/integration servers

A few hundred years ago, coal miners would die because of the build-up of methane and carbon monoxide in the mines. To give early warning of this situation, canaries were brought into the mines. Being more sensitive, the birds would faint first, giving the miners enough time to escape. Consider doing the same for your integration servers in your acceptance environment: deliberately starve them of resources. If they fall over, you will have enough time to review before watching the explosion in production.

Reading the change log of Jenkins

Jenkins practices what it preaches. Minor version number releases occur about once a week. New features appear, bugs are resolved, and new bugs introduced. In general, the great majority of changes lead to improvement, but a few do not. However, when introduced, bugs are generally caught early and removed quickly.

Before updating Jenkins for new features and potential stability glitches, it's worth reading the changelog (`http://jenkins-ci.org/changelog`). Occasionally, you might want to speed up a deployment to production because of a security issue or miss a version due to a stability blooper.

Avoiding human bottlenecks

The simpler your testing environment is, the less skill you'll need to maintain it. As you learn to use the plugins and explore the potential of new tools and scripting languages, the more knowledge the organization needs in order to maintain a stable system. If you wish to go on holidays without random text messages asking for advice, make sure that your knowledge is transferred to at least a second person. This sounds obvious, but in the rush of your daily load, this principle is often forgotten or put to one side.

One of the easiest ways to share knowledge is to send a couple of developers off to the same conferences and events together (`https://www.CloudBees.com/company/events/juc`). Learn best practices from Jenkins user conferences and other conferences too.

This is where managers play a significant role in knowledge dissemination. They need to plan in time and activities for the sharing of knowledge, rather than expecting it to happen by magic.

Avoiding groupthink

It is easy to be perfect on paper, defining the importance of a solid set of Javadocs and unit tests. However, the real world on its best days is chaotic. Project momentum, motivated by the need to deliver, is an elusive force to push back against.

Related to project momentum is the potential of groupthink (http://en.wikipedia.org/wiki/Groupthink) by the project team or resource owners. If the team has the wrong collective attitude, as a quality assurance professional it is much harder to inject hard-learned realism. Quality assurance is not only about finding and capturing defects as early as possible, it is also about injecting objective criteria for success or failure into the different phases of a project's cycle.

Consider adding measurable criteria into the Jenkins build. Obviously, if the code fails to compile, then the product should not go to acceptance and production. Less obvious, are the rules around code coverage of unit tests worth defending in release management meetings.

Try getting the whole team involved at the start of the project before any coding has taken place and agree on metrics that fail a build. One approach is to compare a small successful project to a small failed project. If later there is a disagreement, then the debate is about process and numbers rather than personality.

Training and community

Training and participating in Jenkins and the wider tester community are vital for long-term learning paths that lead to optimized environments. Here are a few relevant resources:

When starting with an online community, it is wise to first review and participate in the mailing lists. This allows you to judge your own standard and gradually become recognized. The mailing lists are summarized at http://jenkins-ci.org/content/mailing-lists. Once you are confident that you can productively participate, consider progressing to real-time interactions through the IRC channel at https://wiki.jenkins-ci.org/display/JENKINS/IRC+Channel. The ISTQB software certification body keeps example documentation on its website for its software tester exams. You can find the documentation at http://www.istqb.org/downloads.html.

Additionally, it is important to have internal trainings in the organization to train resources for end-to-end automation of application life cycle management. To make the resources and stakeholders realize the value and effectiveness of the processes are extremely vital because then only they can identify pain points or repetitive processes and automate them to make productivity better.

Visibly rewarding successful developers

This is a call to resource managers.

Developers and testers specialize in technical matters that are at times hard to explain to the ones outside their problem domain. To reach the highest level of expertise and to keep track of trends requires time (sometimes a lot of their own time), energy, and motivation. Undermining their motivation or underestimating the time required to build their skills will ultimately decrease the quality of your products and will cost more in the end.

Consider what you can do to support them, from pay scale jumps, learning paths, reserving time in the week for developers to read and practice new ideas, to conferences and gadgets. For example, after a pay rise, Kickstarter (`https://www.kickstarter.com/`) is a great place to look for motivational rewards and to stimulate the developers' creative muscle.

Often, the best thing to do is to trust developers and testers and give themselves proper direction to excel to achieve greater heights, and only then they will be able to create a platform to self-motivate themselves.

Train them, challenge them, reward them, and motivate them; get innovations for free. You need to remember that every small appreciation motivates team members and at times you may have healthy competition in the team as well.

Finally, do not make developers do non-development stuff. In general, they need to be highly focused on the complex task of understanding detailed requirements and turning them into rock-solid code.

Stability and code maintenance

This book mentions many plugins and a number of languages and testing tools. It is OK to experiment in development and then push to acceptance, but the more diversity you have in production, the more skills are needed to maintain and especially to write a fluent workflow. Subtle choices, such as pinning Jenkins plugins at known versions and keeping the production version of your Jenkins server stable for fixed periods, help with up-time. Just as importantly, monitoring the load and offsetting most of the jobs away from the master Jenkins ensues a high degree of determinism in the timing of the jobs.

To limit job maintenance implies keeping configuration simple and similar. This is not realistic in a complex organization with a high degree of diversity. Using a test-driven approach helps; conventions also simplify configuration. As the diversity increases, communicating and agreeing to the conventions becomes important. Simple strategies such as one source of documentation wisdom (for example, a communal wiki), regular lessons, learned meetings, and weekly reviews become vital.

Resources on quality assurance

It is a mistake to consider testing to be the sole responsibility of the testers. Coders should feel responsible for the quality of their code, architects for the quality of their designs, managers for the ethos of the project and project planning, and so on. Here are some examples of a range of practical resources on actionable quality assurance-this is not just for the testers.

There are many wise words on avoiding classic mistakes based on years of hard knocks and bruising. A well thought-out set of comments can be found at `http://www.exampler.com/testing-com/writings/classic/mistakes.html`.

If unit tests cover your code thoroughly, then if you break a piece of code during an update, you will know this quickly during the next build. JUnit is arguably the most well-known framework in this genre. You can find the framework's home page at `http://junit.org/`.

The Jenkins home page (`http://jenkins-ci.org/`) covers a wealth of information around the practicalities of configuration, plugins, the community, and hints and tips.

The **Open Web Application Security Project (OWASP)** is a great source of information and tools on security testing. OWASP is focused on improving the security of software. Its mission is to make software security visible so that individuals and organizations worldwide can make informed decisions about true software security risks. You can find the OWASP home page at `https://www.owasp.org/index.php/Main_Page`.

One popular example of a commercial company selling Jenkins infrastructure in the cloud is Sauce Labs (`https://docs.saucelabs.com/ci-integrations/jenkins/`).

There are a number of excellent and free-to-download software testing magazines. The professional tester is one such example and is available at `http://www.professionaltester.com/`.

uTest is the world's largest open community dedicated to professional testers and software testing. Its sole purpose is to promote and advance the testing profession, and the people who do this vital work. For more information, visit `http://www.utest.com/about-us`.

There are more and more free MOOC courses and a number of them support the learning paths of software testers. You can find a full list of currently running MOOC courses at `https://www.mooc-list.com/`.

And there's always more

There are always more points to consider. Here are a few of the cherry-picked ones:

- **Blurring the team boundary**: Tools such as FitNesse and Selenium IDE make it easier for non-Java programmers to write tests. The easier it is to write tests, the more likely it is that the relevant tests capture the quintessential details of user expectations. Look for new Jenkins plugins that support tools, which lower the learning curve.
- **Deliberately adding defects**: By rotating through Jenkins builds and then deliberately adding code that fails, you can test the alertness and response time of the team.
- **Increasing code coverage with link crawlers and security scanners**: A fuzzer discovers the inputs of the application it is attacking and then fires off unexpected input. Not only is this good for security testing, but also for boundary testing. If your server returns an unexpected error, then use a fuzzer to trigger a more thorough review. Fuzzers and link crawlers are a cheap way to increase the code coverage of your tests.

In your development environment, periodically review for new Jenkin plugins. The number of plugins is increasing rapidly and there may be new ways for Jenkins to connect different parts of your organization's infrastructure to Continuous Integration.

Final comments

The combination of Jenkins with aggressive automated testing acts as a solid safety net around coding projects. The recipes in this book support best practices.

Producing quality requires great attention to detail. Jenkins can pay attention to many of the details and then shout loudly when violations occur.

Each project is different and there are many ways to structure the workflow. Luckily, with over 1,000 plugins and the number rising rapidly, Jenkins is flexible enough to adapt to even the most obscure infrastructures.

If you do not have the exact plugin that you want, then it is straightforward for Java programmers to adapt or create their own plugin.

Index

publishing, Jenkins used 302, 310

D

Dashboard View plugin
  screen space, saving 382, 385, 387, 388
data-driven testing 398
Debian security
  reference 158
Denial Of Service (DOS) 163
DevOps 397
disk usage
  managing 82
Distributed Denial Of Service attack (DDOS) 163
Don't Repeat Yourself (DRY) principle 400
downstream job
  about 326
  configuring 327
DropDownViewsTabBar plugin
  reference 379

E

Eclipse
  used, for creating Selenium test case 282, 296
  used, for managing Jenkins build jobs 64
EnvFile plugin
  reference 216
EnvInject plugin
  reference 216
environmental variables
  manipulating 216, 217, 218
errors
  searching, fuzzer used 159
execution
  Android project, configuring for 210, 212, 213, 215
  Ant project, configuring for 204, 206
  Maven project, configuring for 208, 209
eXtreme Feedback Panel plugin
  about 392
  reference 392

F

FitNesse
  about 282
  references 321, 324

testing with 321, 323
Freestyle job
  creating, for Ant project 51, 53
functional testing
  Jenkins, integrating with Selenium 296, 301
fuzzer
  used, for searching errors 159
  used, for searching XSS attacks 159

G

Git
  configuring, in Jenkins 45
global settings
  configuring, in Jenkins 37, 38
GRADLE_HOME
  configuring, in Jenkins 49
Groovy
  Ant, running through 220, 223, 224
  reference 220
groupthink
  avoiding 405

H

Hardware Enablement Stack (HWE) 117
home page
  generating 375
HTML publisher plugin
  reference 376
HTML reports
  creating 376, 377, 378
HTML validity
  verifying, with SonarQube 183, 193
HTML5 browsers
  noise, making 389, 390
human bottlenecks
  avoiding 404

I

information radiator
  setting up 392, 394
ISTQB
  reference 405

77960672R00244

Made in the USA
San Bernardino, CA
30 May 2018